THE
HOTHOUSE
EFFECT

THE
HOTHOUSE
EFFECT

Intensify Creativity in Your Organization Using Secrets
from History's Most Innovative Communities

Barton Kunstler, Ph.D.

AMACOM

American Management Association
New York • Atlanta • Brussels • Chicago • Mexico City • San Francisco
Shanghai • Tokyo • Toronto • Washington, D.C.

※ 52373273

Special discounts on bulk quantities of AMACOM books are available to corporations, professional associations, and other organizations. For details, contact Special Sales Department, AMACOM, a division of American Management Association, 1601 Broadway, New York, NY 10019.
Tel.: 212-903-8316.   Fax: 212-903-8083.
Web site: www.amacombooks.org

This publication is designed to provide accurate and authoritative information in regard to the subject matter covered. It is sold with the understanding that the publisher is not engaged in rendering legal, accounting, or other professional service. If legal advice or other expert assistance is required, the services of a competent professional person should be sought.

Library of Congress Cataloging-in-Publication Data

Kunstler, Barton Lee.
    The hothouse effect : intensify creativity in your organization using secrets from history's most innovative communities / Barton Kunstler.— 1st ed.
        p.   cm.
    ISBN 0-8144-0769-2
    1. Creative ability in business.   I. Title.

HD53.K86   2004
658. 3'14—dc21

                                                            2003012012

Printing number
10   9   8   7   6   5   4   3   2   1

CONTENTS

ACKNOWLEDGMENTS

In writing this book, I have relied on family and friends, and the kindness of those who previously had been strangers to me. Any of the book's shortcomings are solely the property of the author and cannot be laid at anyone else's door, which is too bad but that's the truth of it.

I owe a special debt of gratitude to the people who consented to be interviewed for this work and whose insights provide much of its value, and whose company was always a pleasure to share. Terry Beard and Richard Lazere of Beard Framing and The Big Day, Casey Powell and Mike Jahnke of Sequent and NextGig, Dr. Mara Miniati of the Museum and Institute of the History of Science in Florence, Francesco Coppola and Maria Rossi-Thiebaud of Loop Design in Bologna, Bill Seidman of Cerebyte Inc., Bob Clemence of Hyde Tools, Jim Foley of the Rowland Institute for Science, musician Winard Harper, Bill Ribitch and Jay Boyce of Foster-Miller Inc., Leonard DeGraaf of the Thomas Edison National Site, Arthur Nelson of the Nelson Companies, William Tiga Tita of the Global Management Center and World Trade Network, Giovanni Neri of the University of Bologna, and Jeff Govendo of The Innovative Edge offered their wisdom, experience, enthusiasm, generous portions of their time, and thoroughly enjoyable conversation.

I would also like to thank Adrienne Hickey, Christina McLaughlin, and Mike Sivilli, my editors at AMACOM Books, for their belief in the book, acute suggestions for improving it, encouragement, the mental Gatorade, and for being a pleasure to work with.

Old friends are all over this book. Harris Kagan explained quantum physics and holography—anything I got wrong is definitely due to my own density. Stu Haber provided contacts and a weekly reality check over breakfast at Mel's. Jonathan Gueverra was, as ever, always available to go a round or two over some troublesome idea or passage. Pat Mahoney's thorough commentary on several chapters provided great feedback. Conversations with Andrea Quigley reflected her understanding of the corporate environment and the creative process and, over the years, Maria Mackavey has encouraged my work from her post in her adjoining office.

I owe a profound debt to Joan Dolamore and Susan McFarland on a number of fronts: as my research-oriented division directors at the Lesley University School of Management and as two very close friends who have influenced my views of education, pedagogy, and corporate values. Susan's input as a reader was invaluable, and I could always trust her judgment on whether a given passage was worth retaining.

Joe Romano was invaluable in tracking down and researching photographs, and even more so for the decades of nonstop discussion we've had on many of the book's themes. Douglas Atwood has been and continues to be an inspiration to me, as he is for so many people who knew him, a one-man creative hothouse and one of the most profoundly generous souls one is likely to meet on this journey. My sister, Robin Kunstler, and my brother-in-law, Michael Carney, are, as ever, rock-solid sources of love, laughter, and creative spirit. Florence and Henry Kunstler continue to inspire with their courage, love, integrity, and excitement over each of their progeny's new projects.

Chloe and Remy deserve thanks for patiently putting up with a computer-bound father and for their consistently amazing insights into creativity and life in general. And of course, the greater part of my appreciation of them goes to their very presence, which is all the world to me.

My final thanks and the dedication of this book goes to Holly Pope, with all my love: wife, unerring editor, and complete creative immersion experience in her own right, without whom not only wouldn't this book have been written but the desk I wrote it on would have remained unassembled.

THE
HOTHOUSE
EFFECT

INTRODUCTION

History's most creative communities enchant us with the almost other-worldly quality of their achievements. We may visit the great cities of Europe or trek across harsh landscapes simply to wander through places that are fantastic in their beauty, obscure in their purpose, or haunting in their ruined splendor. Museums display their glory and countless books—travel guides, memoirs, biographies, histories, novels, and art books—navigate us through their mysteries. Any time and place that hosted an extraordinary outpouring of creativity enthralls us. Like exotically beautiful, wildly blooming plants cultivated in the moist, mineral rich, electrically charged atmosphere of a paradisal hothouse, these communities leave behind an unforgettable legacy of creativity, which is why I call the process that gives rise to them the *hothouse effect*.

The idea of the hothouse effect grew out of my curiosity about how such places come to be. Was it an accident of birth, a loaded gene pool that gave ancient Athens its great writers, thinkers, political innovators, builders, and artists? Was fifteenth-century Florence, the heart of the Renaissance, really more creative than Venice or Rome? Or are there different types of creativity, with Florence shining in the arts, Venice in long-distance trade, and Rome in politics?

Perhaps chance or luck determines creative destiny. One place or another is always bound to lead, and it doesn't matter which. Sometimes things work, sometimes they don't, and any suggestion of a pattern to human behavior is wishful thinking. This is a fairly popular way of viewing history even among historians, but a look at any modern organization contradicts it. Most people believe that success or failure in business stems from cogent methods of strategic planning, development, financial management, leadership, and so forth. Certain methods work and ignoring them results in failure. When these methods work over and over, we identify them as *patterns* of effective behavior. Ethical financial oversight, effective planning protocols, and clearly articulated objectives are among patterns of behavior that increase the odds of business success. We distill these patterns into *principles,* statements that demonstrate the applicability of the patterns to diverse circumstances, just as the repeating patterns found in planetary motion can also be linked to the arc of a thrown ball or the stability of a skyscraper via the principles of gravity. Principles of conflict resolution apply, albeit in customized form, to both marital squabbles and international wars. Certain principles of swinging a bat can be used by all ballplayers as well as martial artists, racquetball players, and even a lumberjack swinging an ax. So in this book, we'll be looking at diverse communities in search of the principles that led to outstanding creative performance on their part, which now can be used to enhance the creativity of any organization.

To test whether these principles exist, this book will address the following core questions:

- Why did one community produce numerous creative products that literally changed the world, while equally prominent contemporary neighbors within the same cultural zone generated more modest results?

- Did specific historical factors predispose these hothouse communities to be highly creative? Did they utilize specific techniques to heighten their creativity?

- If we can identify these factors and techniques, can modern organizations apply them to heighten *their* creativity?

- Would increasing creativity improve the performance of today's organizations?

The choice of communities to serve as hothouse models is somewhat subjective, but certain historical groups stand out as obvious examples. Several were independent states, such as ancient Athens and fifteenth-century Florence. Some were, or are, organizations: the early twentieth-century Bauhaus and various contemporary companies. Other groups—such as the American jazz community or the artists who were active in Paris just after

1900—were composed of a loose band of individuals who knew each other and pursued common creative goals.

In a 1959 article, Dr. Edwin Land, founder of Polaroid and the Rowland Institute for Science, made an assertion that might seem to contradict the entire thrust of this book, but with which, in fact, our theme is in total accord. "I think whether outside science or within science there is no such thing as *group* originality or *group* creativity or *group* perspicacity. . . . Profundity and originality are attributes of single, if not singular, minds." After describing the specific ways teams *can* be useful, Land flatly stated, "Teams are not creative as such. . . . For every good idea that has been spawned by a group, millions have been smothered."[1]

Land was wary of overly large companies and disdained mass social movements that submerged the individual in the oceanic flood of "group think," to use George Orwell's term. I couldn't agree more with Land on the conformist and even authoritarian tendencies of large groups acting in concert. The Romans even observed, "The Senators are good men, the Senate is a beast." Granted, the senators often were not good men, but in general, history ratifies both Land and the Romans: Group behavior easily degenerates into the predictable and even violent patterns of the herd or mob.

However, the opposite just as obviously holds true. Many of our greatest achievements occur precisely because a group of individuals acting in concert *elevated* the ethical, intellectual, creative, and social character of each group member. Were this not the case, we would have to conclude that the entire process of socialization served only to reduce human creativity. In fact, there is no such thing as "human-ness" without the vast number of interwoven social processes that allow our individualism to emerge and that inspires us to create things that are beautiful, useful, and new. Land understood this because his whole approach to innovation involved balancing individual and group work. But his generalization about groups reinforces a more deeply held view of creativity as depending on the singular innovator. The hothouse effect, however, asserts that such singular "creatives" are more likely to emerge from within a group of skilled practitioners than from isolation. It also recognizes that the Great Man theory of creativity is no more valid than Thomas Carlyle's Great Man theory of history. Whether man or woman, distinctive leaders will emerge in every aspect of life. However, their brilliance requires a context of numerous other practitioners who, while not as gifted perhaps, nonetheless contribute to the construction of the body of knowledge and practice from which outstanding innovators emerge. As physicist Werner Heisenberg said, "If

Einstein had lived in the twelfth century, he would have had very little chance to become a good scientist."[2]

So, while Land is correct to warn against losing individual creativity in a forest of mediocrity, the hothouse effect demonstrates that such individual efforts derive their power and integrity from social dynamics that generate, nourish, and celebrate the practice of creativity and innovation. Without that, even the gifts of a Beethoven or Leonardo would likely remain untapped. Thus, the hothouse effect is concerned with identifying the factors that make some groups more creative than others, whether one ascribes that creativity to the synergy of exceptional teamwork or the soaring of individual genius, or, as is most likely the case, the delicate but supercharged balance between the two.

The general trend has been for organizations to become more open, but it is still unclear whether timeless factors such as the inertia of hierarchy, the perks of power, the quirks of human nature, or the rules governing the behavior of systems will allow them to change radically. We might also consider whether such systems *should* change radically. Despite the flaws of the modern organization, it has evolved in response to strong cues from the business, human, and social environments that shape it.

One might object that history's societies are "open systems" whose development is fluid and unpredictable, subject only to the constraints of geography, climate, demographics, and human nature. In comparison, business organizations seem to be relatively "closed systems" that marshal resources for highly convergent, task-oriented goals; are quite hierarchal (despite some deeming themselves "flat organizations"); use (presumably) strict self-assessment procedures and standards to monitor and guide performance; encourage conformist behavior and values; and are bound by strict legal guidelines.

Many points of contact exist, however, between those communities that have emerged out of the tumultuous processes of history and modern organizations created to fulfill well-defined commercial tasks. For instance, at key developmental stages—such as the early entrepreneurial phase; major transitions of product, company size, or focus; or integration of networks—operations, objectives, and internal relationships fluctuate radically and the ensuing unpredictability demands bold and creative response. Today's business environment, however, is permanently volatile, serving as a powerful stimulus for reconfiguring basic assumptions about how we conduct business.

We are all aware of the sea-change in the business environment wrought by a broad set of conditions: globalization and the intense competition it engenders; careers being less secure and more fluid than ever; multifunction jobs; the Internet; radical shifts in technology that can make a procedure, product, entire industry, or individual obsolete overnight; and the psychologically disturbing and economically disruptive impact of catastrophic events such as the terrorist attacks that occurred on September 11, 2001. We can also argue that the world is undergoing substantial transformation on many levels. Bedrocks of human life such as the nation-state, the privacy of our innermost thoughts, the human genetic code, the solidity of matter, the stability of our Earth's environment, and even space and time, no longer seem immutable or constant. More and more elements of our lives seem to be temporary manifestations of some greater pattern of universal flux that is, at the moment, at a high-activity phase of its cycle.

Under these conditions, creativity is no longer a luxury of the most advanced organizations; it becomes a necessary instrument in the struggle for survival. And while the notion of "managing creativity" may seem to be an oxymoron, we can definitely cultivate creativity and foster conditions that favor its expression. The leader's role is increasingly to identify creative talent and establish the environment needed for it to operate at maximum power. The hothouse effect provides guidelines for generating a high-performing group of creative individuals, however large or small and organized or informal that group may be.

NOTES

1. Edwin Land, "Thinking Ahead: Patents and New Enterprises," *Harvard Business Review*, September-October 1959 (paper first presented to the Boston Patent Law Association, 1959).
2. Werner Heisenberg, *Encounters with Einstein* (Princeton, NJ: Princeton University Press, 1983), p. 3.

1

THE HOTHOUSE EFFECT

Creativity pervades our every moment. We constantly improvise solutions to problems. We enjoy movies, books, songs, well-crafted objects, witty sayings, or the small creative touches that beautify or simplify our lives. Women and men caught in dull jobs all week prepare superb dinners for friends on the weekend, tell fantastic stories to their children, design clothes, play music, or construct an addition to their house. Sometimes people with similar gifts live in the same community, drawn together by an academic center or industrial enterprise, or the presence of a great teacher, and the region becomes known as a creative hub, such as Silicon Valley and Massachusetts's Route 128, or cities and regions known for their pottery, furniture, or music. Major cities blessed by both geography and history can become central creative forces on the global stage, as have New York, Paris, Rome, Vienna, and Amsterdam at various times during the past several hundred years.

Sometimes lightning strikes and a certain group or community seems to have it all happening at once. As the hub for a dazzling array of creative activities, it is recognized as extraordinary by both its contemporaries and the judgments of history. These hothouse groups, in which creativity flourishes wildly and magnificently, produce results that neither nature nor the usual round of human activity could ever anticipate. The hothouse effect requires a relatively rare confluence of forces to bloom, and their riot of activity generates a lot of heat. And while historical forces impel the hothouse effect forward, careful cultivation by hothouse members amplifies the effect. Any modern enterprise, however, can apply the experiences of these hothouses to increase creativity and heighten performance.

We will be visiting a variety of hothouses, both historical communities and modern companies, and will consider how and why they worked. We'll begin, however, by defining the hothouse, which must meet five criteria to be entered into our lists. These criteria *do not produce* a hothouse, they simply define it. The community that generates the hothouse effect can be identified by its ability to accomplish the following:

1. Sustain a high level of innovative creativity for a significant period of time.

2. Draw on the knowledge and innovations of the broader cultural zone to which it belongs.

3. Spawn geniuses whose achievements climax the work of many other practitioners at all levels of achievement, from the brilliant on down to the work-a-day purveyor of common goods.

4. Establish a new idiom, a new way of doing things that informs its creative products and establishes new standards, procedures, and principles in a variety of fields.

5. Achieve recognition from contemporaries and establish a lasting legacy to which future generations continually return and emulate.

A closer look at these five criteria will illuminate how the hothouse effect operates as well as how the term *creativity* will be used in this book:

1. *The hothouse effect applies to groups or communities that sustain a high level of innovative creativity for a significant period of time.* Innovative creativity refers to the production of objects (whether chairs, poems, or skyscrapers), systems (organizational, political, or philosophical), inventions (helicopters, baseball, or polyester), or behaviors (a new dance, medical treatment, or "secret of success") based on an idea that is either new or had not previously been applied to that purpose. Building a skyscraper that follows a fairly standard design is not—in and of itself—particularly creative from the standpoint of the history of architecture, despite the fact that every construction project requires innumerable acts of creativity, from the architect's plans to the solutions provided by carpenters, HVAC specialists, masons, crane operators, and other workers. But that is true for every structure, and however proud of the final product numerous contributors might be, from the perspective of high-impact creativity, the typical skyscraper doesn't rate.

   However, building a skyscraper with a daring new design, a new way to utilize space, or an innovative use of material raises our opinion of the project's creativity. Developing an entirely new form of architecture whose beauty makes people gasp and that requires new competencies in design, mathematics, engineering, and construction techniques transforms our mental, cultural, and physical environments. That is the level of creativity that marks the hothouse effect.

We might wonder whether a new weapon of destruction or a particularly eloquent con artist expresses a similar level of creativity. Certainly we've always had a soft spot for charming rogues precisely because we recognize the creativity behind their style and skill.

This question compels us to confront the roles of *intention, results,* and *values* in creative activity. By general agreement of most members of the human race, creativity is associated with an intention to improve things. This improvement may be a better mousetrap, a new riff improvised off an old song, a new design for workers' housing, a new use for plant-derived oil in the art of painting, or a creative use of live viruses to prevent disease. Creativity, although closely associated with innovation, is not the same thing. Like freedom or love, creativity is a term that embraces every aspect of our selves and our lives. Like freedom or love—but unlike happiness, sadness, or anger—creativity cannot be easily identified as a discrete cognitive event. We generally know when we're happy or sad, but how free is free? Is it love or just infatuation? Is the new hot painter a creative genius or just a self-dramatizing flash in the pan? I know when I'm angry or happy, but just how free any of us are has been debated continually ever since the notion of freedom was first conceived.

Creativity is a general condition with no clear psychological boundaries. Innovation, however, is more precise. It refers to a new product or process within a specified field, such as industry, art, medicine, or politics. The innovation must become *established* before it is a true innovation; that is, the field to which it applies must accept it as legitimate, as bringing *in* something new, or *nova. In-nova-*tion, however, relies on energies that we deem to be "creative."

Innovation, the fruit of creativity, requires verifiable results. People can attest to the innovation's impact on their lives, such as fewer mice in the house, pleasure in a musical performance, and so on. Without results, there are no lasting effects. While the great ninth-century Chinese poet Li Po wrote poems on leaves and floated them downstream, it is those poems he committed to paper that bore results and had a powerful impact on Chinese poetry and civilization, and twentieth-century American poetry as well.

Ascribing creativity to a product always involves value judgments. A person can twist some metal and wood together and call it a chair: It is new, he loves it so much he's called three friends to talk about how stupendous it is, and it has instantly transformed his life, opening a vista of creativity the fabricator had never before imagined. However, when the next person to sit in it receives a dozen splinters and winds up sprawled on the floor, the new innovative chair begins to undergo re-evaluation. The community, sooner or later (sooner in this case) renders its judgment based on certain values: This piece of junk is not a viable innovation, it doesn't make us feel better about sitting down, it's a threat to life and limb, and it exhibits no structural or aesthetic integrity. Like it or not, they tell the inventor, those are the values by which we decide whether a new innovation is worthwhile. The chair and the inventor's reputation are consigned not to the latest hip design store but to the trash heap of history.

Similarly, the *con* artist may be very eloquent, but his intention is utterly self-serving and generates no chain of response other than anger and the loss of goods or money. Generally, we value more highly activities that produce a ripple effect of appreciative feeling and creative activity. We tend to ascribe little value to activities that benefit one person to another's harm, especially when the beneficiary has tricked the other out of something for which the latter has worked. Because the con man's eloquence exhibits neither creative intention, viable results, nor much creation of value, we don't regard his creativity too highly.

We should also acknowledge that often society itself resists creativity. The artist or thinker may challenge long-standing beliefs or behavioral and political norms. An invention may threaten to throw many people out of work. An inventor or scientist may be so far ahead of his or her time that colleagues cannot accept this person's findings. Copernicus ensured that his description of the solar system was published in 1543 while he lay on his deathbed, probably to avoid the fate that later befell Giordano Bruno, who was burned at the stake in 1601 for teaching Copernicus's claim that the Earth goes around the Sun. Even today, science often yields to departmental politics in determining who receives grants, what research findings are published, and which innovative ideas receive a public hearing. In addition, every society has a certain collective view of creativity: whether it is important, whether it should be funded, whether human life without art is as dull as a steady diet of bread and water, and whether art should be a tame decorative pet of whoever funds it or an independent arena in which we explore the boundaries of consciousness and perception. Do we stop teaching evolution because some religious fundamentalists cannot distinguish between the open, public, *creative* procedures of science and their own private belief systems? A great deal goes into determining relative worth among competing creative visions.

The term *innovative creativity* may seem redundant, but it is intended to contrast with the *maintenance creativity* of cultures whose creative agenda is to nurture tradition. We cannot really ascribe maintenance creativity to Czar Ivan the Terrible, who so admired the newly built St. Basil's Cathedral in Moscow that he blinded its architect to prevent him from ever again building anything so beautiful anywhere else. A better example of maintenance creativity would be the many tribal cultures whose rituals were honed and polished over centuries, even millennia. Their goal was to sustain the conditions that generated new life and energy for the tribe on a predictable, periodic basis, thus enabling it to flourish. They were by no means surrendering to inertia and resignation. Rather, the experience of the landscape of their personal world as an *inscape,* to use the poet Gerard Manley Hopkins's term, and the deeply meditative appreciation for the rhythms of creation, represent an alternative version of creativity to the innovative version embodied in the restlessly seeking spirit of the hothouse effect.

2. *The hothouse effect draws on the knowledge and innovations of the broader culture to which it belongs.* The hothouse community intensifies and invigorates currents of thought and activity flowing across a broad geographical arena, transforming them into something rare and strange that has a stunning impact on contemporaries. Without the extraordinary culture of archaic Greece, there would have been no Athens. Bebop, perhaps jazz's definitive movement, owes its creation to African American thought, society, and literature; global musical traditions; the impact of World War II; the hothouse culture of New York City in the 1940s; the emergence of several gigantic talents from the vast pool of outstanding jazz practitioners; and the entire jazz tradition as well. But just as individual creativity rarely blossoms without stimulation from a network of other practitioners, the same holds true for a hothouse community. Venice, Milan, Genoa, Pisa, and Sienna may have had to defer to Florence in the areas of inventiveness and artistic genius, but Florence's creativity was inseparable from the creativity and mental and behavioral frame-

works of late medieval and early Renaissance Italy and Europe. It may be that some mysterious process leads regional systems to focus their energies on a single community to achieve breakthrough results, a notion to which we will later return.

3. *The hothouse spawns geniuses whose achievements climax the work of many other practitioners at all levels of achievement, from the brilliant on down to the work-a-day purveyor of common goods.* While we tend to view creativity as the fruit of one gifted person's inspiration and dedication, it does not happen in a social vacuum. Even among giants such as Leonardo da Vinci, William Shakespeare, Sir Isaac Newton, Pablo Picasso, and Albert Einstein, only Newton worked beyond the ken of a close-knit circle of practitioners. The same applies to contemporary figures, such as virtually all the masters of jazz and the self-described wizards of Silicon Valley and Boston's Route 128. Most of history's creative luminaries required a community of creators to fully express their gifts.

Solitude still serves as an important component in the creative process of these individuals. Sonny Rollins, the great jazz saxophonist, took a couple of years off from recording and performing to play alone on the Williamsburg Bridge between Brooklyn and Manhattan. Still, this solitude generally complements the richly interactive process of a creative community.

Genius gestates within a social cauldron where ideas and techniques are exchanged at a frenzied pace and subjected to exhaustive experimentation. Genius in the hothouse occupies the peak of a creative pyramid whose descending levels include brilliant practitioners whose achievement is just less than world-shaking, regional figures not quite distinctive or lucky enough to have global impact, local favorites, committed amateurs, and a supportive populace. The pyramid rests on the social structures that support and reinforce this vast effort. But without this swarm of activity, the odds soar against the emergence of the form-shattering Brunelleschis and Leonardos, denizens of the upper levels of creative activity. Unlike the message of the play and movie *Amadeus*, a band of Salieris increases the odds that a Mozart will emerge, and below the Salieris, a host of musicians and music teachers, and below them, countless aspiring young music students, and supporting them all, a society-wide consensus that the music is important.

My examples of genius, to this point, tend to the standard textbook examples such as Leonardo and Mozart. The past several decades have brought to light many talented, previously ignored figures belonging to groups disenfranchised politically and academically from pride of place in humanity's creative history. Women worldwide, Africans, Asians, and Latin Americans, and numerous members of smaller nations or ignored ethnic groups have, today, a greater opportunity to be discovered, if dead, or seen and heard if living. Sometimes these figures prove to be members of hothouses, at other times, not. Certainly the Harlem Renaissance of the 1920s–1940s was a hothouse, but does every studio, town, or region where artists or inventors congregate produce the hothouse effect?

It is not to our purpose to argue the fine points of whether a given cluster of creative people have or have not generated the hothouse effect. However, the hothouse designation rests as much on a group's historical and social impact as on the quality of its products. The fact that quality in large part determines a group's impact on history raises questions of evaluation and standards, but these questions also engender endless, often fruitless, debate. Suffice now to say that the communities that appear in this book meet all five hothouse criteria and have been validated as such by the countless judgments that history makes on the artifacts of civilization. Any exclusion is due either to my own judgment, a lack of data for evaluating a body of work's long-term impact, or simply the limitations of textual space or my own knowledge. For modern organizations, I have reduced history's judgments to whether the company had a lasting impact on its employees and customers, and whether it succeeded while adopting an uncommonly creative approach to the conduct of business.

4. *The hothouse creates a new idiom, a new way of doing things that informs its creative products and establishes new standards, procedures, and principles in a variety of fields.* The artists and architects of Florence invented unique approaches to depicting space and using materials in painting and construction. The Bauhaus artists and designers, the great painters of Paris, the trailblazers of modern physics, and American jazz musicians all demonstrate that outstanding creativity is not only a matter of new products but of an original framework and language that others can draw on to continue the creative work. Many communities have been creative without becoming hothouses. The hothouse effect transforms the underlying rules, roles, and structures governing productive activity. Realistically, of course, modern organizations concerned about the bottom line cannot simply replicate the disorder that often marked historical communities. However, cultivating the hothouse effect in a measured, strategic way can produce striking results.

5. *Hothouses are recognized as exceptional in their own time and establish a lasting legacy to which future generations continually return and emulate.* Hothouses fascinate and inspire entire societies from their inception. Those who live in them relish it while others "want to be a part of it." And others just envy it. Both contemporary and subsequent generations are inexorably drawn to the concentrated energy captured in the hothouse's masterpieces. Invariably, these products enter the bloodstream of other cultures and inspire the further development of those cultures. The art, buildings, technology, ideas, social and political arrangements, and beliefs produced by intensely creative groups define the physical and conceptual landscapes through which future creators travel and upon whose resources they draw.

Ancient Athens, for example, created forms of history, mathematics, democracy, political science, philosophy, drama, architecture, and sculpture that continue to shape our world today. Other societies possessed mathematics or a sense of history, and delved into the meaning of life and the universe. It was Athens, however, that fused these cultural domains into distinctive forms—buildings, literature, political innovations—that inspired an entire civilization and, indeed, provided the raw material from which that civilization sprang.

Two thousand years later, Athens's Golden Age and its achievements entranced Europe and played a crucial role in inspiring the Renaissance. And millions of travelers a year bear witness to the spell still cast by this time and place of old. We might say the same of Florence and Italy in general, of southern France or Paris, the designs and methods of the Bauhaus, and jazz's endless ability to fascinate. Medieval Andalusia, whose hothouse effect flourished in southern Spain for centuries, was called "the ornament of the world" by a noted contemporary.[1] Andalusia's sparkling cities and cultural brilliance achieved fame throughout Europe. People seem to recognize a creative golden age almost immediately and, as poet Lord Byron wrote of the Greek isles, "Eternal sunlight gilds them yet."

NOTE

1. María Rosa Menocal, *The Ornament of the World* (Boston: Little, Brown and Company, 2002), p. 32.

2

THE FOUR DIMENSIONS OF THE HOTHOUSE EFFECT

The hothouse effect, whether blooming forth in an ancient city-state or modern corporation, in a well-organized institute or among informally linked friends, is always the product of a remarkably similar set of causal factors. Some of these factors are developmental, appearing as accidents of history that seem to favor one group over another. Others are technique-driven, comprising the methods that hothouse members employ to cultivate, amplify, and sustain their creativity. We will examine thirty-six of these factors and their role in stimulating the hothouse effect in both historical communities and contemporary business organizations. In so doing, we will also learn how to apply them to stimulate and enrich the creative environment within any group.

The factors are divided into four theme-based groups, or "dimensions": values/mission, ideas/exchange, perception/learning, and social/play. Each dimension contains two descriptive terms. The first term focuses on internal structure and quality, the second on actualization and application. We use the four dimensions in the "Creative" Hothouse Assessment Instrument Tablet (CHAI-T), which enables us to establish a vocabulary and structure for assessing the role of creativity within an organization.

For the sake of reference, the thirty-six factors are listed here, each under their respective dimensions. More detailed explanations and numerous examples of the factors are presented throughout the book.

Values/Mission

1. Values drive organizational goals, strategies, and operations. Values are evident, both explicitly and implicitly, throughout the work environment, and are "lived" rather than imposed.

14

2. The entire community, including leaders, strongly supports and encourages creative expression by all its members.

3. Members are driven by an intrinsic faith that their work is vital to society's well-being and meaningful for how people live their lives.

4. The community conducts in-depth research into the disciplines vital to its work.

5. Members continually challenge and recreate the fundamental assumptions of the disciplines within which they work.

6. The company's mission aspires to universal, even cosmic, application.

7. Firm, safe grievance procedures and protocols allow any employee to challenge actions that seem to them unjust or in violation of the organization's stated values.

Ideas/Exchange

8. Interpersonal conflicts are handled skillfully and serve as opportunities for organizational development.

9. The community provides recognition and respect for thinkers and the products of thought.

10. Intellectual exchange plays an important role in the evolution of group culture.

11. Group members work closely with experts across disciplines and departments, and utilize other fields of knowledge when seeking solutions.

12. Ideas circulate hydraulically throughout the organization.

13. Peripheral or lower-level functions and operations are implanted within the core or upper level of the community.

14. Mastery is accorded the highest respect.

15. Mentorship relationships are cultivated throughout the organization.

16. Hubs of creative activity proliferate rapidly.

17. People are comfortable with enigma and contradiction, and tend to "work" both poles of a dichotomy rather than seeking resolution for its own sake.

18. The organization continually analyzes the impact of core technologies on all aspects of operations, development, and strategy.

19. Innovative educational formats evolve as a response to the exceptional concentration of content and activity in the community.

Perception/Learning

20. Each person is respected as a learner, producer, and potential visionary, and the organization actively promotes education for all its members.

21. Clear, simple, flexible, and effective problem-solving algorithms are taught to and used by all members of the organization.

22. People learn and use a variety of sensory and body-centered techniques to stimulate their creativity at work.

23. Analytic and experiential inquiry into fundamental principles of perception and learning play an important part in the work of the group.

24. Members learn by immersing themselves in surroundings saturated with information and materials.

25. The community has experienced sudden and rapid engagement with a much larger and more complex meta-system early in the hothouse cycle.

26. Members utilize unorthodox structures of thought: metaphor, models, meta-cognitive thinking, meditation, thought experiments, and more.

27. Time is perceived as a palpable dimension and is harvested for its creative energy.

28. The group is open to broad external currents in art, politics, and society.

Social/Play

29. A highly charged vocabulary emerges to describe the group's distinctive creative processes.

30. A strong business model provides the resources and structure that support creative activity.

31. The community continually produces highly effective leaders.

32. Crisis draws the community together and releases hidden reserves of creative energy.

33. Playing with ideas and possibilities pervades many group processes.

34. Social occasions are planned imaginatively and creatively and promote social rapport.

35. The community creates beauty in one form or another.

36. The culture of the organization discourages assertions of power based on an individual's position within the hierarchy.

3

THE FIRST DIMENSION: VALUES/MISSION

The first of the four dimensions of activity that define the hothouse effect is called Values/Mission. The word *values* refers to the qualities that guide social intercourse among human beings. The members of any group that hope to remain cohesive must share a set of values, or a value system. The larger the group, the more room there is for members' values to vary, but beneath it all a shared worldview based on certain fundamental shared values is the central bond of any community. This value system informs, motivates, and inspires its adherents and shapes the objectives they decide to pursue as a group, company, community, or society. Values also deeply influence the *way* a group performs coordinated actions, whether it is honest or cunning, intent on conquest or devoted to the pursuit of détente, willing to cut ethical corners or adhering to a self-imposed standard of integrity. The values-based objectives and standards of behavior are often defined as the group's mission. A mission derives its direction and force from a group's values; any mission that does not actualize a community's values will fail no matter how articulate the mission statement adorning the organizational literature.

The values of any organization have four primary sources:

1. Leadership and values it explicitly promotes
2. Leadership and values it implicitly models
3. Mix of values held by all individuals, whether they clash, agree, or represent a compromise among diverse views

4. Complex interface of group members with their work and work environment

This last factor includes legacy systems embedded in the industry and organizational history, the field's required competencies, and the socioeconomic environment. The messages from these four sources may or may not be consistent with one another. A new manager's values may clash with those of his or her predecessor, company leadership, workers, society at large, or any of the above. Leadership may espouse one set of values while acting in direct contradiction to them, or it may "walk the talk." People with different backgrounds and ethical models can work together as long as certain core values are held in common. Conversely, people born and bred in the same town can be riven with conflict over an issue—such as unionization or affirmative action—that catalyzes two opposed sets of values. Values can be a fuzzy notion, but we instinctively recognize people in synch with our own values and are naturally drawn to them.

The following seven factors describe the framework of Values/Mission shared by all creative hothouses and critical to launching the hothouse effect:

1. Values drive organizational goals, strategies, and operations. Values are evident, both explicitly and implicitly, throughout the work environment, and are "lived" rather than imposed.

2. The entire community, including leaders, strongly supports and encourages creative expression by all members.

3. Members are driven by an intrinsic faith that their work is vital to society's well-being and meaningful for how people live their lives.

4. The community conducts in-depth research into the disciplines vital to its work.

5. Members continually challenge and recreate the fundamental assumptions of the disciplines within which they work.

6. The company's mission aspires to universal, even cosmic, application.

7. Firm, safe grievance procedures and protocols allow any employee to challenge actions that seem to be unjust or in violation of the organization's stated values.

1 . VALUES

Values summarize core cultural expectations and behaviors. Behavioral tendencies do not become values until they have been articulated and understood. Communities may clarify values and facilitate collective access to them by putting them into written forms such as legal codes, the Ten Commandments, the Bill of Rights, or corporate codes of ethics.

Values do not exist outside ourselves as moral meters that we reference periodically—that is, "Are we living up to our values? Are we fulfilling our mission?" Mentally, emotionally, and even physically, values are encoded into the core of our being. They emerge out of patterns of behavior impressed upon us from infancy by primary environmental stimuli such as love, discipline, kindness, choice, disregard, cruelty, or respect.

The hothouse's values inform the daily activities of its members. That doesn't mean that everyone believes the same things or pursues the same goals. It involves a consistent view of the general purposes of the group and the value of each individual as a creative agent. Thus, despite the Bauhaus's variety of arts, crafts, goals, and methods, everyone there understood the institute's greater mission. Similarly, most jazz musicians live the historical legacy embedded in the music. As saxophonist James Carter's album title says, jazz musicians are constantly "conversin' with the elders,"[1] respect for the past that goes beyond the musical tradition; it draws upon values stemming from black musicians reclaiming their history and asserting expressive freedom. This moral force enters into the slipstream of the music and is transmitted to whoever plays it, whether Japanese, Russian, French, white American, or Latin. Thus, values inform our work, but they also emerge out of the work itself, the actions of countless practitioners who have contributed to the integrity of a given discipline. The term *discipline* refers to a field of practice or study; it also refers to the quality required to succeed at it. At the same time, values require discipline, for one tends to violate one's values whenever appetite overcomes discipline. The discipline in the sense of a craft or profession and the values that one brings to that discipline are inseparable, virtually the same entity. In short, values may inform our work, but our work both strengthens and extends the scope of our values.

The hothouse effect only occurs in a community or organization in which virtually all members are committed to a broad set of values and in which the values are implicitly reinforced through the actions of the group members and explicitly reinforced by the leadership. These values reflect qualities such as creativity, openness to ideas, integrity, mutual respect among all members, honesty, dedication, and tolerance. When these values help to shape company objectives, strategic planning, organizational development, operations, behavior within the broader community, and commitment of its personnel, employees are far more likely to pursue their work with passion and to respect their discipline sufficiently to want to pursue the creative implications of their work.

In the descriptions of all the hothouses we will visit in this book, the central role of values will be evident. Yet, it can be difficult to reinforce values without seeming to impose heavy-handed restrictions on how people are supposed to think and create. After all, some people work better alone. Some are gruff and irascible when absorbed in their work. Many do not need to hear about values; they are content to live them every day. And people resent it when a certain set of values is pushed upon them.

Values, however, are not the same as behavior. Having strong, positive values does not mean that one is a nice person, a team player, or lives up to any other superficial expectation. And certainly many creative geniuses had personal lives that were such a shambles as to disabuse us of the notion that creativity always grants a person wisdom and self-esteem. So neither strong, good values—such as honesty or tolerance—nor creativity guarantee the sociability of an individual. They are not, however, completely useless.

Values unite disparate individuals into, if not always a team, a well-functioning community. They generate a common commitment and common language that enable large groups of people to act in a coordinated manner toward the fulfillment of complex goals. Shared values let us accept the idiosyncrasies and even unpleasantness of others because we know that underneath the social persona lie a shared purpose and a shared worldview more binding and important to fulfilling one's work than whether or not the two of us like one another.

Given the general nature and positive tenor of the values that trigger the hothouse effect, it does not require a master of tact to reinforce those values in the workplace. Address values in interviews and employee orientations; it is important that people know how the organization conducts business. Dramatic restorative gestures such as bringing back employees who were laid off in overly zealous downsizing efforts, cutting costs through creative initiatives instead of cutting jobs, restoring lost benefits, and giving up executive perks strongly affirm company values and inspire loyalty.

Clearly explain what you want from the managers and other employees you oversee. Gather key managers together to find their views of creativity. What does the term *creativity* mean in terms of procedure and practice? What's the payoff? What steps will it take to get there? How can broad-based organizational initiatives support creativity? If your managers have given little thought to creativity, restate the problem differently: "How do we increase productivity without burning people out and adding to costs? How can we use technology more effectively?" These questions transition easily into more general issues of creativity.

Managers can receive training on how to conduct similar activities with their own people, a process that can continue on down the line. The leader mandating the program should ensure that the message doesn't become diluted or turn into something strange. Look for small victories first. Let people experience and observe improvements that result from reinforcing values and procedures conducive to creativity. And do not put all your eggs in this basket. The shift toward a more creative orientation need not be presented as the launching of a new era. If it works, people will discuss it and become pumped up for the next stage. Values remain vital when continually reinforced and actualized in the performance of everyday tasks, as evidenced by every hothouse we will visit.

#2. SUPPORTS CREATIVITY

A strong value system inspires dedication to one's work, which in turn fosters the core values in an industry or organization. This dedication and passion for the work often results in broad-based community support for creative initiatives. In musing over fifteenth-century Florence's creative dynamism, Mihaly Csikszentmihalyi notes the engagement of the city's banking and commercial community in deciding major artistic commissions. Brunelleschi's plan for the *duomo* that completed Florence's cathedral, and Lorenzo Ghiberti's commission to design and cast the great bronze doors of the Baptistery right next to the Cathedral, were both solicited and approved by committees of leading businessmen (see Exhibit 1). In fact, even before considering any plans for the Baptistery doors, the leaders of the wool guild, who were most prominent on the Baptistery committee, "wrote to some of the most eminent philosophers, writers, and churchmen in Europe to request their opinion of which scenes from the Bible should be included in the panels, and how they should be represented."[2] The entire approach exhibited the greatest respect not only for the subject matter but for the artistic process as well. The input of Europe's greatest think-ers elevated the quality and vision of the design before the first plans were even considered. The committee solicited drawings from competing artists and selected the five best designs, including those of Ghiberti and Brunel-leschi. The five finalists then had to create bronze mock-ups that depicted the sacrifice of Isaac. In 1402, the committee chose Ghiberti, which seri-ously irritated Brunelleschi, but Florentine genius was never going to be a one-man show.

The consistency, focus, and refinement of the Florentines' aesthetic sensibilities produced felicitous results. One doubts that a similar procedure would yield equal results today. But the broader lesson holds: Florence made a conscious decision to become a beautiful city. Already wealthy, with some of Europe's leading merchant houses, factories, and banks, Flor-ence extended its influence by supporting the creative efforts of its artists, thinkers, builders, and scientists. The city of Dante, Giotto, Brunelleschi, Leonardo, Botticelli, Macchiavelli, Michelangelo, Galileo, and the Medici family never blinked in its commitment to creativity. Incidentally, this out-pouring of creativity generated significant income and industry for the city via the building programs, artistic commissions, technical advances, and visitors who came to view its many wonders.

That decision to be creative, whether made in a spirit of calculation of investment and return or simply for a delight in beauty and invention, looms over every creative person. Many artists and inventors struggle with their decision on many levels. They hear the voice of a disparaging parent as they paint in the studio, or are haunted by images of themselves as a dancing monkey even after a successful performance onstage. After his hundredth failure, an inventor may wonder if he is in fact mad to pursue seeming impossibilities. Certainly, there are those who never doubt them-selves, but even those lucky few still had to decide to take the crucial steps. At some point, Louis Armstrong had to leave New Orleans for Chicago; he knew it, but was still intimidated by the decision. Duke Ellington headed north for New York, suave and confident even at a young age, but even the Duke faced the momentous decision to pursue his gift. Once the decision is made, one finds that creativity generates its own uncanny en-ergy. As a quote often attributed to the great German multifaceted genius Johann Wolfgang von Goethe states, "Until one is committed there is hesi-tancy, the chance to draw back; ineffectiveness. . . . The moment one definitely commits oneself, then Providence moves too. All sorts of things occur to help one that would never otherwise have occurred. . . . Boldness has genius, power, and magic in it."[3]

"Fate favors the bold," it has been said, and the decision to create is bold and risky. This is as true for organizations as it is for individuals. Public support for the arts in the United States, for instance, can be a hard sell, although conditions vary from city to city. Certainly in Italy, as music historian Henry Láng observes,

> Pride in artistic achievements during the era of the Renaissance surpassed even martial pride. Municipalities as well as tyrants and rulers were constantly petitioned by the citizenry for all kinds of artistic projects. . . . The great cities were not alone in constantly endeavoring to enrich their Artistic Treasures . . . many others sought to rival the great centers in their own way.[4]

This broad-based commitment—perhaps *exhilaration* would be a better term—enriched the creative environment of the entire region. Yet even within this broader Italian hothouse zone, Florence emerged in a distinctive position much as Leonardo, within Florence, was recognized as the preeminent genius. And as was the case for Leonardo, who developed amidst like-minded practitioners of uncommon brilliance, Florence soared to its heights in part because the Italian Renaissance had already achieved a high level of creativity by 1400. The same holds for Athens in regard to the rest of Greece. When Florence decided to become beautiful, it activated all its latent powers. As Goethe implied, the decision to be creative has the force of a thunderbolt that animates and awakens unforeseen abilities. For the modern business enterprise, the same conditions apply.

#3. VITAL IMPACT

Strong values often drive one to attempt to make an impact on the world, in part because values by definition demand that we view situations from perspectives other than our own self-interest. The confidence—or faith—that one's work is important to others, that it transcends narrowly focused business objectives, is another factor that inspires creativity because of the inspiration we naturally feel when contributing to the greater good.

Participants in the hothouse effect truly believe they will change the world and they channel all available energies and resources into this task. In contrast, most organizations provide only limited resources and commitment when deciding to "give back to the community" or "be a responsible corporate citizen." These efforts automatically raise a divide between business and values, even with the best of intentions. In the hothouse, social impact is inseparable from the mission and tasks that members practice every day.

At the Rowland Institute in Cambridge, Massachusetts, founded by Dr. Edwin Land in 1980, scientists were thrilled to pursue science for science's sake, even as their work produced marketable technologies. This fusion, difficult to accomplish, attests to Land's rare skills as scientist and manager. He established the vision of science for science's sake by reinforcing the message in conversations and by modeling it himself, carrying out experiments on color and light that had no immediate practical application. Yet he also harnessed this energy by challenging his scientists to "do something important," suggesting industrial problems for them to solve and checking in to keep them on track. Polaroid under Land was a leader in benefits, salaries, and profit-sharing programs that provided substantial additional income to employees. Behind this was a more general sense of responsibility. Jim Foley, a scientist who worked closely with Land, recounts that his employer's philosophy was, "You owe it to those people [the employees] to make the best inventions possible, to do the best work, so they can keep their jobs. There's a certain level of worker that deserves support because they don't have a safety net." Ultimately, we might suggest that Land viewed all corporations as service organizations that should be guided by an intrinsic belief that their work must benefit all stakeholders, not just executives or shareholders.

This belief can be independent of the job actually performed by the company, that is, the product itself may not provide a vital social good. Whether framing pictures, providing software solutions, or designing chairs, a company's potential social impact resides in its entire range of operations: for example, the well-being of employees and customers, quality products, or community goodwill. Some of the work done under Edwin Land's aegis had direct social impact, such as Foley's cancer research (which is covered later in Chapter 15), but it is not the Instamatic Camera per se that made Land such a social visionary. Rather, his impact resided in the treatment of thousands of employees, his advocacy for the invention process and patent protection, many philanthropies, and advancement of the mission of science on many fronts. His companies' chemical and photonic processes contributed to the social good because of their widespread application to countless products.

This commitment translates directly into better performance at work. Every businessperson I spoke with became passionate when describing the motivation, rapport, and dedication of employees who felt invested in both the company and its larger mission. Terry Beard, founder of a chain of framing stores in Portland, Oregon, saw it translate directly into outstanding customer service, while the atmosphere at Sequent Computers Corporation, which we'll describe in Chapter 5, is attested to by the xSequent list serve, which has more than one thousand members years after the company was sold. Participants on the list stay in touch, according to Mike Jahnke, a former Sequent manager, because of the intense loyalty they feel to the Sequent culture and the strong bonds the culture inspired among them.

#4. RESEARCH

As we've seen, the commitment to the fields, or disciplines, upon which one's organization is built, is a major source of organizational values. The deeper one seeks to understand, utilize, and expand the depth and richness of a discipline, the more one reinforces values based on commitment, integrity, imagination, hard work, collaboration, and creativity. This commitment to a field goes even deeper, for it leads one to ratify implicitly the legacy represented by the discipline, industry, or organization, and the continuity of effort and desire that drive a discipline forward. Whether the goal is to "search" or research, the quest for new understanding and knowledge is central to the emergence of the hothouse effect.

Florence had its workshops. In Paris, the cafés, salons, and soirées arose out of the city's dynamic social life. The taverns, parties, delicatessens, and coffeehouses of New York City served the same purpose throughout the twentieth century. And while we take for granted that scientists need laboratories, Edwin Land designed his labs carefully by keeping the needs of his scientists in mind. Loop Design Centre, a multidisciplinary design firm in Bologna, Italy, reconceived its headquarters as a place where research, production, exhibition, marketing, and education all support one another, not only strategically but spatially as well. At Sequent, a company whose chief executive officer (CEO) encouraged creativity at every level, the cafeteria served for weekly gatherings of the entire staff, while Beard Framing Shops, under the auspices of founder Terry Beard, held Friday afternoon salons in which ideas of all sorts were raised for consideration. Jazz had its Minton's Playhouse in Harlem and a host of performance venues. Every business, community, or organization needs space dedicated to inquiry aimed at dramatically transforming the creative fields in which it is active.

5. CHALLENGING ASSUMPTIONS

Providing these spaces is only half the battle. Highly creative groups constantly push against the accepted wisdom of their industry or discipline, and not just to find solutions. The desire to penetrate the secrets of core processes reveals a passionate drive for discovery and creation. While this characterizes the hothouse, it also triggers the hothouse effect by drawing a company or community's practitioners deep into the formative processes that govern a particular field. The insights and access to fundamental principles and processes that deep research entails galvanize further creative activity until the group reaches the critical threshold of the hothouse effect.

Loop Design Centre of Bologna, Italy, researches new materials and approaches to mosaics, architecture, lighting, and corporate communications, but Loop's designers might also get their inspiration from a medieval bell tower or a swatch of color in a Bolognese fabric shop. To facilitate exploration of both the legacy systems of the past and innovative ideas about the future, Loop's laboratories, theater, and multipurpose rooms provide sites where ideas can be tested and products displayed. Dr. Edwin Land's fascination with light and color provided the foundation for Polaroid Corporation, while the Boston-area research and manufacturing firm Foster-Miller relies on the creative verve and fascination with materials that motivates its scientists and engineers. Artists like Leonardo da Vinci and Botticelli not only painted the masterpieces of their era but also studied the mathematics of perspective; experimented with oils, pigments, and adhesives; studied Platonic philosophy; became experts on the effects of light; and absorbed knowledge wholesale from the scholars, intellectuals, and artists who crowded into their city. The workshop of their mentor, Verrocchio, was as much laboratory as art studio. Jazz developed because its leaders always pushed against the most entrenched assumptions of their music: the structure of harmonics, the blend of instruments in a band, the dependence on chords, and the nature of improvisation itself. This, too, depended on research in clubs after hours, at a band member's apartment and in recording studios, and by listening to recordings and studying texts on music theory. Creativity requires research; most creative work is done as a response to other work of like quality within a given field. Inventors examine old patents, painters look at what other painters are producing, and writers study the models that they hope to equal or transcend. They are constantly learning techniques, incorporating ideas into their own work, or rejecting and looking to surpass them.

Such an approach in business would shift training toward a more educational model in which a task orientation yields to inquiry into the broader contexts in which the task is embedded. For example, sales training is already based on a frame-by-frame analysis of the dozens of stages of any given sales interaction, informed by the fields of psychology and even animal behavior. But the sales trainee is only getting the final results of that knowledge, and the purpose of the training is to improve his or her ability to persuade or manipulate the customer. This may suffice for many businesses, but an alternative route could enrich employee development while improving selling techniques and customer relations. Teach trainees about animal and human behavioral psychology, not in the form of glib summaries of questionable research ("Psychologists have found that most people . . .") but in the form of substantive insight into the following:

- The social "meaning" of the sales interaction
- Theories regarding the cross-cultural dynamics of space
- The difference between building rapport and manipulation
- The fascinating choreography of human—and animal—interaction and how it influences the decision to buy
- The salesperson's roles as company representative and community member

Some might object that this type of program could cramp the style of the super-salesperson. However, this is unlikely to occur because that kind of talent can't be sidetracked by knowledge and, as Bill Seidman of Cerebyte, Inc., points out, top performers are expert at factoring into their behavior insights and information of which others are barely cognizant. Is this type of educational approach an example of overkill, a waste of time and money? Will it pay off with increased sales? It may well pay off, but the real benefit comes from salespersons' being so aware of the full breadth of the sales dynamic, which will tend to generate dramatic improvements in learning and performance and unexpected insights. Meanwhile, the outcomes of the usual baseline training are utterly predictable—the good get better or already know the drill, while the training doesn't dent entrenched mediocrity.

6. COSMIC NATURE

The hothouse effect benefits from a group belief in the strong connection between its work and values of a universal, even cosmic, nature. Some members may even assert that their work sustains cosmic harmony and balance. Such beliefs *may* not be taken literally, serving instead as metaphors that propel people to higher levels of creativity. Few composers believe that the galaxy will behave any differently if they write a symphony of celestial quality. What might happen, however, is that the creative act transforms the composer's psyche so that he or she and those who hear the work feel more balanced or in tune with life. This function has always been attributed to art and architecture, whether (according to our assumptions) the twenty-thousand-year-old paintings on the cave walls of Lascaux or the elaborately planned cities such as Angkor Wat in Cambodia, which replicated its builders' vision of cosmic harmony. But we can push this argument: Without art, science, design, mathematics, philosophy, and similar endeavors, human consciousness would have remained bound to the caves. If life on Earth ever reaches out to the stars, or if we ever attract visitors drawn by our civilization ("What are those humans up to down there?"), it will be our creativity that will have changed the universe. Let's not sell it short.

The Bauhaus mission was to transform the way people lived in the modern world. From 1919 to 1933, this German-based design institute transformed the design of practically everything from skyscrapers to teapots. Several of the most prominent Bauhaus masters held a spiritual view of their art and their hopes for what the Bauhaus could accomplish. Consider how the great Russian painter and Bauhaus "master" Wassily Kandinsky encapsulates in the following statement hothouse themes regarding the unity of opposites, the cosmic implications of the work, and even a challenge to accepted norms of space and time:

> You mention the circle, and I agree with your definition. It is a link with the cosmic. But I use it above all formally. . . . The circle is the synthesis of the greatest oppositions. It combines the concentric and the excentric [sic] in a single form, and in equilibrium. . . . It points most clearly to the fourth dimension.[5]

As art historian Roger Lipsey comments, Kandinsky balances the "'soft' intuitive search" with a "'hard' empiricism."[6] Kandinsky was another great artist who balanced artistic intuition with scientific experimentalism, just as so many scientists balance the logic of experiment with artistic flair or subjective intuition.

This exalted view of the Bauhaus mission held true to the Bauhaus's roots in craft tradition. Craft masters throughout the world have always imbued their products with magical qualities: the smoothly finished pipe, rising loaf of bread, cathedral tower, well-honed spear, maiden's wedding dress, shaman's drum—all contain the magic of creation. This appreciation for the miracle of functional beauty is now largely reserved for works of nonfunctional museum-bound art. Picasso, Van Gogh, and Michelangelo are among the more prominent artists whose lives and work have been accorded quasi-divine or magical status.

This link between universal truth and the material product is noted by Uwe Westphal in his history of the Bauhaus: "So in the photography workshop, too, we find the general Bauhaus desire to arrive at statements that would be universally valid and comprehensible to all. And, as Johannes Itten stressed, this was only possible by revealing the true nature of things."[7] The art, inventions, and ideas produced by the hothouse effect serve as highly crafted, high-resolution cognitive tools that encourage audiences and users to perceive reality more clearly and intensely. Many artists would deny any such function for their work, but it is hard to find in the annals of art or science anyone who didn't care if their work found an audience. Even as antisocial a man as Isaac Newton was finally provoked to publish his work years after much of it was conducted when his friend Edmond Halley, famous for discovering the comet that bears his name, strongly urged Newton to publish his discoveries lest others receive credit for them. In eighteen months, Newton wrote the *Principia Mathematica,* probably the most important scientific work of all time.[8] Somewhere that desire to have an impact on the world manifests in the creative act; without it, one wonders whether creative fires have a chance of igniting at all.

Passionate belief in the value of one's work begins with an experience of the power that lies at the heart of creation. The value and impact of art stem from this source. A decorative print doesn't compel us the way a Matisse or Picasso does because the paintings communicate a profound grasp of the elements that define our reality: space, time, light, color, rhythm, shade, drama, balance, composition, relationship, paradox, and technique (the actualization of keen perception). Art may be commercialized, sanitized, trivialized, or politicized, but it remains ever true to itself nonetheless.

Athens exemplifies a community that felt itself cosmically inspired after defeating the Persian Empire in 490 B.C.E. and then again in 480–479, the latter in alliance with other Greek city-states. Victory legitimized its democracy and embodied the triumph of freedom over tyranny, law over violence, reason over pride, and light over dark. This idea entered all of Athens's creative work, most stunningly, perhaps, on the Parthenon, Athena's temple on the Acropolis. Each of the building's four sides contained sculptural panels called metopes depicting scenes from four conflicts in which light or good triumphs over darkness or evil. A sculptural frieze that followed the upper perimeter of the temple's outside walls depicted the Panathenaic procession, a festival in which all community members paraded through the city and up to the Acropolis. The sculptures stated Athens's mission as *the* city-state that overcame the forces of darkness and drew its strength from its democracy. Law was the gift of reason and clarity, and wisdom was no abstract matter, but enabled Athens to defend itself against unjust violence.

This "cosmic connection" can be profoundly disruptive in an organizational setting if used to promote a particular religion or ideology. Its strength lies in its secular nature, its deep roots in the work itself. The more closely we engage the principles and core ideas of a discipline, the closer we come to the sources of insight and creativity embedded in the materials, formulas, history, theory, or product itself. This perspective is an extension of Factors #4 (in-depth research) and #5 (recreating essential assumptions of the discipline); the deeper one goes into a discipline, the more one is likely to tap into this profound source of inspiration.

A few examples will clarify how this sense of cosmic or universal application might surface within a business organization:

- The programmer, software developer, or chip designer who has a seemingly mystical sense of the mathematical elegance of her work. Whether she transmits this idea explicitly or whether it's simply implicit in her work, her vision will inform and inspire.

- The teacher who truly believes that what he teaches is necessary for the well-being of his students and the society to which they belong.

- The manager who views the business environment as a great testing ground and sees it as her duty to teach her people that the lessons of business are the lessons of life.

- A close friend of mine who, when working as a waiter, delighted in presenting food to his customers as if it were a sacred feast, the most important meal of their lives. This feeling came from his generous view of people and his great appreciation for food, but also maintained itself through subsequent endeavors, with significant professional success.

■ The designer whose work derives its power from understanding the history and principles of design and his view that they reflect cosmic principles of harmony and balance; one thinks of the work of Edward Tufte, the world's leading expert on the presentation of data in visual form,[9] or Roger Black, the pioneering Web designer.[10]

■ The finance person for whom numbers have an almost mystical quality and for whom balanced books possess a beauty and elegance of structure equal to that of a well-designed bridge, or the lawyer with a similar sensibility about the deep-rooted structures of the law.

#7. GRIEVANCE PROCEDURES

Grievance procedures may seem to be a pedestrian factor for generating exceptional levels of creativity, but at their best they represent the last internal mechanism for upholding the values of an enterprise. Our entire legal system is one vast grievance procedure, and the development of law is in large part a matter of extending the recourse available for aggrieved parties who have been wronged or are involved in a dispute.

Values mean nothing if *anyone*, whatever their position, is denied the support of law or customary rules. Values are equally meaningless if top people are above the law, the lesson taught to the Athenians by their first great leader, Solon. Grievance committees, much like juries, should include employees from every level of the organization; they cannot be perceived as a management tool and still be effective. In an organization, the ability to bring a grievance is exactly parallel with the recourse to a circuit court, so critical to Athens's organizational development, or the right to counsel guaranteed by United States law. Without it, values seem hollow and a cause for cynicism. One of the signal hothouse-related events in European history, the development of the modern university in the thirteenth century, was inspired in large part by the need to regulate property, wealth, and behavior in an increasingly complex society. As organizations grow in complexity, they cannot leave the adjudication of conflicts over *values*—which every grievance or legal case is—to the same informal procedures that prevailed when the company was small or under the guidance of one person or one small group.

NOTES

1. James Carter, *Conversin' with the Elders* (New York: Atlantic Recording Company, 1996).
2. Mihalyi Csikszentmihalyi, *Creativity: Flow and the Psychology of Discovery and Invention* (New York: Harper Collins, 1996), p. 35.
3. W.H. Murray, *The Scottish Himalaya Expedition, 1951,* very loosely translated from Goethe, *Faust,* lines 214–230. http://www.goethesociety.org/pages/quotescom.html, a Web page of The Goethe Society of North America, contains the full explanation of the quote's origins.
4. Paul Henry Láng, *Music in Western Civilization* (New York: W.W. Norton and Co., 1941), p. 307.
5. Roger Lipsey, *An Art of Our Own: The Spiritual in Twentieth Century Art* (Boston: Shambhala Publications, 1988), p. 211.
6. Ibid.
7. Uwe Westphal, *The Bauhaus,* translated by John Harrison (New York: W.H. Smith Publishers, Inc., 1991), p. 102.
8. W.E.K. Middleton, *The Scientific Revolution* (Cambridge, MA: Schenkman Publishing Co., 1963), p. 77.
9. Edward R. Tufte, *The Visual Display of Quantitative Information* (Cheshire, CT: Graphics Press, 1983).
10. Roger Black, with Sean Elder, *Web Sites That Work* (San Jose, CA: Adobe Press, 1997).

4

ATHENS: SHOWING THE WAY

Around 600 B.C.E., the city of Athens was a cultural backwater, riven by conflict, with free farmers falling into debt and being sold into slavery, and the economy sluggish at best. At this time, other Greek city-states flourished culturally and economically. Yet within a century—not a long time given the much slower pace of ancient society—Athens was a major power in all regards and poised to embark upon a creative endeavor that would literally transform the world. Our ideas of what constitutes history, mathematics, democracy, drama, political thought, ethics, design, logical and analytic thought, sculpture, architecture, and poetry and prose styles all comes through Greece and, to a large extent, Athens. The philosophy of Plato and his followers profoundly influenced Christianity and hence Western history, and in different ways, powerfully informed Arab civilization as well in ways that had a reciprocal effect on Europe at the end of the medieval era.

In this chapter, we will examine the *cultural preparation* that Athens underwent in the sixth century B.C.E. that led to its world-changing golden age of creativity in the following century, focusing on three prominent leaders who exemplify brilliant management. The section on each leader is followed by a fictional account of a modern corporation that translates the Athenian hothouse experience into business terms. In effect, Athens is a model for an organization that made a tremendous turnaround from a condition of total disarray to extraordinary and world-changing success. Let's see how they did it.

SOLON THE MEDIATOR

Enter one of the Seven Wise Men of ancient Greece. These were actual men so revered that their contemporaries anointed them with that impressive title, although other groups of Seven Wise Men dot the ancient landscape. The Athenian wise man was named Solon, an aristocrat and probably a merchant, who apparently was respected by people of all types and class in Athens and its surrounding region of Attica. The highlight of his career as wise man came around 594 B.C.E. when the Athenians, realizing their society was on the verge of civil war, asked Solon to negotiate a compromise among the various feuding groups.

So what did Solon do in this daunting turnaround situation? First, he abolished all debts. This meant that farmers, the majority of Athenians— those who lived throughout the region of Attica of which Athens was the capital—could no longer be sold into slavery once they went bankrupt. Nor could their farms any longer be seized for debt or a portion of their harvest given to the wealthy. These steps were taken to restore balance to a ship of state listing heavily to port. That Solon, an aristocrat, implemented debt reform shows that others of his class were disturbed at the inequities in the system. It also indicates that the impoverished classes were fed up and ready to take action.

Solon realized, as do all good leaders, that a grand restorative flourish would help secure his mission. He found one that also had solid practical results. Using funds from the state treasury, Solon purchased back those farmers who already had been sold into slavery, thus restoring able-bodied citizen-soldiers to Athens and gaining the everlasting love and trust of most Athenians. He also instituted moderate judicial reforms that gave all citizens some recourse against the arbitrary use of power, protections critical to the success of his reforms.

Solon laid the groundwork for the future of democracy in Athens, although he probably had no such thought in mind. He changed the basic political criterion for classifying citizens from the standard of *birth* (nobles, farmers, landless poor) to four new classes based on *wealth*, thus granting successful farmers, merchants, and craftsmen an upward mobility they lacked under the criterion of birth. He established a system of checks and balances, with the Areopagus Law Court, a Council, and an Assembly. As for the executive branch, he turned down the position of absolute ruler, trusting instead to the rule of law. This left a vacuum at the top, but it validated the new system by showing that not even its creator was beyond the reach of the law.

Solon dealt with fundamentals. When the ship is sinking, you don't get fancy. But the direction in which he pushed Athens was critical to its future as a hothouse. His tax relief established a basis for economic growth. The new legal rights of citizens increased their stakeholder's share in the city's future, and the restoration of those sold into slavery won the hearts of Athenians. The shift from birth to wealth meant that Athens was moving away from a superstitious belief in the sacred power of blood into a modern world governed by legal process and grounded in trade and business. Solon's basic sociopolitical structure would last for centuries and provide Athens with the political stability and flexibility that fueled the city's creative impulse. When he turned down the offer of personal power, Solon put the final stamp on the idea that community and justice transcend personal ambition.

Still, Solon's reforms were not sufficient to fuel Athens's creative transformation. They did, however, give the city-state some breathing room. Solon also modeled the direction that effective reforms could take. Although political stability proved elusive for Athens in the decades following Solon's reforms, the living standard improved: Farmers' basic rights were secure, the economy grew, trade increased, and the Athenians learned to live under civil government.

The NowCor Case, Part 1: A Fictional Modern Corporate Solon (parallels to Athens in parentheses)

NowCor, a manufacturer of household goods, has been in the doldrums. Management and staff hate one another, their product line is stale, and their customer base is aging. NowCor's managers seem to have stepped out of the 1950s. Suddenly, however, the chairman of the board dies and his brother, Sol, who now has the largest bloc of stock (his brother's being split among his four children), takes over. Sol is more sophisticated and worldly than his brother, who was twelve years older, and he enjoys sailing and playing trumpet in a jazz band. He believes it is his duty to save the family business, so he takes over as CEO and starts changing things right away.

His first step is to bring the benefits package into the modern age, which wins the loyalty of long-standing employees (Solon restoring the citizens sold into slavery). The company reaches into the till to bring the pension system up-to-date and provide more health insurance and liberal leave benefits as well (Solon's tax relief). Sol does not challenge managers' prerogatives and authority, but gives notice that managers must exceed previous benchmarks of quality and productivity if they expect to stay on (the Athenian shift in political criterion from birth—or long-standing innate authority—to wealth, or performance). He institutes a grievance policy to reinforce accountability (Solon establishing the law courts). There will even be employee representation on the management team, although they will be nonvoting members (increased representation of non-nobles). However, any manager whose group performs well retains the company's full support (Solon not a radical; fairly moderate reforms).

NowCor's performance improves, modestly at first, and not quite enough to indicate a real turnaround. However, the atmosphere is much better and a grateful board of directors votes their chairman a lifetime sinecure and a lucrative golden parachute. And then the astounding thing happens. He turns it down! "My salary will suffice," he informs the board in a succinct note, "and I hope that my example will be followed by all subsequent boards of directors and executives" (Solon refuses to take advantage of his power).

This step reverberates throughout the business world. Sol appears on the cover of *Time* and *Fortune*. *People* magazine publishes a two-page spread on "corporate America's sexiest CEO," as they dub him. *Time* points out that his repudiation of compensation represents a new mood in America, a more Spartan approach to executive compensation. *Fortune* asks Sol, perhaps a bit too slyly, whether he believes his reforms will actually turn the company around, and *Fortune*'s response to its own question is that while some improvement is evident, it'll take more than a grand gesture to help NowCor. *Value Line* and *Standard and Poor's* are unimpressed, and their prognostications regarding NowCor's stock price, which is down in the dumps, are guarded at best (Athens begins its steady rise).

Still, Sol becomes a celebrity and appears on talk shows and at high-level international retreats where he offers sardonic but highly insightful comments that his peers often carry back to their own businesses. Internally, Sol is revered as the man who brought a modern outlook to the company and healed its internal rifts (Solon considered one of the Seven Wise Men). Yet, among management there are still those who do things the old way—that is, sit on a traditional line of consumer goods that are expected to sell themselves. And for some staff, things aren't moving fast enough, and their loyalty to Sol is stronger than to the company (still internal conflict in Athens as the Greek world expands in power and complexity).

And then Sol drops the second bombshell. He retires (as did Solon). This secures his reputation because frankly some people figured he'd stay on for years and become just like the rest of NowCor's executives. Instead, he leaves on a sailing trip with his family (Solon travels to Egypt). One evening, anchored in a cove off a Greek island sipping ouzo and retsina on deck, he explains why he left. "It's up to them now. If they need me hovering over them for the next twenty years, they'll never get it anyway."

PEISISTRATOS THE COORDINATOR

The next leader responsible for Athens's rise was never going to be a contender for Seven Wise Men status. He was considered a tyrant by many Athenians just years after his death, but such are the vagaries of reputation. In truth, he was one of the most capable leaders of the ancient world and not nearly as ruthless as the term *tyrant* would suggest. (The word *tyrant* in ancient Greece meant someone who seized power illegitimately and pursued policies that did not benefit the aristocracy. In other words, a ruler was a tyrant if he used the nobles' methods to promote the welfare of citizens other than the nobles).

This tyrant's name was Peisistratos, a younger kinsman of Solon's, and he strong-armed his way into power in 561 B.C.E. For the next thirty-four years, he was the dominant figure in Athenian life, and his policies prepared the city for its meteoric rise on the Hellenic scene.

Peisistratos's mission was somewhat more complex than Solon's. In Solon, Athens found a steady, bold, and respected figure who could step into the middle of a contentious mess and get everybody on the same page. Now Athens was somewhat more prosperous, but was going nowhere unless it became more politically stable; many Athenians didn't understand Solon's reforms. Achieving stability was also more complicated now. As prosperity, trade opportunities, and the progress of rival states increased, internal pressure came not only from nobles and poor farmers but also from craftsmen and merchants as well.

If Solon can be called the "mediator," Peisistratos's title should be the "coordinator." Peisistratos forged connections between the many pairs of polar opposites that defined Athenian society and coordinated their creative tension to stimulate the economic and political growth of the community. These polarities were both demographic and structural in nature:

- Peasant versus noble
- Rustic villager versus city dweller
- Athens versus outside world
- Tradition versus innovation
- Clan justice versus civil law
- Land-based versus sea-based economy

Peisistratos found unique ways to trigger creative reactions between these opposing forces. Of course, every other city-state contained similar dichotomies, but because Athens developed so late compared with its rivals, the tension between the poles of Athens's dichotomies was more extreme. When Peisistratos created links between these cultural oppositions, they produced an almost electric energy that drove the Athenians to creative heights.

One of his first acts established public wells so that the nobility could no longer control the peasants' critical access to water; this also generated a so-called watercooler effect that inspired people to gather freely and schmooze. Peisistratos established circuit courts that dispensed law to all corners of Attica, thus securing the rights that Solon established and strengthening the people's loyalty to the community. Peisistratos himself traveled throughout Attica to assure rustics that they belonged to the same community as wealthy landowners and city-dwellers and also to show his commitment to upholding their rights. He extended loans to the poor, which stimulated the economic recovery begun under Solon. Yet he also won over most nobles by rarely abusing his power, refusing to redistribute land, and maintaining Solon's governmental structure.

In this latter regard, Peisistratos performed a critical organizational function. *He gave everyone time to practice new behavior patterns.* The Athenians used Peisistratos's reign to practice the new forms of government and habits of mind ushered in by Solon. The inherently dynamic and expansive transformation that Athens experienced was balanced by the stability provided by the benevolent tyrant.

By asserting the rule of law and his own authority on behalf of the poor, and allocating seed money to stimulate economic activity among the poor and the artisan and merchant classes, Peisistratos used the analytic, legalistic, and centralized mind-set of Greek city-state culture to upgrade the standing of the poorer, more marginal citizens. In effect, he transmitted aristocratic values of autonomy and freedom to the lower classes. Yet he went further than simply "educating" Athens's marginal citizens. He took the far more radical path of implanting energy and institutions from the *periphery into the core,* or from *the lower levels to the top,* a powerful step in generating the hothouse effect.

Rather than simply bringing so-called executive culture to the lower orders, Peisistratos lured the poor peasants and woodcutters of Attica into the city of Athens. To do this, he built impressive limestone temples on the Acropolis (see Exhibit 2). These temples, later destroyed by the Persians in 480 B.C.E., were the predecessors of those marble ruins we so admire today. Many rulers have erected monuments to their own glory to intimidate their subjects. In Athens, as throughout Greece, the temples served as public monuments expressing the unity of the citizenry. The building program stimulated the economy by providing work and raising demand for skilled craft persons, while both employment and the temples themselves attracted Attica's poor to the city. Visible to all from miles away, the dramatic Acropolis cliffs sported the new temples proudly, as if beckoning to all of Attica. The flashy precinct of the gods drew greater numbers of people into the psychological, political, and economic orbit of the city.

But Peisistratos still had other tricks up his sleeve to forge a bond between rich and poor, city and countryside, future and past. He honored Dionysus, a deity popular among women and poor country folk, a god of wine, intoxication, and wild dancing (see Exhibit 3)—in other words, everything normally suppressed by central or higher authority—by establishing a shrine to the god at the base of the south face of the Acropolis. At this time, Dionysian celebrations consisted of primitive, comedic, drunken "goat dances" in which two figures mimed a battle over a wine-filled goatskin. Yet under the influence of Athens's urban and cosmopolitan worldview, the rough Dionysian celebrations on the south slope evolved rapidly into the magnificent art form of Athenian drama whose masterpieces, such as the *Oresteia* trilogy, *Oedipus the King*, *The Trojan Women*, *The Bacchae*, *Clouds*, and *Lysistrata*, are still frequently performed today. There the Greeks created the basis of modern theater out of the highly charged interaction between Dionysus's cult and the new urban and cosmopolitan world into which it had been transported.

True to Peisistratos's genius, the incredible quality of Athenian drama is due largely to how it compressed and resolved the tensions inherent in key dichotomies in Athenian society. Plot, character, and conflict emerged in classic mythic terms involving rites of passage and mystical experience. Meanwhile, the themes, dramatic action, and characters' concerns often revolved around civic issues such as the role of authority, the nature of law, the way sophisticated language can both obscure and reveal the truth, treatment of prisoners of war, and so forth. The plays' audiences attended in an inebriated Dionysian state, and Aristotle stated that the drama's main purpose was "cathartic," well in keeping with Dionysus's original mission.

Planting the Dionysian aspect of rural culture in the heart of the city and its festivities was a masterstroke, because it ensured a constant circulation of cultural energy. Impulses, ideas, information, and insights moved back and forth between city and country and rich and poor. The sophisticated language of both Greek poetry and urban life fused with the earthy, vibrant language of the countryside, just as the rational mind-set of merchants and politicians fused with the more emotional, tactile, organic impulses of the country. Athenian creativity drew much of its strength from the dramatic festivals, whose potency in turn came from primitive sources still nurtured and revered. Peisistratos also reestablished the Panathenaea festival, a joyous celebration of the city and its people that drew all of Attica to the city. Once again he brought marginal community members into the center and elevated energy from the roots of the culture into a position of influence over its most sophisticated elements.

Athens possesses an excellent natural harbor and was well-situated to thrive commercially. Yet it did not fulfill its economic potential until Peisistratos set in motion aggressive mercantile policies. By designating certain city neighborhoods for production of weapons, pottery, jewelry, and other crafts, and encouraging shipbuilding, Peisistratos opened Athens to the currents of a civilization that extended from Babylon in the east to Marseilles (the Greek Massillia) to the west. The concentrated studio areas facilitated intensive exchange of materials, ideas, and applications. He also standardized Athens's currency, and the drachma soon became one of the standard coins of the Hellenic orb.

The NowCor Case, Part 2: Pi Stratos Takes Over at NowCor (parallels to Athens in parentheses)

Eight years after Sol stepped down as CEO, NowCor was in trouble again. The old guard executives, while not rolling back Sol's reforms, did their best to slow them down. Young managers inspired by Sol's approach left the company, frustrated by their inability to fulfill his mission (political conflict flares in Athens after Solon retires). As they argued at meetings, Sol hadn't been concerned only about getting the company on its feet again. He ignited a spirit of excitement and entrepreneurship, and they wanted to build on that. They also wanted to continue his policy of keeping people informed about the company's goals and how they could contribute to them. But they could not overcome the inertia of those who argued that NowCor sold unglamorous goods that appealed to the common sense of everyday housewives (continuing power in Attica of the conservative land-based aristocracy). The old guard's strategy focused on maintaining shareholder dividends and trusting to those brands that Sol's policies had revived. Conditions were better than in the old days before Sol's reforms. But while gross income had followed the economy upward, profit margins gathered downhill momentum with morale right behind.

Sol's nephew, Phil "Pi" Stratos, was an ambitious young man looking for a suitable challenge (Peisistratos was a kinsman of Solon's). His nickname came more from his devotion to Boston cream pie than mathematics, but he worked off the calories as an all-American hockey player at Boston University. He was a fanatical student of the martial arts and had traveled widely. Pi believed in the power of effective leadership and his whatever-it-takes philosophy could be seen as arrogance by those who didn't know him well. Sol's own children did not want to be involved in NowCor, but they did hold, along with Pi and his sisters, a controlling interest in the company. They were close with Pi and also worried about the company. So one day, along with Pi's two sisters, they all marched into a board meeting and made the other directors an offer they couldn't refuse—purely financial, of course.

For the next twenty-two years, contrary to all initial expectations (including his own), Pi Stratos ran NowCor. The company grew tremendously under his direction, but that is not why he stayed. He stayed because, in a development that surprised him more than anyone, he found that he cared passionately about NowCor's thirty-eight thousand employees and the company itself. He saw himself as steward of a family legacy and also steward of the people who depended on his leadership so they could pay their mortgages and send their kids to college.

Pi saw no reason to change the formal arrangements Sol had instituted (Peisistratos gave Athenians the opportunity to practice Solon's newly created institutions). He figured they just had to be updated. To start, he pushed half-a-dozen key executives into retirement and filled their posts with younger women and men, all with MBAs, savvy about global trade, willing to lead by example, and loyal to Pi (Peisistratos's aggressive mercantile policy). Still, Pi understood that lower down the organizational chart worker productivity was suffering. Departments lacked direction and supervisors spent their time covering their tracks and keeping a low profile rather than taking risks or challenging accepted practice. The changes at the top would help, but it would take time for most employees to feel their impact. Pi thought hard about how to tap their talents and energies to benefit the company and everyone who worked there.

Pi started by initiating a pilot program of monthly discussion groups that were attended by nonmanagers. He laid out clear ground rules for the meetings. No two people who worked together could attend the same group; Pi didn't want the groups to become outlets for departmental complaints or gossip about particular bosses (Peisistratos didn't overthrow nobles). No line managers could participate (public wells, the chance for the poor to congregate in Athens). Taking a cue from Plato's *Symposium,* in which a group of prominent Athenians gather to discuss a chosen topic (but providing coffee, tea, and juice instead of wine), Pi gave each group a topic related directly to work but general enough to stimulate creative thought. First topics assigned included "NowCor's Innovation Environment—Who Are We Kidding?" "Work-

place Accidents Waiting to Happen," and "Where Aren't We
Heading—And Is That a Good Idea?" Topics rotated from one
group to another in successive months. One person from each
group underwent facilitator training, and group secretaries rotated
week to week. Discussions had to last for two hours and they were
not to take place over lunch: NowCor dedicated real work time
to them to demonstrate their importance (greater public access to
political office; training and practice in mechanisms of empowerment).

Pi made it clear that only he would see the discussion results;
even though participants were not *supposed* to complain about
bosses and similar matters, he knew that employees would speak
more openly if he guaranteed confidentiality. Pi selected the ideas
he thought most valuable for review with other executives. He
knew this could be seen as a waste of time, but he wanted to make
a point: Every idea was potentially valuable and every member of
NowCor was viewed as a talented contributor whatever their actual position.

Pi delegated the best ideas to the appropriate managers to implement, while others entered the company more informally
(strong central leadership on Peisistratos's part). Some ideas went
nowhere. Over the next two years, the discussions would include
almost every employee, a seemingly tremendous investment in
time and money. Yet, benefits dwarfed costs. Employee turnover
and absentee rates declined and morale improved, slowly at first
and then more rapidly as people saw their ideas benefiting the
company (Athenians' confidence increases in all respects). Responding to one group's suggestion, Pi dedicated an entire suite of
offices to special projects groups. Known as The Plaza, this area
became a hotbed of innovation and "the tailwind," as Pi called
it, that drove NowCor's stock to ever loftier heights (the newly
established neighborhood craft centers that stimulated the Athenian economy). When Pi expanded benefits and profit-sharing ra-
tios, the company went on to achieve record profits.

CLEISTHENES THE INTEGRATOR

After Peisistratos died, his sons ruled Athens, but they did not have the old
man's skill. Athens and the Peisistratid family suffered economic losses

when the Persian Empire conquered Ionia (the collection of wealthy Greek city-states along Asia Minor's coastline and on the Aegean islands), and internal tensions flared. Hipparchus, the younger son, was assassinated in 514 B.C.E., an event remembered in Athens as a heroic blow for freedom. Hippias, the elder, was overthrown in 510 B.C.E. and eventually took refuge at the Persian court. After various power plays, Cleisthenes, an aristocratic leader of the democratic party, became Athens's leader. In 506 B.C.E., he instituted a brilliant mathematically based revision of the political system that represented a quantum leap in organizational development.

Solon had mediated a truce among contending interests that allowed them to at least function together. Peisistratos had coordinated powerful internal tensions to produce dramatic results in business, economics, art, and politics. Cleisthenes's reforms integrated the political activities of all Athenian citizens, going far beyond his predecessors and setting Athens apart from other states whose size and potential were similar to its own.

Cleisthenes knew he had to break down the old political alliances that once again had destabilized Athenian politics. He used his hard-earned popularity to disband the four traditional tribes to which all Athenians belonged, simply wiping the slate clean. In their stead, he created ten new tribes. He also created three new political clusters based on geography: city, coast, and hills (the poorer region of the Attic interior). Every Athenian citizen—each free male—and his family thus belonged to one of the ten tribes *and* to one of the three clusters.

Cleisthenes then divided the Athenians into thirty groups, or "thirtieths," by dividing each of the ten tribes into thirds. In each tribe, one third came from the city, one third from the coast, and one third from the hills. Thus, conversely, the city, coast, and hills clusters were each divided into ten different groups of citizens, each belonging to a different tribe. One could belong to tribe 1/city group, tribe 3/hills group, tribe 6/hills, tribe 6/coast, and so forth.

The integrating effects were electric; loyalties were entwined in a way replicated in no other city-state. Geography bestowed on the people of each region a certain commonality of interest; for example, most city dwellers would benefit from certain policies, while most hills people from others. Yet the hills people were spread out across ten of the thirtieths, each of which belonged to a different tribe. The formal tribal allegiances played an important part in the political system that Cleisthenes established, because certain offices rotated from tribe to tribe.

Thus, by 506 B.C.E., among the more populous city-states, only Athens granted citizenship and political participation to such a high percentage of her men. Solon's wealth-based categories still prevailed, which meant that some people were more equal than others, but no one could lose their basic rights because of financial failure or be convicted of a crime without a trial. At the very least, one remained in the lowest group, the *thetes,* which participated in politics via the assembly and eventually the council, the courts, and other positions of state. Only Athens reached out to the poor and drew them into continual engagement with the political system and urban culture. While women and slaves were excluded, the fact remains that Athens's citizen body soon numbered more than forty thousand men, a vast number to tap into compared with the more exclusive city-states that operated with 20 to 25 percent of that number of full citizens. The impact upon Athens's creative, political, and military development was stunning.

The NowCor Case, Part 3: Clyde Sinise Gives NowCor Wings

Pi always suspected he would exit this life with a bang, but it was the "bang" that he prevented that made his end so noteworthy. One day, on an undivided four-lane highway, he purposely drove his car in between a swerving truck and a bus carrying a local high school team. As he'd intended, the bus was spared the collision but Pi was not. The last thing he saw was the bus braking to a safe halt on the shoulder of the road.

With Pi gone, two of his nephews took over the company, but one was a playboy who never attended to business and the other was a spoiled young man who believed his task was to micromanage everyone from the CFO to the cafeteria workers—who worked for an outside contractor anyway, but he didn't know that. An economic downturn hit the company hard; perhaps it needn't have, but Nephew Number One panicked, decided to close a manufacturing plant to cut costs, and then when the economy perked up again, NowCor missed the rebound. At this point, the board threw the nephews out and replaced them with an executive that Pi Stratos had recruited out of Stanford some fifteen years earlier (overthrow of Peisistratos's sons; after maneuvering, Cleisthenes assumes power). Now a seasoned corporate infighter and respected VP of overseas operations, Clyde Sinise came in with a reputation for a mind as sharp and sparkling as diamonds. Four years of the nephews' incompetence had crystallized his ideas about how to turn NowCor into a global business powerhouse. Once in, he wasted no time.

Clyde decided on a complete organizational overhaul. Over time, the domestic and overseas branches of the company had become hopelessly entangled in some areas and completely out of touch with one another in others. Finance viewed the company as a unified operation while the overseas operation always felt short-changed. Product development was handled by a separate division but differences between overseas markets—South America versus Asia, for instance—were frequently ignored, and packaging was handled solely stateside. Clyde realized that despite Pi's brilliant marketing and organizational innovations, core problems still needed to be addressed.

Clyde created three new strategy groups: New Initiatives, Business Intelligence, and Education, each recruiting employees from across the corporation. Looking to develop both leadership and collaborative skills, he suggested that the role of coordinator rotate daily. Each day's coordinator met with the next person serving in that role to prepare them for the transition. Clyde also informed the twenty-five members of the three groups that they were to continue with their regular jobs while meeting for three hours twice a week; he would arrange with their managers for a clearly defined portion of their workload to be distributed elsewhere (formal integration of geographic areas into political system, greater access to political office).

The plan worked. The three groups addressed issues long ignored by the conservative hierarchy that still wielded some power (major shift in balance of power within Attica). The Business Intelligence group eventually purchased, customized, and implemented a full-scale system that tracked hundreds of variables in countless combinations and was made available to all employees. Managers received special training on how to utilize the program for maximum impact. The New Initiatives group actually took a step backward, urging the company to clarify its objectives before kicking off any new product lines. As they drilled deeper into what this would entail, they converged with Business Intelligence and developed an analytic algorithm capable of isolating product impact region by region, including "secondary synergies" generated by the success of any specific product. The Education group decided to provide training on cross-cultural issues that affected product design and marketing. It offered seminars on various problem-solving models. As its scope expanded, the group offered courses throughout NowCor that enhanced the analytic skills and global perspectives of all employees. As more and more people rotated on and off the committees, serving on them proved to be a source of pride for employees and an incredible career, leadership, and skills development experience. Morale soared and new product launches proved to be stronger than ever. Within five years, NowCor became one of three global leaders in a product line that had expanded to include home improvement, financing, and educational software (proliferation of initiatives in the new Athenian economy).

By then, Clyde realized that the committees had become almost superfluous because their methods were so integrated into NowCor's culture that they no longer functioned as a primary source of innovative ideas. The organization had become more responsive to changes in the business environment. Yet Clyde made sure the three committees continued on, because he felt they helped integrate the corporation (maintaining formal integrative structures, even as individual roles expanded in scope and power). He also had something in mind for them called the (Loops) Accelerated Counter-Entropic Systems Upgrade, or (L)ACES-UP. His goal for (L)ACES-UP was to streamline every important operational loop, including product development, shipping, intelligence feedback and analysis, and even the way employees learned both on the job and in the outside courses the company paid for. He charged the three committees to fulfill that objective but made no other announcement to the company, and he let them figure out how (L)ACES-UP would fulfill its mandate.

FACTORS

As we observe a number of historical communities and modern companies, an increasing number of the thirty-six factors come into play, offering us a deeper view of the four dimensions of creativity and their contributions to launching the hothouse effect in a modern business context. The hothouse factors, described below, that were prominent in Athens's preparation for the hothouse effect are grouped thematically for the sake of clarity, and the specific factors are listed at the end of each subsection. First and foremost, for Athens, is the actualization of values, but factors from all four dimensions nourished the Athenian florescence, so we will have a preview of many of the other factors here as well.

- *Strongly Articulated and Actualized Values.* All of Solon's reforms reinforced his core commitment to the basic rights of all citizens under the law and the primacy of law over the desires of any one group. Peisistratos's core values were practical in nature: promote economic growth and political stability and create a dynamic balance between key constituencies within the state. Cleisthenes's values can be easily read in his constitution: a belief in the ability of all citizens to conduct the business of government. Although Peisistratos was a master manipulator who always looked out for himself and Cleisthenes sought to advance his family's ambitions, values still determined their strategic directions and Athens flourished because each leader expanded on his predecessor's vision. When men took power who sought to reverse the leaders' policies, as Peisistratos's sons did, the community rebelled. Their leaders' values emerged in large part from the Athenians' worldview. Despite its former backward nature, Athens had always viewed itself as the parent city of the brilliant Ionian cities that dotted the Aegean islands and the eastern Aegean coast. The long period of oppressive aristocratic rule and their region's backwardness probably fueled a fierce desire for liberty among the Athenians. But its isolation also helped. It lay beyond Sparta's sphere of influence, which enveloped southern Greece. It was isolated even from Ionia and was cut off from the more primitive north and west by forbidding mountain ranges. So even among the individualized Greek communities, Athens was especially distinctive. The fact that the city was blessed with three great leaders who amplified these tendencies demonstrates the critical role played by leadership, values, and a committed populace in generating the hothouse effect. (See Factors #1, #2, #7, #8, and #31.)

- *Cross-Pollination of Polarities.* Peisistratos was gifted at reconciling polarized elements of society and sustaining creative tension between each pole. Even the dichotomy that defined all others, innovation versus tradition, became a source of Athenian pride and energy. The most important dichotomies left unresolved by the Athenians—man and woman, freepersons and slaves, and Athenians and non-Athenians—became a source of weakness for the Athenian state. But other polarities gave it power: mercantile policies that fused local and cosmopolitan aspirations; the expansion of the citizen body by linking country and city; the powerful juncture of rural tradition with the abstract, universal, and empowering quality of the law; and the cultural maturation that came from uniting ritual and art in drama. (See Factors #13 and #17.)

■ *Open Discourse.* From Peisistratos's wells to Cleisthenes's matrix of interdependency, multiple conversations and debates were taking place all over Attica across boundaries of class, profession, geography, and political interest. In the political unrest that preceded Cleisthenes's ascendance, local taverns became hotbeds of new ideas and political change. The constant circulation of ideas, energy, and information is vital to every hothouse, occurring in taverns (Cleisthenes's Athens and the United States in Revolutionary times), cafés (Paris), workshops (Florence), clubs (the jazz community), informal conversations (early twentieth-century physicists), celebrations (the Bauhaus and physicists), salons (Napoleonic-era France), libraries (medieval Andalusia), and informal lunches (Silicon Valley). Today, the Internet is a global gathering place in which countless individuals exchange every level and type of idea. (See Factors #10, #12, and #16.)

■ *Cross-Functional Units.* Each Athenian citizen belonged to several overlapping units within the organization, and hence filled multiple roles. As Athens's political system evolved over the decades following Cleisthenes's reforms, this cross-functional aspect intensified. Almost anyone could hold most political offices and almost everything was subject to debate. The council presidency rotated *daily,* by lot, although each tribe held the presidency for thirty days in a row, which balanced the daily rotation with monthly stability. This is a more integrated model than is generally found in business, because it superimposed four definitive matrices: tribe, region, birth, and wealth. (See Factors #11 and #20.)

■ *Whimsy, Play, and Festivals.* The Panathenaea and Dionysian festivals played central roles in Athenian life. They both expressed the spirit of the democracy and unified the entire region. Playfulness and celebration are critical to creativity and actually represented the substance of Greek culture itself, shaping the values and behaviors of everyday life. As the Bauhaus leader, Johannes Itten, said two and a half millennia later, "Play becomes party—party becomes work—work becomes play." (See Factors #13, #33, #34, and #35.)

- *Symbolic Vocabulary.* The presence of judges in the countryside; the Acropolis monuments depicting religious images and narratives; the renewed festivals; the form and content of the newly invented drama; and the reformed tribal and political systems, all established a vocabulary of profound richness and fluidity that excited the Athenians' creative faculties. These symbols, images, and terms in Athens included the following:

  - Names of the new tribes and political offices
  - Place names of Athens's new trading partners
  - Memorable lines from the tragedies performed in the theater of Dionysus
  - Language of the festivals and the meaning of their rituals
  - Images that adorned temples and shrines throughout city and countryside
  - Language of the law courts
  - Philosophical and proto-scientific concepts and terms
  - Mathematical terms and geometric metaphors
  - Metaphors based on sailing, farming, and trade

  Fresh vocabularies act almost as magical incantations. They reflect a unified set of values and goals and stimulate a high level of instant rapport among those who can demonstrate familiarity with it. This type of vocabulary cannot be manufactured synthetically in an effort to engineer corporate culture. Or rather it can, but it won't produce creative results. It generally rises out of the crucible of experience and from a need to express new ideas and processes for which existing language is inadequate. (See Factors #5, #19, #21, #26, and #29.)

- *Sudden and Rapid Engagement with Meta-Systems.* During the fifth and sixth centuries B.C.E. in which Athens achieved its highly unlikely florescence, the city came into intimate contact with the vast and ancient civilizations of the eastern Mediterranean and Middle Eastern worlds. In that regard, it trailed dozens of other Greek city-states, which had regained contact with Egypt, the sea-faring Phoenicians, and Babylon, the civilization's greatest city, during the ninth to seventh centuries B.C.E. When a small community that is entering a major phase of cultural development suddenly and rapidly comes into close, extended contact with highly sophisticated meta-systems, the hothouse effect thrusts forward with rocket intensity. A meta-system is several orders of size and complexity greater than the smaller emerging system. For the Greek world, the meta-system was Mesopotamia and Egypt, which by 1,000 B.C.E. had experienced urban life for at least three thousand years, a longer time than that which separates us from Athens itself. (See Factors #25, #27, and #28.)

5

A HIGH-TECH HOTHOUSE: INSPIRATION MEETS ORGANIZATION

The steps that led to the full-blown creative flowering of an ancient city-state may seem remote from the experience of modern corporations. Yet some business leaders have used similar methods to promote creativity in their companies. They have gone beyond discrete steps such as encouraging employee feedback, holding brainstorming sessions, or using open-space offices, to a more thorough integration of creativity into the design and function of their companies.

The Values/Mission dimension saturated the culture of Sequent Computers from the beginning. Casey Powell, founder and former CEO of Sequent, decided to establish the company's creative orientation before the company even opened, and he sustained it through periods of dramatic growth that culminated in IBM's purchase of the company in 1999. Sequent developed and marketed open client/server systems for commercial computer applications and systems that supported enterprise-wide applications and information services. Sequent was the market share leader in large UNIX systems and installed thousands of large-scale systems worldwide. The experience at Sequent was unusually positive for its employees as demonstrated by one rather astonishing fact we've already noted: Four years after Sequent was absorbed into IBM, 1,100 ex-Sequent employees still keep in touch on a Web site devoted to the spirit of their former company. As Mike Jahnke, former vice president of worldwide sales operations at Sequent, said when I interviewed him, "The Sequent culture was very unique. Lots of Sequent people tried to replicate it but it's very hard to do. In 20-20 hindsight, we discovered how unique Sequent was."

From Sequent's beginnings in 1983, Powell had a clear vision of the company becoming a major provider of data-management solutions. Trained as an engineer but a self-professed professional manager, Powell consciously set out to establish a workplace in which creativity could flourish. A key step, he believed, lay in encouraging employees to circulate and seek one another out for advice and collaboration. Jahnke notes that "There was lots of cross-talk between cubicles. It fostered teamwork and an internal competitive spirit. There was nothing we didn't think we could accomplish. Everyone looked forward to coming to work." As in Athens, stimulating public discourse across department, function, and level was vital to fomenting a creative environment of highly motivated people.

However, simply telling people to go forth and circulate is like announcing at a slow cocktail party that all guests must talk to five other people. Powell, therefore, decided to design the workspace so that employees would *want* to walk across the physical plant to confer with others. He hired a behavioral engineer who suggested painting the sky-bridges connecting Sequent's buildings with bright colors, inside and out, thus making the sky-bridges more inviting to use. The window mullions were even painted black so they'd be invisible against the glass. As Powell explains, he wanted the design to draw the eye *along* the length of the sky-bridges to make them more inviting to use. And, in fact, people constantly walked around Sequent, seeking input on projects and connecting with members of other project- or function-based teams. Another illustration: When Sequent was only a small company with a few dozen people, one coffee pot sufficed for all employees and, like Attica's public wells, it became a central hub for people to meet and discuss workplace issues. When the company grew larger and several coffeepot sites sprouted up, Powell initiated weekly lunches in the company cafeteria so the entire staff could gather regularly, one of those informal ceremonies that keeps any culture vital.

Powell wanted to encourage Sequent staff to interact with as many coworkers as possible, so when the company grew to fifty employees, he suggested everyone wear a name tag bearing their first names to encourage people to address one another as they passed in the halls. They were not part of some "rah-rah" company initiative, but one piece of an overall strategy to maintain open channels among Sequent's growing number of employees.

All of Powell's efforts to encourage the flow and circulation of ideas and information (I&I) reinforces a powerful creative principle: (1) the more sources of I&I that feed into a group's creative process; (2) the greater the volume of I&I flowing from those sources; (3) the more paths along which I&I are transmitted (that is, people discussing ideas, sharing information); and (4) the less time it takes to transmit I&I, the more creative, useful, and valuable will be the new ideas that come out of this process. In algebraic terms, Value (V) = *Number of Sources of input (S)* + *Average Flow per source (F)* + *Links (L)*/TIME (T) or V = (S + F + L)/T. Quality is left out of the equation to reinforce the point that *even amplifying purely quantitative factors can increase creativity and the qualitative outcomes of a given development path.* For example, in the open source process that created the Linux operating system, thousands of programmers worldwide focused on a powerful, preexisting core UNIX program that was already the product of an intensely creative process. The product's value was so extraordinary because of the thousands of sources, the continual high-volume input from a large number of participants, the intensively integrated interactional paths among so many participants, and the relatively short amount of time it took to develop. The Linux open source methodology has become a model for product development and problem solving precisely because it generates so much circulation of I&I in such a short time.

Powell, reflecting back in a recent discussion, said he wanted Sequent to develop as a "knowledge-based, not a power-based hierarchy" where value and values lay in acquiring and sharing knowledge. In a sense, this echoes the Athenian shift in defining political status from birth to wealth; in both cases, the leader replaced a traditional and rigid criterion with a more flexible, merit-based standard. The many young people working at Sequent understood that knowledge was the currency of recognition and respect. Hence, it was clear that it paid to be a continuous learner. As both Peisistratos and Cleisthenes seemed to know, it is easier to shift behaviors by setting up conditions that allow people to act in more naturally satisfying ways than simply prescribing change. If the conditions that promote creative behaviors are built into the explicit values and design of the workplace, people will want to learn and share what they know.

Powell was hands-on in promoting vertical communication within Sequent. He personally delivered every orientation for new employees, articulating company values and lending his presence as guarantor of those values, much as Peisistratos's tours of the countryside validated the values implicit in his reforms. Sequent's vice presidents were ensconced within their own groups rather than with one another, and an unspoken rule barred managers from clustering together in the cafeteria. Jahnke recalls that everyone, Powell included, worked in cubicles, which shocked Jahnke when he first started working there because he was used to executives living on "mahogany row."

Powell believes that "if everyone believes in the cause, they'll find a way to get it done," an axiom expressed by every CEO in this book. Sequent actively encouraged people to make decisions and stand by them. When the CEO counterintuitively advises staff to forget about the so-called best decision, the specter of failure dissolves. Instead, Powell championed "the right decision," the one that a person truly believes will work most effectively, which grounded decision making in the individual sensibility rather than in a preimagined template of what "best" should be. Encouraging personal responsibility, however, only made sense if employees at every level felt empowered to make suggestions *upward* in the organization, if their presence, to use our Athenian language, was implanted within the upper corporate levels. Powell insists on the same point that, again, every CEO in this book reiterated: To make a company or department work, you need to get the right core people, get them to agree about what they want to achieve, and let them run with it.

An organization can only achieve this level of communication if its value system supports an upward flow of ideas, even when they challenge accepted practice. Powell established the company's values and wrote Sequent's code of behavior so that everyone was treated respectfully as a person and employee. Powell made it a point to regularly and explicitly reinforce Sequent's culture. At his new job as CEO of NextGig Inc., a manufacturer of database accelerators in San Diego, Powell posted a six-point list of core values throughout the plant. At Sequent, Powell delivered all orientations for new employees, and at job interviews he and his staff were quite clear about Sequent's core values and the type of person they wanted. When I asked Powell how an interviewee could be sure Sequent or NextGig actually lived up to that code, he noted that the behaviors— honesty, hard work, empowerment, a disdain for workplace "cowboys," and total commitment to customer service—are so pervasive, a new hire gets a feel for the culture right away.

At NextGig, as at Sequent, new employees are assigned sponsors who contact them before they begin work. The sponsor helps the new person get set up, makes sure they have everything they need, and advises them on cultural norms and taboos. Sponsors may hold any position in the company but they cannot be the individual's manager. The bond between sponsor and new hire, according to Powell, becomes very strong and often lasts beyond employment.

Also as at Sequent, employees learn during orientation that NextGig's culture empowers people to make the right decision and the goal is to take care of customers first. The message is: "This is what we want to be. You have the power to help us become that company." Managers encourage employees to speak up with suggested improvements. If they have problems, they can send Powell an e-mail and he'll address the issue without putting the employee in a tough position with his or her manager. This in no way encourages a backbiting culture, but rather one in which people can both transmit innovative ideas without worrying about repercussions and have some recourse in the case of abuse of trust. "A boss," states Powell, "helps you get your job done. It's not their job to do something to you." At the same time, employees are responsible for asking supervisors for any help or resources they need. The upshot is that people were not afraid to speak out at Sequent, and they are not afraid to do so at NextGig either.

Sequent culture encouraged employees to challenge and improve any aspect of the operation. The company's basic assumptions were periodically questioned and reviewed. When Sequent grew to fifty employees (on its way to an eventual three thousand) and Powell suggested the use of name tags, people grumbled that the company was becoming too corporate. In response, Powell asked everyone to list all the things they thought were good and bad about being "big" and about being "small." In the ensuing conversation, Powell pointed out that the real issues had nothing to do with big and small, but with good and bad. "Why not simply work to achieve what's good about both rather than getting tied down to whether we're behaving 'big' or 'small'?" he asked. The discussion also reaffirmed the original objective of Sequent becoming a large company, a goal that is often unexamined in a growing organization.

Hothouses always find a way to promote meta-cognitive processes, that is, people thinking about their own thought processes (see Factor #26). "Life is simple. Reducing life to simplicity is the hard part," says Powell, who admires the clarity that comes with simplicity. To encourage an elegant simplicity of thought at Sequent, he promoted a common-sense algorithm for reviewing and analyzing all operations: There is only one "best" decision but there may be several "right ones." Find what works, make your decision, and live with it. Assess whether you obtained the outcome you were trying to achieve. Jahnke points out that this freed people to be flexible in developing their solutions. In Jahnke's view, "The big thing that differentiated Sequent in a cultural sense was that it was very customer driven. Whatever it took to make the customer happy was seen as identical to generating revenue. It was a very sound business model." If a customer needed service, Sequent employees felt completely empowered to initiate the solutions as well as improve the customer's operations any way they could.

Jahnke notes that perfectionism can work against service providers because customer needs are always changing; to provide that extra 10 percent to get the "best" or ideal solution rather than the "right" one increases customer costs disproportionately and risks missing the target. Sequent devised solutions that worked and then followed through with twice-yearly meetings with all their top customers. The meetings were small enough to allow for two-way give-and-take. Customers shared information and the company could troubleshoot across a broad-based platform. That was when the extra 10 percent became an extra 20 percent or more because the company could refine its systems to meet the most specific customer requirements. "If you don't project that, people don't want to work with you," Jahnke says about Sequent's customer-oriented, problem-solving focus.

Sequent's ability to respond to customer crises played a major role in defining its culture. As we'll see when discussing Factor #32, crises often prove to be defining moments for the hothouse effect. Jahnke notes that it's one thing to do well under good circumstances, but crisis provides the true test of a company's commitment to customer service: "Sequent was exceptional at deploying and focusing resources on customer crises and coming out with a more positive relationship than you went in with." Every major customer had an executive sponsor and the sponsor relationship enabled customers to address potential problems early, before they became serious. This helped to account for the high percentage of repeat business that Sequent earned. When asked if this approach generated business, Jahnke replied, "Absolutely yes. People like doing business with creative counterparts. Bringing customers to the home office for presentations and value analysis energized us as well." Sequent generated exceptional customer loyalty because customers enjoyed working with people dedicated to their interests and to their own jobs. The energy and mutual commitment fed on each other and resulted in outstanding customer relations and service.

After IBM purchased Sequent, Jahnke worked as an executive at a billion-dollar-plus company and a smaller start-up. He found employees receptive to his efforts to implement the Sequent approach inside the company, but considers the biggest roadblock he faced to be the entrenched attitudes of control and micromanagement among top leadership. Ultimately, Jahnke believes, people have a deep-seated vision of what they want the culture of their company to be. The Sequent—and Jahnke—approach was to establish employee accountability for achieving goals and to encourage them to pursue those goals. Despite a feeling that he had a favorable influence on these companies, he eventually left to rejoin Powell at NextGig.

According to Powell, at Sequent and NextGig "decision making was pushed way out into the organization." Empowering employees requires strong leadership at least equal to that of centralized or hierarchal models. A manager needs to monitor decisions; even Dr. Land, noted for the latitude he gave his research scientists, checked in periodically to make sure they weren't headed down a dead end. In a knowledge-based hierarchy, states Powell, the decision maker at any level seeks input and then makes the decision. If he or she can't make the decision, the decision maker should conduct a vote of the team. Except in extraordinary situations, however, that vote marks a failure to focus in on the *right* decision rather than the best one. It is the manager's job to frame the objectives correctly, which means being absolutely clear about details and goals. We all operate within limits in all we do, and the clearer the limits, the more confidently we can assert our freedom, for without limits we have no sense of our objectives or the relative importance of any given action or goal.

One of the strangest yet most powerful hothouse characteristics resides in a multisensory approach to problem solving (see Factor #22). At Sequent and NextGig, Powell circulated an upside-down organization chart with the customer at the top and Powell at the bottom, which he feels helped shake up the corporate mind-set. The visual disorientation of the upside-down chart gave the message more impact than any speech or memo, and reinforced core company values such as two-way vertical communication and deemphasis of position power. Next to Powell's Sequent office was a room with wall-length white board at which employees conducted frequent brainstorming sessions. Although brainstorming is an obvious concession to creativity, it is a useful tool. The location of the brainstorming room at Sequent also sent the message that at the top level of the company, brainstorming's open, noncensorious style was the norm.

Like many hothouses, Sequent recognized the value of thinkers and masters of their craft or discipline (see Factors #9 and #14). "We brought in whatever we needed," said Powell. Once he read an article by Jay Galbraith of the Wharton School on the problems that arise at each stage of a company's growth. He called Galbraith and asked him to spend time at Sequent. But Powell did not want employees to simply hear about Galbraith's theories, he wanted Galbraith to tell them about the *next* big problem Sequent could expect to face. The company also encouraged employees to take college courses, and its internal courses became part of its culture.

Sequent's values–driven culture also sought to have an impact on the outside community but again, as in so many hothouses, the impulse came up through the roots of the company itself. Any interested Sequent employee could sit on its charitable board. The board decided to fund issues that Sequent employees were already involved with and in which their donations could make a significant difference, a major focus being kids at risk. Many companies, of course, have large charitable campaigns. The difference at Sequent lay not in its social commitment, but in having that commitment initiated and organized by the employees themselves.

Powell and his coworkers actualized many of the same hothouse factors we'll see in action elsewhere, and they operated across all four dimensions of the hothouse effect. Powell set out to promote the Ideas/Exchange dimension from the beginning, building the circulation of staff and ideas into the design of the Sequent campus and reinforcing it via the mentorship program, the invitation to outside experts to share their knowledge with Sequent staff, extraordinary employee empowerment, and the promotion of the company as a knowledge organization. The Perception/Learning dimension was exemplified by the expectation that each person was a creative engine within the company, the active promotion of Powell's problem-solving algorithm, and an imaginative approach to organizational development. Powell's leadership, the company's strong business model, the readiness to meet any crisis, and the general creative spirit that animated the place all strengthened Sequent's position in regard to the fourth dimension of the hothouse effect, that of Social/Play.

Many organizations activate one or more of these principles. By implementing so many of them, Sequent achieved a critical mass of behaviors that enabled the company to maintain its creative flair through numerous stages of growth. Sequent is one of the organizations that proved that placing creativity, knowledge, ethics, thinking skills, and employee empowerment and engagement at the top of the chart is no starry-eyed dream, but a highly satisfying way to achieve success. The lasting impact it has had on so many of its employees demonstrates, as well, the professional and personal enrichment they experienced there.

6

THE SECOND DIMENSION: IDEAS/EXCHANGE

The second creative dimension that produces the hothouse effect is called Ideas/Exchange. This dimension describes how ideas and information—the currency of the human mind—pass from one person to another. Because the medium, style, and context of exchange can modify the information being delivered, ideas and exchange are linked; ideas are the product, while exchange is the delivery system. If ideas move only downward through an organization, they will develop differently than if circulated throughout the entire system. The tone or style of an exchange can also modify the message: An evaluative comment delivered with a sneer carries a different message than the same comment offered in a helpful tone. In effect, the information differs because the medium of transmission—in this case, its emotional conductivity—alters it.

The hothouse community organizes itself to use information and ideas efficiently, as many systems do, but also imaginatively, expansively, and in seemingly nonutilitarian ways. Most organizations establish networks so that they can function as cost-effectively and responsively as possible. The hothouse does this too, but its exchange network takes on another function entirely—to expand and enrich the operations of its members' minds and creative instincts. In remarkably similar ways, hothouses have always been highly sensitive to how ideas and information circulate throughout the community, and nearly all hothouses are nurtured by common patterns in the cultivation and transmission of ideas, as described in the following list.

The Ideas/Exchange dimension can be described by twelve factors (Factors #8 to #19) that play a powerful role in triggering the hothouse effect.

Ideas/Exchange

8. Interpersonal conflicts are handled skillfully and serve as opportunities for organizational development.

9. The community provides recognition and respect for thinkers and the products of thought.

10. Intellectual exchange plays an important role in the evolution of group culture.

11. Group members work closely with experts across disciplines and departments, and utilize other fields of knowledge when seeking solutions.

12. Ideas circulate hydraulically throughout the organization.

13. Peripheral or lower-level functions and operations are implanted within the core or upper level of the community.

14. Mastery is accorded the highest respect.

15. Mentorship relationships are cultivated throughout the organization.

16. Hubs of creative activity proliferate rapidly.

17. People are comfortable with enigma and contradiction, and tend to work both poles of a dichotomy rather than seeking resolution for its own sake.

18. The organization continually analyzes the impact of core technologies on all aspects of operations, development, and strategy.

19. Innovative educational formats evolve as a response to the exceptional concentration of content and activity in the community.

#8. CONFLICT RESOLUTION

The ability to successfully resolve conflict is an important measure of any group's functionality. Good conflict resolution is not simply reactive; rather, conflict is viewed as a high-energy event that offers opportunities for personal and organizational growth. While artists and other creative people are often competitive with one another, bitter or angry conflict drains the energy and desire from any creative endeavor. People skilled at conflict resolution tend to be comfortable with their own responses to conflict and thus tackle situations early on, when resolution is easier and requires less drastic intervention. Devising creative ways to deal with conflict also reinforces the general tone of innovation and creativity within a group.

Leaders usually take on the responsibility of dealing with conflict, and it is by resolving conflicts that leaders learn to lead. When leaders remain unflustered in the midst of conflict, they in effect reconfigure how the members of their groups experience the conflict. Instead of conflict defining the situation, the leader's calm, focused intervention defines it. The conflict's "mental scale" shrinks. Everyone grows calmer because the leader becomes the focus of attention. The dog owner who jumps into a dog fight screaming and yanking the chain is subsumed by the fight and makes it worse. The person who stays cool, quickly sizes up the main danger point, and calmly disengages the dogs is far more effective and adds nothing to the dogs' frenzy.

Leaders who understand their own relationship to conflict can better address conflict in a calm, focused way. Dr. Richard Lazere, a psychologist and entrepreneur who has worked closely with Terry Beard on the latter's Lust for Life program, pointed out in an interview that conflict resolution is as much about managing conflict *avoidance* as resolving incipient or actual clashes. Lazere cites a presentation about revenue in which listeners nodded agreement because they wanted the meeting to end and didn't want to confront the brutal reality that the presenter was also avoiding. Lazere's response was to ensure that participants confronted the issues. As Lazere pointed out, conflict avoidance includes resolving conflict too quickly. Avoidance takes several forms, such as the intimidating loudmouth whose way of avoiding conflict is to overwhelm the other party with a thunderous barrage and drown out his or her own insecurity about conflict.

Whatever methods one employs, *everyone* must be subject to the same protocols, whether the CEO, a large investor, or a young rising star. There are also many excellent books and advisors on conflict resolution so we don't need to repeat their lessons here. But we should say a word about using conflict to energize a group.

Conflict provides a chance to break tired reactive habits of dealing with issues, and it can reveal important things about an organization and its procedures. Let's say John and Mary aren't getting along. We can reverse the "figure–ground" relationship—that is, shifting the main figures (John and Mary) to the background and bringing broader organizational issues up front. What does their conflict say about departmental or company objectives, or how people communicate? Why did the conflict erupt? Anything that grows comes out of fertile ground, so what is the fertile ground here? However it is handled, shifting John and Mary to the background defuses the most personal, and hence volatile, aspects of the conflict. The figure–ground reversal taps into data embedded in the conflict. Even if it does not provide a solution, it offers a useful alternative view of the problem.

Preventive techniques include interventions by mentors and periodic communication between groups or individuals on either side of organizational fault lines. Terry Beard counsels managers to chat informally with employees about expectations to ward off misunderstandings that can turn into disputes. Lazere notes that service providers such as attorneys, consultants, and bankers are often reluctant to raise the tough issues because they depend on good will for their business. Usually it's the entrepreneurs and investors who ask the tough questions. Thus, it is important to have gadflies around who are willing to challenge anyone, including leadership, on the issues. Many creative interventions can address disagreement and conflict. Theater productions and artistic endeavors, such as group mural projects, not only build teamwork but allow groups to address the source of conflict directly through the art process itself. These projects generate multifaceted results, including the promotion of a creative mind-set, and can often defuse uncomfortable tensions before they erupt.

At the Bauhaus, founder and director Walter Gropius invited the competing but similar group of artists known as "de Stijl" to participate in the Bauhaus, thus generating creative synergy rather than sterile competitive relations between the two groups. Athens turned to its legal system for conflict resolution, which stimulated mental growth in all directions: the application of logic to problem solving; the structure and language of drama; philosophical inquiry; and the complex dynamics of the political system. It even transformed Greek religion, demonstrating the creative force inherent in innovative institutional responses to conflict. CEO Casey Powell at Sequent gave the green light to anyone who went to extraordinary lengths to deliver customer service. If challenged by a superior over their right to take action, employees were told to say, "Casey said it was okay." Just knowing that the mandate for independent customer-oriented action came from the top served to dissipate conflict and empower employees. The leader who acts as a lightning rod to channel potential conflict harmlessly into the ground instills confidence throughout the organization.

#9. RESPECT FOR THINKERS

Resolving negative situations before they descend into dysfunction does more than restore equilibrium, it releases passionate energies and inspires creative solutions to problems—solutions whose benefits extend beyond the immediate situation. Yet it is equally important to take advantage of positive events that, rather than lingering as conflict does, flash across the landscape and are gone before they can be utilized. One of the great wasted resources in any organization resides in the large number of good ideas lost because they represent enhancements to the system; acting on them is naturally less urgent than responding to systemic threats. Yet, the hothouse effect often generates procedures for capturing these otherwise transient insights and turning them into valuable intellectual capital.

The key to this ability lies in the group's essential respect for thinkers and thought and reflection. Every workplace has people who deliver reflective comments in meetings, see a bit farther than anyone else, produce insights that trigger ideas in others, and simply seem to see dimensions of a situation that other people miss. This is a tricky but important skill to manage, akin to tending the embers of a company's creative fires. How can we follow through on such ideas instead of having them evaporate, as often happens? Recording these ideas, identifying those people who frequently have them, mentoring or placing these people in mentorship positions, using them as sounding boards to gain alternative perspectives, and giving them the go-ahead to follow through on their ideas, all represent ways to liberate the inherent creativity of a company's thinkers.

Management is undergoing an important shift from managing people to managing ideas. The two paradigms are far from mutually exclusive, but just as an earlier shift from managing operations to managing people changed the benchmarks of good management, so too will the shift from people to ideas. Respect for thinkers shows an understanding of the critical role played by theory and ideas in energizing and expanding the practical. The Rowland Institute set aside space in its library specifically for people to think in; Edwin Land's rule was that no one could be disturbed while there. The Bauhaus, Rowland, and Sequent all regularly brought in lecturers to share ideas. Thinkers can be found anywhere in an organization, and when recognized, it is more likely ideas will be captured by and transmitted throughout the culture. The terms *information management* or *knowledge management* are meaningless unless a company creates an environment in which ideas can be cultivated and those who generate them rewarded.

#10. INTELLECTUAL EXCHANGE

Extending the reach of this respect for thinkers propels us into the more rarefied realms of the hothouse effect. The notion that intellectual exchange should play a role in any business might seem quixotic. Of course, many intelligent people have many intelligent conversations when accomplishing a job. But the idea of intellectual exchange could easily seem irrelevant. Can you imagine calling a break during a marketing meeting to discuss the evolution of *chiaroscuro* in sixteenth-century Italian painting? Not likely to happen.

This is a tough one so we'll approach it obliquely. The students I teach at the Lesley University School of Management in Cambridge, Massachusetts, are on average thirty-five years old; most are already managers and those who aren't expect to be soon. One of the elective courses, called World Views, garners enthusiastic reviews from students. One recurring theme in their evaluations strikes me as particularly interesting: "This course should be in the core management program." The students have nothing to gain by saying this; they are always honest in their evaluations and they can express their rapture with a course without asserting that it should be required.

Well, it's a good course and they think it should be required—what's so strange about that? First, a few more words about our students. They are bright, motivated, and for the most part, have a limited background in the liberal arts. They are in school to improve management skills and rightfully resent anything they consider to be a waste of their time. The World Views course is thus not a likely candidate for the core management program, because it covers archaic origin myths, ancient Greek philosophy, the Gothic cathedrals of Europe, the great astronomers of the late Renaissance, and issues in technological innovation—and relates these topics to organizational change. Class members remark how refreshing it is to approach management issues from a perspective outside a management-centered approach. The experience does more than revive them, however; it stimulates thinking about their careers and companies in new ways. We analyze Gothic cathedrals, which began gracing Europe in the twelfth century, as intensively coded, high-density databases. These arouse wonder not only for their visual splendor but also for the care, precision, quality, and technological innovation embedded in everything from carving a gargoyle three hundred feet in the air to distributing the weight of stone via complex, decorative structural elements. Rather than focusing on the cathedrals as works of art, we analyze them as embodiments of the worldview of their time. The two most startling aspects of the cathedrals' space—the interior volume and the spires that rose thirty to forty stories—required specialized knowledge in mathematics, architecture, and technology, not all of it understood today. These dimensions of space, volume and height, reflected the awakening of the European mind and the rapid expansion of cultural horizons.

The gigantic stained-glass rose windows and rows of pictorial windows added luminosity to volume and height as a third spatial element that also reflected the mind's awakening. Setting so much stone above a large glass window required specialized solutions for the distribution of force. The colorful glass itself demanded advances in chemistry and optics, knowledge derived from the Arabic culture, which was enamored of optics, courtesy of their access to the ancient Greek texts of Plato, Euclid, and their heirs. The countless individual sculptures that adorn each cathedral depict an entire cosmology of personalities both noble and monstrous, and might have inspired Dante, at the end of the Gothic era, to create the multitiered universe of dramatic personages that inhabit his *Divine Comedy*. The rhythm of the architectural ribs echoed the new rhythms of the complex gears that drove the rapidly evolving technology of clocks that were being installed on bell towers all over Europe. Complex patterns and rhythms were also becoming evident in everything from music to economic activity.

The cathedrals stimulated local and regional economies and drew people to the cities much as the Acropolis building programs did in Athens. Paradoxically, they not only stood as monumental testimony to the Church's power but also expressed the new, revolutionary, humanistic spirit emerging within the growing cities, especially in the university towns. The sculptures of saints and sinners and gargoyles and kings depicted individual personalities and passions; who they were as people began to matter apart from the status of their faith. More abstractly, the celebration of voluminous, soaring, and luminous space gloriously expressed the falling away of the medieval age's physical, intellectual, and spiritual restrictions.

It is impossible for anyone to engage ideas like these without viewing afresh their own technological, cultural, and business priorities, workplace, hierarchies, and society. Throughout the World Views course, students and instructors alike are fascinated with the incredible processes that must occur to generate breakthrough innovations, whether in architecture, astronomy, or thought itself. They begin to view both innovation and their own careers from far more open, expansive, and challenging perspectives than most organizations cultivate.

Terry Beard's framing company embraced this approach by spending more than $100,000 a year for employees to attend cultural events and bring discussions of their experiences into the workplace in the form of regularly held salons. The historical hothouse communities, of course, all exhibited a relentless intellectual curiosity; perhaps the Florentines and medieval Andalusians were most striking in this regard. Corporate initiatives could take the form of salons, discussions, lectures, and especially courses. Courses can be linked to specific organizational concerns such as innovation or the history of technology, or they can address areas of general employee interest. College and high school degree programs fulfill this purpose as well. The most creative workplaces benefit from the broadest set of skills, knowledge, interests, and passions that its employees possess. These companies get the most from their employees because they enjoy bringing all they have to offer into work. Encouraging intellectual exchange sends the message that the entire range of knowledge and ideas can be applied to workplace challenges, thus enriching both the individual and organizational stores of creativity.

#11. TAPPING OTHER DISCIPLINES

One constant of the hothouse effect is the interdisciplinary exchange that occurs among its members. Every company I visited promoted interdivisional and interdisciplinary conversations, both formal and informal, among all the staff. Loop Design Centre, Foster-Miller, and NextGig all encourage employees to wander through the company to trade ideas with whoever may be helpful. Entrepreneur Arthur Nelson's divisions in the Nelson Companies maintain close contact with one another. Thomas Edison's laboratory explicitly promoted the "mucking about" method, at least in his earlier years at Menlo Park, and he called his staff "muckers." Edison constantly consulted the many technical experts he employed and the various storerooms and workshops contained endless inventories of chemicals, animal hair, tools, machine parts, stones, gems, plants, metals, sonic and electrical devices, and who knows what else. Leonard DeGraaf, archivist at the Edison National Site in West Orange, New Jersey, points out that Edison was intent upon turning out inventions quickly on a regular basis. Edison wanted to ensure that any material he needed would be readily available, which, in those days, meant onsite at the lab. The availability issue was especially important, DeGraaf notes, because Edison worked on inventions for a wide range of industries, so he never knew what he might need. Edison was always thinking about the invention process and how to make it more efficient. He laid out the West Orange laboratory, which succeeded the one at Menlo Park, to increase his people's access to whatever they needed. As DeGraaf explained, "Edison want[ed] to work on a diversity of things, he want[ed] to work quickly, and he want[ed] his lab ready to do all of those things. He had a well-stocked research library, chemical labs, and stock rooms, and the machine shops to produce any model he needed." Edison worked, in large part, before the era of plastics, which were invented during his lifetime, and the huge stockpiles of materials in his lab reflected the Victorian era's belief that "nature will provide" whatever is needed. Thus, the entire structure of the most productive invention lab in history was predicated on facilitating interdisciplinary access to materials and the sharing of expertise among the men who worked in the shops, labs, and storerooms. And while this approach is very stimulating from the point of view of creativity, for Edison it clearly met several pressing business needs as well.

Florence was the great clearinghouse for the most advanced ideas of its time, all of which entered into the creative processes of its greatest artists. Athens played a similar role two millennia earlier and its greatest leader, Pericles, cohosted with his paramour Aspasia salons for leading scientists, writers, and artists of his day. In early twentieth-century Paris, writers and painters mingled together quite conscious of their mutual artistic symbiosis, while the Bauhaus represents as complete an integration and cross-fertilization of disciplines as one could expect in a formal setting. Jazz musicians fed on one another's styles (which could be strikingly diverse). Many looked outside the world of jazz for musical ideas, while others had been classically trained early in their lives.

The thoroughness with which this factor permeates the hothouse effect demonstrates its vital role in fomenting the effect. Casey Powell *started* Sequent with a policy of encouraging close interaction among all departments and employees. Eugene Foster *started* Foster-Miller so that design and engineering could constantly inform one another. The interdisciplinary approach of the Italian workshops during the Renaissance not only maintained the era's creative momentum but was also in large part responsible for its achievements.

Why is this factor so powerful? The exchange of ideas triggers more ideas among people passionate about them and fascinated with where ideas might lead. Ideas know no boundaries. We don't think only with the part of our brain devoted to marketing, managing, silicon, or paint—and no painter, for example, knows only about paint and no engineer knows only about metal or mathematics. The realm of ideas is like a vast society in which ideas cluster in neighborhoods, towns, and cities, while some live lonely lives deep in the woods. Ideas may be drawn from the (figurative) remote countryside to the city, where they excite a whole new cycle of creative activity, much as New York City's daunting record of creative activity has always been fueled by immigrants arriving not only from over-seas but also from the American South and Midwest. When two or more "cities," or entire fields of ideas, combine—such as writing and painting (Stein's Paris), physics and visual metaphor (the physicists), engineering and design (Foster-Miller), industry and art (the Bauhaus), music and social change (jazz), art and politics (Athens)—creative energy rises dramatically. When four or five individuals, or several departments within a company, exchange ideas regularly, the impact is analogous to that of a trade net-work's effect on prosperity among its member communities. Every set of ideas, every field of knowledge, is built on certain methodologies, patterns of thought and behavior, assumptions about the world, agreed-upon goals, an ethical model, a shared view of how things work (such as people, mate-rials, or machines), and a fundamental way of organizing knowledge. When people from different disciplines exchange ideas, a good part of these ele-mental ideas, feelings, insights, beliefs, systems, and time-tested truths are transmitted along with them. The more interwoven the exchange among practitioners from different fields, the more dynamic, numerous, and po-tent the ideas that emerge from this activity.

#12. CIRCULATION OF IDEAS

Establishing these connections and encouraging the exchange of ideas and information across the links is only half the job. The other half involves creating the systems and environment to support this exchange, using a more informal, ongoing dialog among all participants that transmits what-ever is useful to whoever needs it, whatever their position in the hierarchy. Hothouse members usually have the freedom to establish and utilize these channels of exchange, while managers facilitate rather than monopolize the initiative. Informal interactions and gatherings, design elements such as Sequent's skywalks, multifunctional teams assigned to all projects (even when assigned to a specific department), spaces set aside for the sharing of ideas, symposia at which employees examine important workplace issues, seminars by outside experts, educational programs, and cultural events, all promote the circulation of ideas. Managers who converse with out-of-the-way community members can discover a wide range of perspectives they won't find in their offices. Opportunities to implement this factor will often present themselves.

Jazz offers numerous examples of this free, circulatory flow of ideas. In November 1929, Coleman Hawkins played a few solos and ushered in the tenor saxophone as jazz instrument *par excellent*. As Gary Giddins wrote, "In early 1929, not a single tenor saxophone solo on record could equal the maturity of Bechet's soprano on 'Cake Walking Babies,' let alone Hodges's alto on 'Tishomingo Blues.' By early 1930, that was no longer the case. Hawkins had established for all time the stature of the tenor during two weeks in November with a handful of solos that require no apologies."[1] In other words, jazz musicians took up Hawkins's insights immediately, taking advantage of the jazz world's wide-open system of exchange. The musicians accessed their industry's intellectual capital with absolute efficiency. Despite often being cheated by an industry hostile to their personal interests, the musicians—black, Latino, and white alike—retained creative control over their music and hence missed no chance to extend its incredible range of beauty and invention.

#13. IMPLANTING PERIPHERAL FUNCTIONS

Implanting elements from the periphery into the center, or from the bottom of an organization within its upper levels, requires strong support from leadership and illustrates what organizational development guru Barry Oshry calls a *power move*: a bold, high-risk bid to reconfigure power relationships within a group.[2] Its dramatic nature draws the community together at the outset to cushion the shock of the move itself. Casey Powell's turning the organization chart upside down at Sequent and NextGig relies on the mildly dramatic humor intrinsic in "turning things upside down" to transmit the notion that hierarchy is far from sacred. Nonetheless, the gesture will not work unless clear protocols and procedures *support, structure*, and *sustain* the lower and peripheral elements in their new position.

These protocols existed at the Bauhaus, where procedures encouraged students to communicate with Gropius and the other masters. As we have seen, Powell established protocols that ensured that everyone could be heard from without fear of raising the manager's ire. Even with good intentions, old hierarchal habits die hard. It is difficult not to be aware of power differentials, or to refrain from using them when one can. To overcome such habits requires strongly supported procedures. Importing the Dionysia to Athens, as wild as it may have seemed at first, represented an organizational framework that guaranteed the input of primitive rustic energies into the life stream of the region's capital city. Such a result, if supported by top management, can give any organization the same edge it gave Athens and

Sequent: more brainpower, imagination, motivation, loyalty, and spirit, and better results.

The more people who are involved in organizational discourse, the more links and hubs they create in the network of communication. Links are channels or pathways that connect different members of a network and different regions within the network.[3] Hubs are junctions—concentrations of processing capacity—that receive information from existing links or that send forth new links to transmit information to another hub. Hubs can be people, cities, offices, computers, labs, cafés, mobile communication units, or any link's terminal destination. In general, the more connections flowing in and out of a hub, the more important the role played by that particular hub. Exceptions abound. A gatekeeper, for example, overseeing highly classified information, with one link flowing in and one flowing out, may still play a critical role in a network. But from the perspective of the entire organizational ecology, isolated hubs tend to be less important than well-connected hubs. Ideas moving upward come out of a different realm from those that travel down—we can say the latter come from the canopy while the former come up from the roots. If the links between roots and canopy are obstructed, the canopy dwellers lose touch with conditions down on earth and root-dwellers feel suppressed. The emerging hothouse relies upon all members functioning as vital, well-connected hubs empowered to establish links as necessary.

One cannot simply impose new modes of thought and behavior on a community. It makes more sense to change the conditions in which communication takes place so that this hydraulic network establishes itself naturally. This involves encouraging managers to trust the perceptions of those below. Model a culture in which anyone may pose questions or suggestions to anyone else. Defuse the paranoia that arises when one manager's staff members are seen speaking openly with the manager's boss or peer from another department. This does not involve nurturing or indulging people or any other condescending approach; it is about fostering mature discourse that can make a difference. Whether one creates an entire culture where that can happen, as at Beard Framing, Sequent, the Bauhaus, or in the jazz world, or whether initially the leader models this behavior and shows that he or she expects it from other employees, this dynamic model of exchange is critical to establishing a more creative work environment.

#14. MASTERY

All these ideas, energies, and data pulsing through the system still does not mean that all hubs are created equal. Every organization has its masters, and hothouses offer them explicit recognition and view their knowledge and experience as a key community resource. In Athens, Florence, the Bauhaus, and the jazz community, mastery was accorded formal or semiformal status. In the jazz world, there was usually little doubt about who earned the accolade of mastery, and these musicians—whether Charlie Parker, Duke Ellington, Louis Armstrong, or Billie Holiday—were widely emulated. In the workplace, the masters establish best-practice benchmarks and make them real as opposed to being abstract concepts. In a competitive workplace, one of the jobs of leadership is establishing the role of mastery without creating jealousy among driven, ambitious people. Verrocchio, Leonardo's mentor and head of his own workshop in Florence, and Duke Ellington managed to do it, and the best sports coaches do it as well. Great practitioners inspire us to perfect our craft, whether trading currency, framing pictures, playing music, fishing, or designing new molecules. Mastery represents an efficient method for transmitting the highest levels of creativity, thought, and technique from one person to a group of promising practitioners. When one works in close contact with a master, one absorbs the master's habits and skills by osmosis.

Mastery is the ridgepole of the tent; without it, standards and expectations lose shape and definition, and frequently the tent collapses. If masters are managed at all, it is with a light, collegial touch (barring serious personnel problems). They can be evaluated just like any other employee; if they do poorly, address it. Jim Foley said about Edwin Land, who was the master among masters at Polaroid and the Rowland Institute, "He talked to you all the time—not to tell you what to think but to keep you excited and to make sure that you weren't following a dead end. Land figured that if you were bright, dedicated, and in love with your subject matter, you could run with it." His faith in scientists was absolutely logical to him. Thus, at Polaroid, he let scientist Howard Rogers sit quietly for two years while mulling over a problem because he knew Rogers's capabilities with the certainty that an older master has regarding a younger one, and it paid off. It is almost impossible to imagine any executive willing to risk two years of nonproductive activity in a key employee, but Land and Rogers both knew that external evidence was not relevant and that the work *was* being done. Duke Ellington, another master among masters, used this management style every time his band played a song. His associate Billy Strayhorn, who wrote or cowrote many jazz classics, said about Ellington,

> Watching him on the bandstand, the listener might think that his movements are stock ones used by everyone in front of a

band. However, the extremely alert may detect a flick of the finger that draws the sound he wants from a musician. By letting his men play naturally and relaxed, Ellington is able to probe the intricate recesses of their minds and find things not even the musicians knew were there.[4]

Contrary to popular belief, creativity has everything to do with copying and repetition. Absorbing lessons from the masters is an incredibly efficient way to learn the most powerful techniques. Hunter S. Thompson, a wildly innovative writer, copied passages from the elegant styles of F. Scott Fitzgerald and William Faulkner just to internalize their technique. Frank Sinatra would write and rewrite the lyrics of songs he was about to record to study their inherent possibilities of phrasing, at which he was a master. The great jazz musicians almost always started off their careers by imitating the sound of a master whom they admired.

Creative people, of course, go well beyond simply copying. They adapt the techniques of the master and also challenge them, seeking their own original discoveries. In his autobiography, Miles Davis describes his frustration at continuing to sound like trumpeter Dizzy Gillespie, whom he greatly loved and admired.[5] Nonetheless, Miles was obsessed with developing his own sound, so he was not content to play in the "footsteps" of even the greatest of the era's trumpet players. Because the techniques of mastery include mental preparation and creative strategies, the bond between master and learner becomes very powerful, and that bond itself becomes a creative factor in stimulating the hothouse effect, in the form of mentorship.

#15. MENTORSHIP

Mentorship is a teaching or advising relationship between two mature practitioners for whom the master/student relationship is no longer appropriate. Mentorship creates a two-way vertical connection within a group. These high-capacity connections transmit a lot of concentrated energy and information. The mentor benefits as well because the best way to learn is by teaching, which forces the mentor or teacher to present ideas clearly and coherently. Mutual mentoring between equals from different departments or disciplines is equally powerful. Thus, mentorship can create a network of powerful *horizontal* as well as *vertical* links. A truly hothouse approach to mentorship would be strategically developing a network that connects all elements of an organization via these high-powered links.

Mentoring may seem similar to receiving lessons from the masters, but the masters' knowledge can be disseminated in many ways, mentoring among them. Mentoring, even between equals, provides validation and confidence, which, like gasoline additives, increase the propulsive force of the hothouse effect. It is often the mentor who gives a person the courage to strike off in an uncharted direction, and who provides the innovator with strategic advice born of experience and detachment from the situation. It is extraordinary how many exceptionally successful people look back to one or two teachers or mentors they met early in their careers who changed their lives. The role of mentorship at Sequent and NextGig, as we have seen, attests to the power these relationships have to energize and strengthen an organization.

#16. HUBS

When I interviewed Massachusetts entrepreneur Arthur Nelson, I started thinking about the various creative hubs he had created. Nelson believes that if an idea proves successful, creative hubs proliferate as a natural outcome of the human impulse to launch out into other companies and areas. Similarly, Edwin Land believed scientific and industrial progress were best served by small companies of two thousand employees, which he considered to be the ideal size for a research-oriented firm. As they grew, these companies would spin off other like-sized organizations, proliferating into a powerful network of creative companies.[6] Nelson sees the spinning off of new ventures as a natural outcome of business success. This idea comes naturally to a man who started nineteen enterprises divided about equally between for-profits and nonprofits.

The proliferation of creative hubs can refer to founding cities or institutions, hiring new scientists, establishing new labs, attracting artists to a downtown neighborhood, or spinning off a new company. The Greek city-states followed this course as soon as they became viable. Beginning in the late eighth century B.C.E., even small-sized towns sent out colonies to found instant city-states in northwestern Greece, the north African coast, Italy, southern France, and along the shores of the Black Sea where they perched "like frogs around a pond." These colonies were independent but maintained close ties with their mother cities, although these ties could turn into the bitterest of hostilities. The Greeks were so immersed in the integrity of the political unit that governed their lives, and in the role of citizen, that the *idea* of the city-state functioned as a database instantly transferable to its chosen site. Harnessing the power of the resulting formidable network of creative hubs had a monumental commercial and cultural impact on Greece.

Organizationally, encouraging creativity means establishing and promoting as many creative hubs as possible. Rather than managing, this process is more like orchestrating, as illustrated by Billy Strayhorn's description of Duke Ellington's command of his orchestra. The paradox is that the more freedom and recognition Ellington gave his superb musicians, the more intrinsic authority he had over the entire band. The more creative people in an organization, the more potential hubs the company can support.

New hubs proliferate because the creative impulse within a group is drawn to a perceived need and seeks to meet that need. Hubs should not proliferate because a particular manager decides to split a department in half or set up a division or follow a new management paradigm that he or she has heard about. The group itself knows when it is ready to generate a spin-off, which brings us back to our orchestra leaders, because it is actually more difficult to conduct than to manage. The game suddenly becomes much more strategic. How much independence does the new hub have? What is its objective? Can the organization afford it? Are the old position descriptions obsolete? Is the network becoming too complex for the management team to oversee? These problems arise frequently anyway, but a *creative* hub is a different beast; it is formed precisely *because* it can operate at a high performance level. Yet, it invariably pays off. Whether the many artists' workshops that sprang up in the Renaissance or Dr. Land's vision of proliferating research firms, the proliferation of hubs is a central process in the emergence of the hothouse effect.

#17. CONTRADICTION

As Peisistratos demonstrated, the ability to weave connections between opposing forces taps a profound energy source. As in brainstorming activities, the key is not choosing between the two forces but in allowing them to inform one another. We can compare this with an electric current flowing between two poles. When the two sides of opposition transmit their perspectives to one another instead of ending at loggerheads, a current of activity opens up. The two opposites are really only at different points of perspective along the same linear path of activity. One side can show the other where it is headed (for example, up or toward the "light"), the other can remind its mate where it has come from and what it left behind (down or toward the "darkness"), or vice versa. Yet, the power of this engagement lies in the immediate, charged quality of the interaction between the two poles. When the rustics began visiting Athens regularly, the city must have astonished them, and yet they too provided the city with their excitement and energy. Operating under seemingly contradictory circumstances forces one to utilize all available perspectives and data. It is also a powerful mental exercise—one must employ different parts of one's mind, perhaps even different regions of the brain, which awakens the creative faculties. Holding seemingly contradictory points of view reduces the tendency to select automatically the one that best fits our own preconceptions.

One of the toughest problems today in advancing a career or even assuring oneself continued employment involves navigating our way through the daunting contradictions that mark the current business environment. Are lower-level and middle-level managers really leaders, as they are often encouraged to be, or virtually powerless implementers of commands sent from above? How can we be agents of change at work if *change* often means extensive lay-offs, including laying off ourselves? Continual expansion within an economic system bound by definite limits is a dilemma faced by all companies, yet managers and workers are pressured to produce results against steeper and steeper odds. How do growing companies maintain the characteristics that brought them success as they become larger, more impersonal, and more bureaucratic? Is there a conflict between personal ethics and the compromises one must make for a business to succeed?

At the Bauhaus, Kandinsky, Grunow, Moholy-Nagy, and Itten explicitly used the principles of opposition and contradiction in their workshops. They talked about how tensions entered into the creative process, and they conducted creativity exercises to bridge the gap between movement and thought, imagination and reason, form and color, and so forth. The Bauhaus fused art and design and technology into one master discipline, while Dr. Eugene Foster was inspired to found Foster-Miller as a fusion of the disciplines of engineering and design. Some creativity tricks help promote this approach in the workplace. Contrarian solutions involve moving in the direction opposite to the obvious one. Is everyone focused on streamlining processes? Perhaps, instead, the solution lies in *adding* procedures, which often clarifies the steps required to complete a task most efficiently. People can be encouraged to withhold judgment on competing viewpoints until the best aspects of both have been tapped. And, as at Foster-Miller and the

Bauhaus, project teams might draw from departments with different views of project needs and objectives—that is, engineering and sales, finance and research and development, or information technology (IT) and lower-level management (who must implement and live with IT's solutions). As Athens demonstrated, unifying these different stakeholders, even for a limited time, will produce dramatic results.

#18. TECHNOLOGY

Technology plays a special role in the formation and exchange of ideas because it is not simply another aspect of work or personal life: It is central to human society and economy. Over millions of years it has become, by virtue of the relationship between human beings and our tools, another facet of human nature. It extends our animal capacities: a spear extends the reach of our arms, a gun still farther; a horse increases the speed of our legs, a car even more dramatically, and airplanes give us wings; dogs extended our senses of smell and hearing and placed fangs and claws at our service instead of tooth and nail; a computer speeds up certain mental acts; television, binoculars, and telescopes extend the range of sight; and so on.

Many social critics have noted technology's other impacts on our lives: We become alienated from ourselves by performing dull, repetitive tasks that deaden bodies, minds, feelings, manual skills, and aspirations. The care and feeding of expensive machinery takes precedence over the care and feeding of human beings, especially those who work the machines. Technology constantly mediates our experiences of society, nature, and one another until we lose the immediacy and authenticity of our responses. The machine imposes its own rhythms and behaviors upon us. To drive a car, we sit inside a bubble of glass and steel and glide obliviously through our environment, spewing toxic gases along the way. That experience shapes our reality and determines interactions with our neighbors, streets, passengers, and landscape. The computer achieves this no less than the assembly line. The irony is that machines give us the illusion of control over our world and our own lives, both because they create so much wealth for us and because of their display of the immense power required to illuminate cities, move mountains, tunnel through the earth, or fly jumbo jets. So control becomes a central feature of what it means to be human—we control the air, earth, sea, and all things that live in and on them. But our own lives are largely controlled by the same machines that allow us to exercise this power.

Every organization should periodically reassess all equipment and systems in order to establish more effective and seamless interfaces among them. Analyzing the impact of technology on initiative, customer service, adaptability to new situations and conditions, and creativity realigns key operations with business need but also provides an efficient approach to investing in technology. This analysis is emphatically not a performance review and is best done with full participation of employees; it is a way to make technology "smarter," which is not always achieved by upgrading systems or equipment.

The ratio of investment to benefit includes qualitative factors. Organizations have learned to be more selective in their upgrades, but as systems become more complex, it becomes more difficult to predict such things as obsolescence, actual depreciation of value (as opposed to formulaic predictions that may be based on out-of-date standards), the interface of new systems with those still in use, the degree to which investment in one system commits a company to the same supplier for others as well, or the features of a system an organization will actually use.

Sometimes, automating a function causes customer and collegial relationships or specific procedures to fall through the technological cracks. Because technology is both an extension of ourselves and yet definitely "other" than us, its use is riddled with contradiction. Yet this very contradiction makes it such a creative medium: to address the "shadow side" of technology while exploring its potential makes it more likely that an organization will take full advantage of it, while reducing its downside.

Hyde Tools and its sister company, Dexter-Russell, manufacturers of metal tools located in Southbridge, Massachusetts, have implemented a model, award-winning environmental program aimed at recycling metal filings and the large quantities of water that production requires. According to Bob Clemence, an executive with multiple duties with the company, Hyde is a family-owned business with deep roots in the community. After being in business for 127 years, Hyde expects to remain in the area for at least an equal number of years. Its commitment to the environment is driven by its commitment to the community and its employees. Clemence's sentiments are strikingly similar to those of Edwin Land when the Hyde executive states: "Either people care or they don't. We're not just responsible to ourselves but to the 535 families we employ. We're responsible for a lot of people. It goes beyond just being a responsible company, it's about being a responsible citizen."

Clemence describes how the entire production process comes under continual scrutiny for ways to reduce any waste produced and to minimize the use of natural resources. The results have been outstanding. From producing 800 tons of metal filings, Hyde now generates less than 400 tons, and all of that tonnage is recycled into blacktop for highways. Hyde saves 27 million gallons of water a year by using closed loop chilling systems and low temperature evaporation to recycle the water that contains production residues. This approach requires an ongoing engagement with technological issues that directly affect production. "Anytime we look at materials, we ask is it environmentally sound? Can we remove it easily? Replace it?" Clemence states. Sometimes it can be done, but some processes are prohibitively expensive. Environmental responsibility seems to imply fiscal irresponsibility. But, as Hyde has demonstrated, continual assessment of technology's role in all operations can be integrated into sound business practice, and it will pay off in numerous ways.

One often hears from the corporate frontlines that far too many IT people don't know enough about management, and that too many managers know too little about the technological systems they oversee. This can be termed the Second Digital Divide, and it continues at immense cost to businesses, schools, government, and other organizations. Oddly enough, although more and more people in all fields are growing increasingly adept at using technology, the increasing complexity of the systems serves to maintain the gap between management and technology. Closing that gap requires people on both sides to learn important lessons about their organization, industry, and colleagues, and thus enriches the fund of ideas and insights available to all. And, needless to say, the process should result in more efficient and creative use of these incredible machines whose implications we are only now beginning to grasp.

#19. EDUCATIONAL FORMATS

Elizabethan England, whose capital hosted the hothouse in which William Shakespeare, Christopher Marlowe, and Ben Jonson flourished, boasted a burgeoning nationwide public school system that steeped its students, who included the three aforementioned innovative geniuses, in the history and literature whose historical and legendary characters entered stage left in so many plays. Italy's cities and towns also possessed excellent lay (as opposed to church) schools attended by middle-class boys. The education emphasized the mathematics and practical geometry the boys would need when they became tradesmen or merchants, and these schools played a vital role in shaping the Italian Renaissance.[7] The schools founded in Athens by Plato and Aristotle, one can argue, still operate today after undergoing transmutation from one civilization to the next. The schools and libraries of medieval Andalusia played an important role in inspiring the Renaissance. Centuries later, the education received by the gifted physicists of Europe laid the basis for the most astonishing scientific advances in known history. The Bauhaus developed revolutionary methods for teaching creativity and for teaching creatively. Many great jazz musicians had excellent childhood music educations, and their educations continued onstage and in rehearsal via an informal but concentrated mentorship process.

The message is clear: An educated population is best able to utilize the rich and various inputs necessary for any creative endeavor. Education doesn't only teach us *more* knowledge, it transforms and expands the cognitive and conceptual structures through which learning and discovery take place. Education and the foundation of innovative educational formats are critical to the hothouse effect. At Beard Framing, Terry Beard's sponsorship of tickets to cultural events and in-house salons at which employees discussed books and ideas was intended to increase the intellectual capital of everyone in the company. Beard's example is exceptional because it recognizes that the entire organization benefits from intellectual excitement and discovery. Beard saw immediate returns in customer service, but he didn't implement the program with those returns in mind. Rather, he knew that a staff alive with ideas and exposed to creativity would be more motivated, creative, and adept at fulfilling customers' requests.

Corporate universities and online learning programs are attempts to meet increasingly complex learning demands. Neither, though, is generally designed with creativity in mind, and most educational and training models simply deliver pedagogy as usual. Business and industry alone do not have the ability to inspire, transform, and sustain the level of innovation required to overcome outmoded habits of thought. There is a world of ideas and invention out there that modern organizations desperately need. Many businesspeople thirst for fresh ideas and the freedom to seriously play with those ideas. Ultimately, intellectual capital is not only about patents and university degrees but also the mental enrichment of every employee.

NOTES

1. Gary Giddins, *Visions of Jazz* (New York: Oxford University Press, 1998), p. 123.
2. Barry Oshry in the *Power and Systems* seminar, 1999, Cape Cod, Massa-

chusetts. Oshry's experiential seminars are renowned throughout the corporate world, and his books, such as *The Possibilities of Organization* (Boston: Power and Systems, 1992), supplement the workshops.

3. For an excellent introduction to the science of networks, see Albert-László Barabási, *Linked: The New Science of Networks* (Cambridge, MA: Perseus Publishing, 2002) and Mark Buchanan, *Nexus: Small Worlds and the Groundbreaking Science of Networks* (New York: W.W. Norton and Co., 2002).

4. Eric Nisenson, *Blue: The Murder of Jazz* (New York: St. Martin's Press, 1997), p. 93.

5. Miles Davis with Quincy Troupe, *Miles: The Autobiography* (New York: Simon and Schuster, 1989), p. 90.

6. Edwin Land, "Research by the Business Itself," in *The Future of Industrial Research: Papers and Discussion* (New York: Standard Oil Development Company) from a paper presented at the Standard Oil Development Company Forum in New York, October 5, 1944.

7. Michael Baxandall, *Painting and Experience in Fifteenth-Century Italy* (Oxford: Oxford University Press, 1972), pp. 86ff.

7

RENAISSANCE À LA FLORENTINE: "DISTURBERS, AGENTS OF THE NEW"

The European Renaissance was one of those hinges on which the gates of history swing open to welcome a host of new human energies. The onset of the Age of Exploration, with its ocean voyages, colonialism, and exponential growth of wealth and knowledge, is preeminent among these energies. Others include advances in key industries such as mining, metallurgy, optics, ballistics, construction, and agriculture; the growth of complex financial institutions and universities; sudden exposure to the knowledge of the ancient Greco-Roman world, lost to Europe for a millennium; emergence of the nation-state; renewed interest in the realm of the senses and objects of luxury; the emerging power of cultural symbols such as Romantic Love, the Virgin Mary, and the devil; the invention of the printing press; discontent with the Catholic Church culminating in the Protestant Reformation; and an absolute explosion of activity in all the arts and sciences. No corner of the world would be left untouched by this legacy, whose actual dates vary from locale to locale, but can be very roughly dated from 1300 to 1600, with the 1200s as a transition period. Perhaps Shakespeare's death in 1616 in Europe's western borderlands can serve as a fitting finale to the Renaissance.

If one country is given pride of place in the European Renaissance, it is certainly Italy, both in terms of its achievements and its primary role in triggering this profound historical transformation. And the heart beating at the core of the Italian Renaissance was a land-locked city, and not a particularly large or militarily powerful one at that: Florence. How can we claim to locate the source of the Renaissance in that single place? One clue lies with a principle we have already mentioned: The hothouse effect is often the culmination or *expression* of a broader cultural movement. We can almost imagine an unconscious system-wide decision that the system itself is too dispersed, with interests and agendas too diverse, to climb the steepest creative slopes. So the regional system concentrates its energies on one community to maximize creative innovation, much as the human brain, at 2 to 3 percent of a person's body weight, uses 20 percent of the body's oxygen intake.

STILL MUSIC EVERYWHERE . . .

One day in Florence an odd jazz quartet sets up on the side street near our hotel, a renovated Renaissance-era stone tower. Around the corner, Dante's house still stands near his local church in which chamber music was performed last night and Beatrice, Dante's infatuation and inspiration, married another man seven hundred years ago. The church predates Dante by more than two hundred years; but in Florence, centuries crowd together just as the ancient houses on their tiny streets. And there's this quartet: two guitars, an accordion, and an alto sax. The musicians themselves are, physically, an intriguing mix. The lead rhythm guitarist is about thirty and plays with a *joie de vivre* that includes one of the most delighted, infectious smiles I've ever seen. This smile is directed largely at the alto player, a short, moderately stout fellow with a calm, buddhistic face. The accordionist possesses musical abilities well beyond the other practitioners of his instrument who wander Italian cities seeking tourists to serenade. In contrast to the beaming guitarist and serene saxophonist, the gaunt accordionist appears to have been recently roused from the dead; to say he is expressionless is to ascribe a level of animation his features could never sustain. On the other side of the alto scowls the second guitarist, with sharp, brow-shaded eyes and hawk nose. He often doesn't play but watches the street and confers with another fellow who seems to be involved with the group in some undefined way; occasionally the second guitar plays a bass line on the low strings.

It is the saxophonist who keeps me there. He is sensational, in the style of Johnny Hodges. Later I inquire about him from a waiter in a café whose walls are lined with pictures of local jazz musicians. He knows whom I mean and nods vigorously when I say how good the alto is, but the waiter doesn't know his name. His playing is fluid and his improvisations move over, around, and under the scales. All the while, his guitarist is whipping away on rhythm and beaming like sunlight at the music emanating from the horn. The accordionist plays interesting chord changes behind them; he's tuned into the frequency but gives no sign other than the movement of his fingers on the keys and the slight shifting of his wrists working the bellows.

I'd listen all afternoon, but two police officers come and politely tell the band they cannot play on the side street, although they are welcome to perform in the piazzas. There's some discussion. I call out, "Loro sono fantastico," and the policewoman smiles at me—or at my Italian. They leave, but I don't see them in any of the piazzas after that.

The record store near the Duomo plays opera to lure customers inside. There is opera everywhere, it seems: in Rome's Piazza del Popolo where a troupe rehearses for the next night's performance, in a park near Santa Maria Novella in Florence, in the Uffizi courtyard where a lone tenor sings beautifully and sells his CDs, and in an ancient watchtower in Umbria, where a young opera singer performs songs of every century from the fourteenth to the twenty-first. In Perugia, the international jazz festival boasts some big names, but it is the brilliant energy of bands such as Ray Gelato's and Johnny Nocturne's that drives the weeknight crowds wild.

There is nothing like wandering an Italian city at night. Whether Florence, Perugia, Rome, Venice, Bologna, or countless others of all sizes, you walk among ghosts—ghosts with secrets. In a world before cars and Vespas, the sound of boots and hooves and carriage wheels clattered tellingly across the cobbled stones between the closely set walls of the alleyways or across the empty spaces of the courts. Occasionally, you hear only that older city and you know each sound tells a story. But whose story? A poor shepherd boy who sketched beside his flock when the era's leading painter noticed him while passing by and made him his apprentice (Giotto discovered by Cimabue)? An illegitimate boy from a town a few miles from Florence (Leonardo)? A stonecutter's son whose knowledge of the quarries was transmuted into the *Pieta* and the *David* (Michelangelo)? The story of families spending their allotted time in history and passing beyond memory, leaving behind the timeless city they helped to sustain? Beggars and cutthroats, geniuses and princes, proud, passionate women and bold, conniving men. Exactly five hundred years ago, Leonardo and Machiavelli collaborated on a project to divert the course of the River Arno, challenging destiny and geography at a time when to do either inspired terror and religious guilt.[1] A millennium before the Renaissance, merchants calculated as they paced these streets in a Europe traumatized after the fall of Rome; a millennium before that time, traders walked these same streets in Etruscan times, selling Corinthian pottery or Spartan bronze. At night, everywhere you go, you pass briefly through another time zone where the shifts are counted in centuries, not hours.

THE GRAND BAZAAR OF IDEAS

So, then, why Florence? Or rather, how Florence? Why and how did this city pass through the vanishing point of human thought and emerge out the other side as the center of a matrix of ideas that not only changed the world but actually created one? The home of great traders, their city had been among Europe's wealthiest since at least 1300. As the year given for Dante's *Divine Comedy,* 1300 might claim the honor of launching the Renaissance. Or perhaps the curtains went up a few years earlier when Cimabue painted the Madonna in a style with "something of the draughtsmanship and method of modern times," according to Vasari, the sixteenth-century painter who wrote about the lives of the great Italian artists. The Florentines were so in awe they carried it through the streets to Santa Maria Novella in a celebration that Dante could have observed.[2] Or perhaps the Renaissance began in 1402 with the competition, won by Lorenzo Ghiberti, for the commission to create the north and east doors of Florence's ancient Baptistery. The committees that chose the winning designs solicited ideas from the greatest minds of Europe. Also, several talented sculptors worked with Ghiberti on the north doors. The magnificent doors may have been cast out of heavy bronze and spun from Ghiberti's genius, but the far-flung network of ideas blanketing the continent imbued the doors with their vitality as well. This was equally true of the even more stupendous east doors (see Exhibit 1), which Ghiberti created after finishing the north doors. At any rate, whether Dante, Cimabue, or Ghiberti—all three men and associated events are Florentine.

Florence "discovered" oil painting and perspective around the same time as the Dutch did. Oil paint developed through experimentation while perspective was arrived at through mathematics, another interesting polarity linking the concrete with the abstract. Oil paint articulated the substance of things, perspective the space in which they came to be. They were well suited to one another. Together, they created an illusion of realism that called into question the evidence of the senses, as the appearance of three-dimensional figures on a flat painted surface tends to do (see Exhibit 4).

Oil's richness stemmed from its ability to let light through translucent under-layers of paint and then to trap it there, creating effects that a master orchestrated using optics and color theory, studies of light's behavior in nature, and the effects garnered from the interaction of materials. Oil was perfect for depicting in exquisite, lush detail the luxury objects of nouveau-riche merchants, dukes, and kings, and the emotionally charged scenes commissioned by wealthy cities, churches, and monasteries. Perspective opened up horizons of space and thus possibility, and enabled painters to chart the complexity of the new architecture that adorned the expanding cities. Together, oil and perspective were perfect for portraying the social mobility, complex social dynamics, expanding intellectual horizons, and increased wealth that marked the era. With art, philosophy, and architecture, the artistic innovators both secured the new vision and, at the same time, extended it. This is a critical function of creative work: It anchors in the real world what was previously just a vision, and provides a substantial platform for further development.

We are all children of Florence. As novelist and critic Mary McCarthy mused in *The Stones of Florence*, "The Florentines in fact invented the Renaissance, which is the same as saying that they invented the modern world—not, of course, an unmixed good."[3] Without the Renaissance we simply wouldn't be us. And just as Athens represents the core cultural achievement of the ancient Greco-Roman world that flourished for two thousand years, so too does Florence serve the European Renaissance. As with Athens, this does not detract from the many other centers of cultural activity in Europe during this era. Nor does it imply that cultural florescence radiates primarily from one single source. Certainly Italy and its cities can be considered one big hothouse effect, without which neither Florence nor the Renaissance would have flourished. However, even within such a matrix, one dynamic hub harnesses the power of a continent's worth of ideas and plays the pivotal role in a defining historical moment.

McCarthy calls Florence "a turning-point," not simply in terms of artistic achievement, but in the growth of what McCarthy considered "a gigantism of the human ego," that is, a momentous change in how human nature was experienced and viewed.[4] It is, after all, the city of Machiavelli as well as Leonardo. She notes that the "Florentines introduced dynamism into the arts, and this meant a continuous process of acceleration, a speed-up, which created obsolescence around it, as new methods do in industry."[5] Published in 1959, her words can stand as a description of the computer's impact on business and daily life. "The *last word,* throughout the Renaissance, always came from Florence."[6] McCarthy describes the Venetians, in 1433, as being "amazed by these advanced persons" when a contingent of Florentine artists, intellectuals, and architects took up residence in the island city: "Wherever the Florentines went, they acted as disturbers, agents of the new."[7] This was precisely the charge hurled at the Athenians throughout their golden age in the fifth century B.C.E.: They were restless, disturbers of the natural balance of Greek politics and economics, they were a different *type* of person. Even some Athenians felt this way. The conservative politician, Thucydides (not the historian of the same name) accused his rival, Pericles, of costuming Athens "like a whore." What was he referring to? Nothing less than the newly built magnificent temples of the Acropolis, including the Parthenon itself. It can be tough living inside the hothouse effect.

What forces shaped this hothouse effect, and how did the Florentines themselves nurture and sustain this powerful energy? Why did Florence, of all places, produce a man who designed helicopters and painted the Mona Lisa; another who figured out a radical method of building the world's still-largest dome; and a third who designed St. Peter's, painted the Sistine Chapel, and sculpted the *David*? Near the beginning of it all, Giotto shatters centuries of tradition in painting and his exact contemporary Dante creates the watershed literary work of modern European civilization even as he plays a prominent role in Florentine politics.

THE GOLDSMITH'S WORKSHOP

Athens showed us how a sequence of internal reorganizations laid the groundwork for its hothouse effect. The Florentine artists' workshops, on the other hand, show us the hothouse effect at its culminating rather than preparatory phase. The workshops demonstrate that creative communities have an unerring instinct for growing their own talent. Celebrated workshops included those of Pollaiuolo and Ghirlandaio in Florence, Squarcione in Padua, and Bellini in Venice, but by far the most stellar example is that of Andrea del Verrocchio (1435–1488). Many of the best Florentine artists were skilled in a variety of disciplines, and Vasari, the sixteenth-century Florentine painter and chronicler of other artists' lives, noted that Verrocchio "was at once a goldsmith, a master of perspective, a sculptor [in metal and marble], a woodcarver, a painter, and a musician."[8] Verrocchio's most-gifted student was Leonardo da Vinci, but others were almost as renowned such as Botticelli, Perugino, and, according to one writer in 1490, "almost all those whose names now fly about the cities of Italy."[9] Leonardo came to Verrocchio through his father, Piero, a well-respected lawyer. Leonardo was illegitimate and Piero had his own family in town, but he seemed to have cared about and for Leonardo, although they had their difficulties. Piero showed Verrocchio drawings done by his adolescent son and Verrocchio was so impressed, he offered to take on da Vinci as his apprentice.

In the mid–1460s, Florence was already seething with Renaissance energy. Men such as Cimabue, Giotto, Brunelleschi, Donatello, and Massaccio predated Verrocchio, but

> When Leonardo became his apprentice, Andrea's workshop was in the process of becoming a meeting place of all the artistic youth in Florence—it was a crucible in which the principles of the new "modernity" were being hammered out. Here everything that went on in the city was subject for discussion. There was talk about dissection, antiquities, philosophy; artists exchanged models, plans, sketches, recipes for varnish or binding agent; and it was a place of recreation, where music was played.[10]

This brief passage by Serge Bramly, Leonardo's biographer, identifies several key building blocks of any hothouse effect:

- Concentration of youthful (not necessarily young), innovatively restless talent
- An exhilarating sense of mission often associated with overturning the strictures of convention and tradition
- Immersion in analyzing and examining the universal ideas derived from great systems of thought; in Florence, these included those inherited from the ancient Greco-Roman world; new discoveries in science; and the vast web of Arabic, Byzantine, Hebrew, and ancient Greek learning flooding into Italy at the time
- Lively exchange of innovative ideas and techniques within numerous creative disciplines
- Analysis of those disciplines at their most fundamental levels—that is, painters developing the actual paint used in producing their masterpieces, pushing the limits in regard to the metallurgy of large objects and sculptures, discovering secrets of perspective, etc.
- Indulging the festive spirit and integrating it into the daily round of work (Verrocchio himself was a musician)

The city beyond Verrocchio's workshop was equally stimulating:

> In Florence, Leonardo was at the heart of refined human-
> ism—a brilliant world of literary and artistic ferment and an
> extraordinary melting pot in which Tuscan tradition was en-
> riched with a revival of interest in classicism and by new in-
> fluences from the North and from as far away as Byzantium
> and Asia. He was inspired by his Florentine predecessors, the
> revolutionary painters Giotto (1267?–1337) and Masaccio
> (1401–1428).[11]

In Verrocchio's workshop, Leonardo sought the best oils to mix with
the pigments he produced by crushing plants, beetles, shells, and stone.
Inventing varnishes, gesso, and glues was all part of his grounding in the
underlying chemistry of his art. His lifelong interest in light and optics was
reflected in his innovative use of oil paint. Rather than merely bouncing
off the pigment, as it did with tempera paint, light bounced around and
refracted inside the tiny globules of oil, creating a luminous variety and
richness of color to which Renaissance painters were acutely sensitized.
Leonardo in particular used oil to its maximum potential to create a warm,
emotionally expressive patina of light over his figures, and a mysterious,
mystical, moisture-laden atmosphere that hung over his background landscapes as if the world he painted were already lost—or not yet discovered.
In the course of his life, Leonardo applied lenses, glass balls, and mirrors to
the study of vision, and drew complex polyhedrons to illustrate a friend's
mathematics book.[12] He designed flying machines and waterworks. Vasari
tells us that Leonardo loved animals and would often buy caged birds and
set them free; his notebooks offer a veritable bestiary of animal sketches.[13]
Geography, astronomy, mathematics, anatomy, hydrology, fortifications,
weaponry, the apparent physics of light, the mysteries of sight—experts in
all these fields abounded in this city of seething intellects and Leonardo
learned from many of them and outstripped all of them in some pursuits.
Long before Galileo, Leonardo analyzed the physics of weight, motion,
and inertia. He is credited with the first landscape drawing in the Western
tradition, a tribute to his passionate study of nature, especially the Arno
Valley, home to Florence and his own native village of Vinci. While no
rational explanation can account for someone like Leonardo, we can make
two broad assertions: (1) He seemed to channel the entire range of Renaissance activity through his extraordinary consciousness, and (2) Verrocchio's

workshop offered the ideal training for a youth capable of assimilating and synthesizing the knowledge of so many disciplines at once. From Verrocchio, for instance, he learned metallurgy for the workshop's architectural commissions, and the tolerance of various alloys undoubtedly came in handy in his engineering projects. And as art critic Arthur Danto noted in a recent article, Leonardo owed Verrocchio the debt of his teaching him *sfumato,* the depiction of an object's three-dimensionality by modulating light and shadow.[14] As in everything else, however, Leonardo used the technique to almost unreal effect.

The mentor must have been a superb manager. When one considers the talent collected around Verrocchio, the variety and scope of the projects his workshop handled, and the loyalty he inspired in those he mentored, including Leonardo, it is clear he understood how to manage creativity. Verrocchio likely had Edwin Land and Duke Ellington's ability to keep the many gifted people around him excited about the next project. All three men inspired personal loyalty based on fairness and respect, and they allocated work in a way that kept jealousy and pettiness at a minimum. All three were also good businessmen, as well as natural leaders of younger men, their authority stemming from competence and character, rather than position.

Verrocchio's spirit was clearly inquisitive, generous, and scientific. He led his apprentices in the search for ever more effective materials for their work. According to Vasari, Verrocchio often switched back and forth between painting and sculpture in order not to grow weary with either.[15] This aspect of his character was well in accord with his native city. Florence was the center of the quattrocento's (fifteenth century's) spirit of exploration. Christopher Columbus was a contemporary of Leonardo's and Florence, although not a seagoing state, possessed the same expansive spirit of exploration that seized many European states.

INFORMATION EXPLOSION

The transoceanic expeditions were not solely responsible for Europe's information explosion. Johannes Gutenberg's invention of the printing press by 1448 showered knowledge over all economic classes. Suddenly, literacy was no longer only the province of monks poring over the Bible or a few ancient texts preserved from the fall of Rome a millennium earlier. Many of the pamphlets and books circulating throughout the continent contained prints and information about plants, animals, ancient history, and distant lands. While books were more readily available to the wealthy, information had become not only vastly more voluminous but also more democratic. Oddly, it was Venice that dominated the printing trade in the second half of the quattrocento, in part because the Medici rulers of Florence feared that printing would undermine the value of their manuscript collection.[16] Still, books were available to all, especially the educated scholars and artists most attuned to new currents of thought.

As da Vinci biographer Bramly points out,

> Of all the men of the quattrocento, it was the artists—and Florentine artists in particular—who most believed in progress, for they always had before their eyes the works of preceding generations. . . . The scientific spirit that inspired Pippo Brunelleschi [builder of the Duomo] was also found in Verrocchio's studio. Leonardo inherited it: his art and all his knowledge stem from its principles. Observation, analysis, deduction, experiment: "Science is the captain, practice the soldier," he wrote.[17]

Such clear, simple guiding algorithms (such as "observation," etc.) are surprisingly common to many hothouses, as Sequent and the Nelson Companies illustrate. Leonardo certainly proved that a general yet focused approach to invention, business creation, or problem solving need not limit creativity.

The discoveries of Columbus, the subjection of the Americas, and the sea routes to the East all expanded the horizons and possibilities of space in the Renaissance mind. The entire mental landscape was transformed as a result, the new lands across the Atlantic mirrored in the new regions of the mind. The proliferation of settlements was mirrored in the proliferation of interconnected hubs of knowledge contained within these new mental regions. Every physical and geographical extension and connection was reflected in the inner landscape of tens of millions of people, many of whom had more than a taste of the spirit of scientific inquiry that permeated the lives of the most advanced thinkers. Meanwhile, as the Gutenberg-generated information revolution pervaded Europe, equally powerful springs of knowledge were flooding *into* Europe from the outside, as though the exchange of information and ideas were moving at warp speed through dimensions of thought previously unimagined. But to understand the power of this knowledge, it is necessary to understand something of its source.

FLORENCE MEETS BYZANTIUM

After the fall of Rome in the fifth century C.E., Europe was cut off from the vast treasury of ancient knowledge for eight hundred years. Meanwhile, the Arab lands, resurgent under Islam from the early seventh century C.E. on, inherited many of the ancient Greek texts. For example, Arab scholars studied and expounded upon the works of Plato, and seemed particularly interested in his theories of optical vision and music, and learned advanced mathematics from India. The Crusades, which began in 1095, brought European nobles and knights into close contact with Arab culture, especially during the Crusaders' occupation of Jerusalem throughout virtually the entire twelfth century. The Crusaders brought back to Europe many Arab cultural forms: the songs that inspired the early European troubadours, a tradition of courtly love, architectural techniques and designs, various mystical doctrines, geographical information, and perhaps fragmentary knowledge of the Greek philosophers and scientists, some of whom, for example, believed that the Earth was a sphere that circled the Sun. In Spain, the Islamic caliphate of Andalusia flourished as a major cultural center from the eighth to fifteenth centuries, with vast libraries and a class of scholars and thinkers drawn from the mixed Muslim, Jewish, and Christian population. The region provided Europe with ancient learning and the poetry, philosophy, science, and engineering methods then current in the Arab world.

At the same time, north of the Holy Land, the Turks' dominion crept ever closer to Constantinople, capital of the Byzantine Empire, which was actually a direct continuation of the ancient Roman Empire. Before Rome lost control of Europe, Constantinople (present-day Istanbul) became the eastern capital of the Empire around 300 C.E. It adhered to Orthodox Christianity and ruled Asia Minor (modern Turkey), the Balkans, northern Syria, and territories east of the Holy Land, although the Empire's borders fluctuated significantly throughout the centuries. It was the legitimate heir to the Roman Empire, its language was Greek, and it survived the fall of ancient Rome by a thousand years. The Byzantine government was a theocracy no more interested in scientific inquiry than was the Roman Catholic Church in the West. But its libraries contained much of what remained of antiquity's written heritage, and its scholars knew more about Greek and Latin texts than anyone alive.

Over the centuries, as the Turks advanced, many Byzantines fled west, among them a host of scholars and bibliophiles carrying their precious books. Italy, because of its proximity and the spiritual kinship of a Roman heritage, lured many as a final destination. By the early 1400s the Byzantine Empire consisted of a plot of land surrounding Constantinople, a global center of trade and manufacturing. The Italians had a major stake in maintaining the eastern trade routes that passed through Constantinople and politics swirled like a whirlwind around the empire's plight.

In 1438, the fate of the Byzantine Empire converged with Florentine history. A great embassy of seven hundred Greeks, including both the Byzantine emperor and the patriarch of the Byzantine Church, arrived in Florence to meet with the papal court and Italy's leading diplomats, scholars, and merchants. The Greek leaders hoped to win pledges of military support against the Turks. Their scholars made the argument that the two great intellectual traditions that diverged when the Roman Empire fell should be reunited, and the various churchmen poked around the issue of reuniting the Eastern and Western Churches.[18]

"As far as the inhabitants of Florence were concerned the impact of the Council was not doctrinal but cultural and ceremonial. It exposed them to an influx of visitors—a veritable crowd—from an utterly different yet highly sophisticated and exotic civilization."[19] This was not the only instance of Florence's exposure to the meta-system that existed beyond the Adriatic Sea, but it did inject into the city a massive dose of the character and perspectives of a meta-system. It is fascinating, too, that we can pinpoint a single event that had such a dramatic impact on Florentine culture and thought.

The Council of 1438 was all for naught. On May 28, 1453, the Turks broke through the city walls of Constantinople and renamed the city Istanbul, the new capital of an Ottoman Empire that survived until 1917. Florence had already benefited for two centuries from the refugees fleeing the advancing Turks, and a large portion of the information revolution that inspired the Renaissance came from the fallen Byzantine Empire. So the Genoa of 1451 into which Christopher Columbus was born, or the Florence of April 15, 1452, whose nearby town of Vinci recorded the birth of Leonardo da Vinci, were at the center of massive changes that were global in scope. These changes destroyed the Byzantine, Inca, and Aztec empires, ravaged African and Asian kingdoms, and cemented the system of national states that still dominates the world. Out of this turmoil grew a truly global economic system that is being knit ever more tightly together by the threads of technology and finance. As historian Lisa Jardine states, "The surviving records of visitations like the 1438 Florentine Council remind us that East and West were in constant—if sometimes tense—dialogue, and that the very instability of the Mediterranean political scene led to percolation from one culture into the other."[20] However, for the relatively provincial Florentines, ensconced among the Tuscan hills (however more sophisticated they were than other Europeans), the revelation of Byzantine learning and global perspectives was probably a one-way inspiration. The Byzantines, after all, were staring their own extermination in the face.

FLOURISHING IN THE IN-BETWEEN

As with Greece as a whole and Athens especially, the hothouse effect in Florence emerged out of an information revolution wherein Florence, a small, contained system of tremendous internal kinetic energy, interfaced with and absorbed what a far larger, more complex system could teach it. The meta-system would seem a likely candidate to overwhelm the emergent system, but in fact, it is the smaller more vital system that transmuted the huge data bank of the meta-system into fuel for its own vision.

Like Athens, Florence had strong local traditions. Although this could apply to any community, it does not occur equally. Rome, for instance, by 1500, had pursued a policy of transcontinental conquest and conversion for two thousand years. Rome's mission was always universal and its perspective global. Venice developed as a trading corporation almost from the beginning. Its fortune was the sea, not the land, and its worldview embraced caravan routes to the distant east and even the fabled kingdom of Cathay visited by Venice's native son, Marco Polo. Milan always operated in the shadow of the great northern European powers, such as France and the Holy Roman Empire. Florence, however, like Athens, lay just outside the reach of the superpowers of its age and (unlike Athens) its inland location reinforced its localism. Even in the fourteenth century, many Tuscans broke with the Roman Catholic Church, because they were fed up with its corruption. While retaining the religion of Catholicism, many people simply conducted their own services and sacraments. The ambitious thrones of France and the Holy Roman Empire always had their eyes on northern Italy as a path to expansion, while Spain exerted pressure from the south through the Kingdom of Naples, which it often controlled. But as art historian Arnold Hauser notes, the Florentines resisted both the political and artistic influence of court-based societies during the fourteenth century, finding their artistic expression to be too frivolous.[21] It was its "in-between" geographic position that afforded Florence the luxury of its own artistic style and that protected it politically. Florence was solidly middle class, too, and evinced the more secular, pragmatic, and direct character of the merchant and artisan class.

Hauser asserts that

> [A]n objective, realistic, unromantic attitude to life now [ca. 1400] predominates again in Florence, with a new, fresh, robust naturalism, against which the courtly-aristocratic conception of art can make its way only gradually. . . . The ["imposing realism"] of Massaccio and of the young Donatello is the art of a society still fighting for its life, albeit thoroughly optimistic and confident of victory, the art of a new heroic period in the development of capitalism, of a new epoch of conquest.[22]

This perfectly expresses the release of creative energy experienced after overcoming crisis and its associated feeling of renewed possibility. Not that Florence's quattrocento was a period of license and pure celebration. As Hauser and Mary McCarthy note, the Florentines were often subject to fits of puritanical angst. The hothouse effect can be exhilarating, yet challenging. Athens, the Bauhaus, the jazz community, the physicists of the twentieth century, and Florence all balanced pleasure against the seriousness of their work. A controlled and calculating purpose on the part of those driving the economic and social engines mingles with a vigorous, skeptical, and often exhilarating bohemian atmosphere.

Florence possessed the mind-set of a modest military power set inside a highly competitive environment that included some big sharks and in which even secondary powers threatened the city's well-being. In such conditions, it is natural to adopt a shrewd, calculating, analytic approach to the world to better ensure one's survival. This came easily to the merchants of Florence, but it was also reinforced by its exceptional secular educational system. As discussed briefly in Chapter 6, throughout Italy the lay schools emphasized geometry and algebra, which best prepared students for mercantile life. Historian Michael Baxandall explains that merchants did not use containers with standard measures. Sacks, barrels, baskets, and bales of infinite variety were used to transport goods. So a merchant had to be expert at gauging the volume of the goods he was buying or selling. In Germany measurement relied on complex rulers and measuring tools handled by a specialist; "an Italian, by contrast, gauged his barrels with geometry and pi."[23] Baxandall points out that while Florentine mathematical knowledge was not extensive by our standards, the sophisticated and thorough use of what they *did* know was extraordinary. This facility with formulas of proportion and measure was central to Florentine culture and nourished the cognitive framework that inspired artistic breakthroughs in perspective and the treatment of complex spatial forms.

TWIN PEAKS

Florence and Athens already exhibit commonalities in regard to the respective development of their hothouse effects. Both emerged from a period of crisis and absorbed the learning of a contemporary meta-system whose temporal dominion matched the vastness of its geographical span. In both cities, a dynamic creative community engaged in intensive analysis of artistic and intellectual disciplines. The role of the mentor, the sense of mission, and the weaving together of cultural polarities contributed to the creative energies of both cities. In addition, both Athens and Renaissance Europe created intensive concentrations of information-rich, analytically driven energy in the form of institutes, universities, and schools of philosophy. The first modern university was founded in Bologna in the twelfth century; today, the University of Bologna has 110,000 students and 7,000 faculty members. The European universities arose to handle the influx of ancient learning that the Byzantines and Arabs had preserved since the fall of the Western Roman Empire, and to formulate and bring sense to the welter of legal issues that an expansive, mercantile, increasingly urban society demanded. The universities became major processors of information and ideas that drove the momentum of creative change.

Festivals and whimsy played central roles in both cities; perhaps it is no accident that Botticelli and Leonardo da Vinci were both practical jokers. Vasari recounts how one of Botticelli's protégés had just completed an important commission and eagerly went to fetch his patron to admire the work. While he was gone, Botticelli and friends attached (with removable wax) paintings of the city officials' hats on the heads of the angels in the painting. When the painter returned with the patron, he was ready to panic. The patron, however, who was in on the joke, simply expressed delight at the work, never once mentioning the angels' absurd headgear.

He then asked the painter to leave the room to discuss payment and Botticelli had the hats removed. When the poor painter returned, no one let
on that anything had been amiss.[24] Brunelleschi, too, designed even more
elaborate practical jokes, one that was so maddening to its target that the
man left Florence for Hungary, where, it turns out, he amassed a great
fortune.[25]

Both cities thrived on conversation and debate, a predilection evident
in Athens' law courts, assemblies, and dramatic and Platonic dialogs. The
Florentines debated all the current ideas and were famous for their sharp,
irreverent manner of speech. Both cities were hotbeds of experimentation
with materials and ideas. Both relied on generous patrons for their support
of the arts, in Athens' case the city coffers themselves, which included
substantial "contributions" that were expected from the wealthier citizens,
tribute from the cities that joined (often involuntarily) the Athenian League
after the Persian Wars, and Athens' silver mines. In Florence, the patrons
were the fabulously wealthy ruling Medici family, rich merchants, the
churches, and the city itself. Both cities were infatuated with the quest
for universal principles of beauty, perspective, mathematics, and political
morality.

In other ways, too, they were similar. Both operated in highly treacher-
ous political landscapes, with betrayal and shifting alliances commonplace,
and numerous independent states engaged in intense military, economic,
and political competition. Internal political conflicts could be savage; creativity does not guarantee political stability (although neither does it rule
stability out). Athens and Florence both struggled against destiny in the
form of geography. Athens' greatest military leaders did their best to convince the Athenians that they were not really a land-based community, that
they could sacrifice their farms and countryside for the sake of the city and
its ships, a shift in thinking whose equivalent in any nation today would
still be deemed wildly radical. Two thousand years later, Machiavelli and
Leonardo pushed against geographic destiny with their plan to divert the
Arno.

Both cities erected architectural wonders that welcomed the populace
into their spaces, rather than monuments proclaiming the remote and awe-
some domination of their rulers. Both were intoxicated with mathematics,
which they felt gave them a direct line to the Divine and regulated the
perfection they actively sought to express in their art and architecture. One
city produced Plato, the other virtually worshiped him. Athenian painters
were famous for their uncanny realism, as were the Florentines. The latter's
intensive studies of vision and optics were matched in importance by the

real-world observations of Aristotle and his students. Mastery was highly respected in both cities, but no one was immune to petty political back-stabbing. Neither state succeeded in establishing good government beyond its cultural florescence, though despite the petty jealousies and astonishing betrayals, both did sustain viable and relatively benign political systems for a significant period of time during their respective golden ages.

Many of the cultural factors that prepare a community to achieve the hothouse effect are evident in the history of Athens in the sixth century B.C.E. In the Florentine workshops and the atmosphere of the city's daily life, we can witness the dynamics and methods—both consciously and unconsciously applied—that the most-talented members of the community used to enhance their own creativity and to amplify the collective effort of their colleagues. Both remain favorite destinations of travelers still entranced with the productions of these two extraordinary hothouse communities.

NOTES

1. Roger D. Masters, *Fortune is a River: Leonardo da Vinci and Niccolo Machiavelli's Magnificent Dream to Change the Course of Florentine History* (New York: The Free Press, 1998).
2. Vasari, *Lives of the Artists,* translated by George Bull (New York: Penguin Books, 1965, 1982), p. 53.
3. Mary McCarthy, *The Stones of Florence* (New York: Harcourt Brace Jovanovich, 1959), p. 121.
4. Ibid., p. 121.
5. Ibid., p. 122.
6. Ibid.
7. Ibid., pp. 122–123.
8. Vasari, p. 232.
9. Serge Bramly, *Leonardo: Discovering the Life of Leonardo DaVinci,* translated by Sian Reynolds (New York: HarperCollins Publishers, 1988, 1991), p. 74.
10. Ibid.
11. Alessandro Vezzosi, *Leonardo da Vinci: The Mind of the Renaissance,* translated by Alexandra Bonfante-Warren (New York: Harry N. Abrams, Inc., 1996, 1997), p. 28.
12. Ibid., p. 81.
13. Vasari, p. 257.

14. Arthur C. Danto, "Reading Leonardo," *The Nation,* volume 276, April 7, 2003, pp. 32–35.
15. Vasari, p. 236.
16. Michael Olmert, *The Smithsonian Book of Books* (Washington, DC: Smithsonian Books, 1992), p. 128.
17. Bramly, pp. 77–78.
18. Lisa Jardine, *Worldly Goods: A New History of the Renaissance* (London: Macmillan Publishing, 1996), p. 50.
19. Ibid., p. 52.
20. Ibid., p. 56.
21. Arnold Hauser, *The Social History of Art,* vol. 2, translated by Stanley Goodman with Arnold Hauser (New York: Vintage Books, 1951), p. 32.
22. Ibid.
23. Baxandall, p. 86.
24. Vasari, p. 228.
25. Ross King, *Brunelleschi's Dome: How a Renaissance Genius Reinvented Architecture* (New York: Penguin Books, 2000), pp. 79–81.

8

THE ART OF THE IDEA: FOUR ENTREPRENEURIAL INNOVATORS

Any entrepreneur will tell you that the companies they started began with an idea. Because starting up companies requires at least one good idea and a lot of improvisation, it tends to be a fairly creative task. The four entrepreneurs discussed in this chapter all share a profoundly creative approach to the development of their businesses. Each one of them demonstrates that it's not just an idea that lies at the core of a successful enterprise, but that at its core, business is actually about managing ideas themselves. Managing ideas successfully requires, of course, a host of other business competencies, but keeping one's eyes on these ideas has a galvanic impact on creativity and the effectiveness of strategic planning. The ideas run like a current of mineral-rich water through the heart of the enterprise, feeding it, enriching it, and stimulating growth. Creative, highly effective management is always aware of how the current is flowing and ensures that nothing is done to interfere with it. There are many ways to utilize this energy.

BEARD FRAMING: A 1990s HOTHOUSE IN PORTLAND, OREGON

In 1993, Terry Beard, founder and then-CEO of Beard Frame Shops, instituted a project he called "Lust for Life" for his company of thirty-plus stores in Portland, Oregon. Beard envisioned his company actively promoting the personal development, "lust for life," and cultural awareness and creativity of its 250 to 300 employees. The program, with full employee participation, organized salons on the first Friday of each month to discuss books or cultural events people had attended. Other topics taken up at the salons included community service, the environment, fitness, and public education policy. The company spent $100,000 a year on tickets for employees to attend concerts, visit museums, and participate in classes. For a time, each job applicant filled out an autobiographical self-assessment whose main purpose was to identify employees with a zest for personal growth and excitement about life's possibilities.

In several conversations with Beard, it occurred to me that he really wanted his employees' work life to be as fulfilling, challenging, and creative as any other part of their lives might be. That sort of decision is never made for business reasons alone. It is simply how creative people go about their lives. They earn money because it is necessary, and they are creative because that is the only way they can be. The challenge is to bridge the world of survival and business on the one hand, and the realm of visions and imagining on the other, a theme that runs through all human society. For Beard, the bridge involved enriching his staff's environment with the excitement of art, knowledge, and conversation. He didn't believe that it was a gamble, just something that seemed right and could not fail to have positive results.

When asked if he saw any real causal link between the Lust for Life activities and positive business results, Beard pointed immediately to "team building, team spirit, and the élan that emerges from the very intense and exciting time together. The team that grows together, grows *together*." This connection between individual and organizational development paid off in all areas, according to Beard, including "working on the mission statement, sales approaches, and cultural details. The program created solidarity and team spirit. People worked together exceptionally well." Beard recalled that ideas flowed constantly from the salons into the workplace. Morale was exceptional at the company during the period Beard calls its golden age, from 1993 to 1996. Turnover was reduced because staff members saw purpose in their jobs arising from the "lifelong development of people" that Beard described as a central commitment of the program. Morale and commitment translated into an exceptional level of customer service, especially important in a framing shop, where people bring in treasured photos and art works, or prints to beautify their living spaces. Along with some design sense, framing also involves a level of craft and the company's intellectually and culturally lush environment reinforced employee creativity, which translated into high-quality customer service and exacting standards of work. Beard dubbed the impact of this creative input the "synergistic multiplier effect," alluding to how a buildup of creative energy achieves a critical mass that triggers something akin to the hothouse effect.

The mission of Beard Frame Shops was not simply articulated as a set of goals infused with high-sounding values. It was felt and acted upon by all employees, embracing their intellectual life and social vision as well. The atmosphere attracted high-quality workers; about half were artists and virtually all turned their creativity to improving both business and technical processes. Customer service was outstanding because the Lust for Life program extended into personal interactions between staff and customers. The company's commitment to its people was evident to all, and staff regularly went well beyond expectations when troubleshooting, filling orders, and improving product.

In 1996, a large framing chain challenged Beard Frame Shops on its home turf, and competitive pressures led Beard to turn operations over to a capable management team that, nonetheless, did not support Lust for Life. He eventually sold the company to Northwest Framing, although he still retains an interest and the shops still operate under his name.

Beard remains committed to the Lust for Life philosophy and applies its principles in his Rotary Club activities and his new company, The Big Day, an online wedding registry that allows the newlyweds' friends and family to buy elements of the couple's honeymoon such as dinners, massages, nights in a hotel, airfare, and so on. The Big Day is a start-up with a small staff, very different from Beard Framing, yet Beard and his business partner, Dr. Richard Lazere, who worked closely with Beard on Lust for Life, find the same principles apply. Lazere calls it "business with a soul" with values, accountability, standards, and responsibility as the platform upon which, as Beard says, "We can have real fun with challenging ideas."

Beard's advice to others interested in engaging in similar initiatives is to "begin at the top—it has to start there." He believes that it is especially important to achieve buy-in by demonstrating the program's impact on individuals, one person at a time. Beard cautions against claiming that any such program provides a panacea for the entire organization, and he states what I feel is the first law of cultural change: *People need to feel it for themselves first.* You can't tell people what is supposed to happen or how it is going to work. Just go about it quietly and let them feel the impact themselves. Then they tell their friends and the level of receptivity begins to soar. Beard emphasizes that the path to organizational super-performance is through the individuals within the organization, not in imposing a template on the existing culture. Creative initiatives attract people who are capable and desirous of operating at a high level. Beard suggests "taking it piece by piece." Start people off by asking employees to try something new and having the company support their initiative, even financially. It may involve taking a class or volunteering in a new context. Employees can then share their experiences at a salon held inside work, on work time.

What struck me most about Beard Framing was not the owner's commitment to his employees or even how he backed up his encouragement with significant funding. It was not even his recognition that a creative atmosphere would be good for business. I found it fascinating that a business owner would extend staff development into the realm of so-called pure culture—that is, concerts, museum visits, and so forth. Beard guided his employees directly to the source of creativity. What better place to find it than through art? He trusted people to get something out of their experiences and to bring it back into the workplace. The salons gave people a chance to reflect on what they had seen or read, and this reflective component is very important. Had Beard infused the events with a specific business agenda or with a need to make it "relevant," it would have killed the creative spirit the experiences brought to people's lives and then to the framing shops. As it was, everyone could live creatively on the shop floor even if stuck with a less than inspiring task because the job embraced the larger creative world outside their doors. Beard simply had faith in the power of creativity and that faith was transmitted to his employees, and it worked.

THE GOLDEN NET

As a friend of William Tita, I am used to his encapsulated descriptions of a typical week's itinerary: "I'm flying to Paris for a conference this evening after I teach downtown, then I'll visit my mother in Cameroon on Tuesday. Wednesday I go to Karachi, then Cairo, and I'll be back home Sunday so let's talk then. Monday I fly to Pittsburgh to teach . . ." Along with being a much sought-after professor and consultant, Tita is president of the Global Management Consortium (GMC), which owns one third of the World Chamber Network along with the International Chambers of Commerce and the Paris Chamber of Commerce, which each own a third. Until recently, Tita was visiting nearly one hundred countries a year; he's cut back, but still annually logs more than most of us visit in a lifetime. Although a business advisor and entrepreneur, Tita's energy does not come primarily from the excitement of building a successful global enterprise, although that is clearly a passion. Rather, he has an overriding values-driven objective, which is to use the Internet to promote South–South trade, that is, trade among the G-77 nations (which actually include the 133 developing nations plus China) via GMC's online World Trade Network. To that end, GMC established technology centers in fifteen nations and close partnership with the G-77 Chambers of Commerce, which, with the technical support of KPMG, provide the Digital Certification and validation for all businesses that join the Trade Network, providing members with a powerful assurance of credibility. The company's objective is to link the entire developing world into a fully functional trade network through which members engage in commerce regardless of the boundaries of geography, thus stimulating growth, development, and economic viability throughout the less advantaged members of the global system. Exchange is the key for the network: exchange of goods, currency, and most of all, the core idea of the entire enterprise—that businesspeople across the globe believe in the idea itself and its power to generate trade and create wealth.

Tita's vision derives its strength from the values he imbibed growing up in Cameroon within a large but close extended family. Like many of his peers, Tita was indeed raised by a village, and he feels a powerful commitment to the global village that is linked by technology and commerce. As befits someone trying to establish a commercial hothouse, Tita's values were forged by rigorous training in several disciplines. For Tita, creativity is a central element in this undertaking. Given his background in mechanical engineering, economics, entrepreneurship, social ethics, and international development, it is not surprising that he sees creativity as a coordination of science, technology, and development (or economic growth). He describes science as "the discipline of the natural state of things whether involving the physical world or the realm of human endeavor, and it is intrinsically inventive. Technological innovation is the application of science to the solution of problems relating to the creation of goods." For Tita, innovation comes from many sources. Organizational innovation involves different ways of arranging things, such as a production line, procurement methods, or managerial responsibility. According to Tita,

> Economic growth or development occurs when you purposely put innovation to the production of goods and services, which become the engines of sustaining employment and improving the quality of life. The entrepreneur applies science and technology to the purposes of production. The entrepreneur also mixes in other ingredients, like capital, with science and tech-

nology to create an enterprise that becomes an engine of
growth.

Tita believes that "creativity provides connectivity, ideation, and innovation to the process. Everybody in that loop is playing some role—
entrepreneurs, scientists, technologists, workers, politicians, economists."
The creative drive leads different stakeholders to connect with one another
and develop innovations that generate growth. And when such a process
achieves a critical mass of activity, it becomes self-sustaining for a very
productive activity cycle. As infrastructure in much of the developing
world rapidly improves, the hope is that millions of online businesspeople
will explore the potential of intercontinental trade associations, multiparty
deals, and other productive and economic synergies that the network can
help to coordinate. The developing world is ripe for such an expansive
vision, not only because of the level of need but also because the lack of a
well-entrenched system allows businesses to act more nimbly and fluidly.
Economic growth begins with small- to medium-size businesses and is
fueled by entrepreneurs investing locally and cultivating local workforces.
Because the superstructure of current stakeholders is relatively thin, even in
countries dominated by a few corporations, the army, a dictator, or several
families, the Internet can work as a great leveler.

One of Tita's concerns is the so-called digital divide between rich and
poor people and industrial and developing nations. Because the Internet
can function as a global leveler to some degree, Tita notes various examples
of how the Net has democratized the flow of information worldwide.
However, using technology to close the digital divide requires creativity
and significant investment to build capacity, extend training, and ultimately
to persuade businesspeople to trade with one another. The tremendous
potential for a global network to offer online training and education to
underserved areas can play a major role in providing the expertise—
whether in the form of education, business methods, or health information—that can stimulate development. Information *is* power, as Tita's
account of the failure of international and government agencies to stimulate
trade relationships among the G-77 nations between 1964 and 1985 indicates. "By 1985, [the agency programs] were all bankrupt because govern-
ments don't trade, businesspeople do. Bureaucracies are more into
structures and bureaucracy than they are into trade." Soon after, the United
Nations Center for Trade and Development (UNCTAD) asked the Chambers of Commerce to help by involving the business community, but at

various international trade conferences, Tita noted that the G-77 nations lacked commercial information about one another. At that time, in the mid-1980s, Tita owned a Cameroon-based software company called Infomatics whose software applications enabled corporations to transmit data. Tita realized the developing world needed a trade information system and he saw his own business's needs in that framework. Because of his computer expertise, he was able to influence the various chambers and international development agencies to support this type of network.

When Tita first witnessed the Internet in operation in 1989, he immediately grasped its potential as an engine of growth for the developing world. He hopes to move the Net from the status of innovation, which it still is, to the primary medium of commerce. To become economically viable, the developing nations need to sell their products to other developing nations. They cannot rely on the industrial nations as a market for resources and goods because they will lose out in the former case and can't compete in the latter. An Internet-driven trade network can overcome the gaps in language, time, and distance among developing nations.

Tita noted that the frequently stated proverb that a chain is only as strong as its weakest link applies to any global trade network. He explained that if one is serious about creating a global network, "the Gambian Chamber must be equal [in importance and integrity, obviously not size] to Paris. It can't count as one tenth of a Chamber." This notion has practical implications. Tita flatly asserts that one must establish a *global* network first and only then build the loops within that network to connect online "regions" of natural common interest. One cannot start with the loops and then expand into a global network because the large-scale institutions will freeze out certain loops and the network never becomes global. Ultimately, the human networks are what make any trade network a success. Without countless individual decisions to break out of traditional paradigms of business and trade, little progress can be made. However, in preparing people to make this leap, a network can serve as an important tool.

Despite having many talented people working for and partnering with GMC, the organization is currently so new, wide-flung, and loosely connected, that it doesn't yet have a company culture cohesive enough upon which to impose a creative vision. For now, the hothouse effect resides in Tita himself. Already, however, many of the core themes of the hothouse effect are evident in the network's development.

The values component is vital to the hothouse effect because it overrides the tendency to seek quick returns or circumvent the work needed to generate outstanding results. A story from the beginning of Tita's career more than three decades ago illustrates how the synergy between business results and values-driven initiatives can work in surprising ways. For his senior project at Duke University, he wanted to build inexpensive housing for some of the poorer African Americans living near campus. However, his department felt that it wasn't a stringent enough test of engineering ability, so its members insisted he work on the design of a cooling system. After returning to Cameroon as an engineer, Tita sought to design an office complex with air-conditioning in order to increase productivity and boost economic output. At that time, however, air-conditioning in Cameroon was primarily used for storage of hard goods and no one was interested in cooling offices with it. Soon after, he went to IBM as a research engineer where he focused on climate's impact on computers, especially as heat affected computers in Africa. Tita ordered a weather-simulating oven to test computers under extreme conditions. However, he drew some internal flak for what was viewed as a quixotic expense. Just before he was to face the heat over the oven, Proctor and Gamble canceled a $27 million order (late-1960s dollars) in Florida because IBM's computer electrodes had broken down. Florida's heat had activated the gases used in manufacturing the electrodes, which corroded as a result. Tita's research provided the solution and, as he says, the experiment became a big deal and his career was propelled onward and upward.

Today, he considers it ironic that the path of research that deflected him from his desire to work on a community-based project, and which then was thwarted when he tried to apply it to economic development in Cameroon, wound up to be so helpful to his career. In 1969, he went to the University of Pittsburgh for his MBA. The social dimension of his work was driven home by the fact that he and his wife couldn't get a house within six miles of campus because they were black. His commitment to his earlier goal was still undiminished, and at Pittsburgh he was able to support the African American community's small business enterprises via applied technology. The entire sequence of experiences led him to a post-doctoral position in social ethics at the University of Southern California.

Specialists in problem solving often point out that "playing" with materials and ideas leads to surprising solutions. Tita's experience shows that a tenacious commitment to ethics also produces surprises in terms of solutions and career development. Every hothouse has a strong values component that is actualized in the pursuit of its objectives. Part of the hothouse effect's inherent creativity comes from a willingness to rearrange the accepted order of things for the sake of solutions that serve human beings rather than account ledgers. And as Tita's true-life fable shows, profits and people need not be exclusive concerns.

The ability to think, plan, and act across boundaries represents another dimension of the hothouse effect embodied by the World Trade Network (WTN), because it is truly global. Although national cooperation is essential to the WTN, the service itself is borderless. Tita's expertise reaches across numerous disciplines and the WTN is an engineering, management, cultural, ethical, and business challenge all at once. Although GMC has technical centers, it is a virtual organization. Yet, Tita's vision is rooted in the open, all-embracing perspectives of many traditional African societies and their powerful resonance with the open, expansive, global character of the Internet and the twenty-first century's global trade. Tita, like many figures at the center of a great notion, draws together seemingly contradictory forces and orchestrates them toward the fulfillment of a common goal.

"AFTER THE FOURTH OR FIFTH TIME, IT BECOMES EASY"

Arthur Nelson, founder and CEO of the Nelson Companies, has started nineteen companies and nonprofit organizations since 1954 and was cited as 1999's Master Entrepreneur of the Year for New England by Ernst and Young. His office in Prospect Hill in Waltham, Massachusetts, looks out over Route 128, which is second only to Silicon Valley as a high-tech center. Nelson feels very connected to this area, considering he has built one of its signature hotels, office buildings, and other developments. But he is tied to the area in other, more curious ways. In 1987, a group of MIT engineers were tramping around the wooded hills to the east, seeking a line of sight from their transmission tower on a hilltop to a convenient building so they could establish an Internet connection. At that time, only Digital Equipment Corporation and IBM had Internet service in the area, according to Nelson. Nelson's office building lined up perfectly with the tower and Nelson welcomed the engineers' offer to set up a receiver on his roof. The Nelson Companies thus became one of the first organizations in the region to have Internet service. Odd things like that happen when you're connected to a place.

When discussing his approach to business, Nelson frequently returns to a single clear algorithm. Nelson tells a good story and his description of the entrepreneurial process begins with a metaphor. He says that at first, you find a need, but that can be like wandering in the fog looking for a mountain. When you find the mountain, says Nelson, "You know something no one else in the world knows. Now you can walk toward the beautiful mountain." The first step in Nelson's algorithm, then, is identifying the need. Second, you decide what kind of organization can fulfill that need, or, stated another way, what kind of business you will be going into. The third step is to surround oneself with people who believe passionately in the project. Fourth, describe the new organization's mission in crystal-clear terms; fifth, establish a business plan; sixth, get everybody aboard; and as a last step, let them run with it.

Nelson reflects that "after the fourth or fifth time [starting a company], you learn enough to make it simple." An algorithm's power lies in its repetition as a kind of mantra that orients and guides you during high-risk behavior. A rock climber, for example, internalizes rituals that guarantee that he or she will check the safety of every hold on the way up a rock-face. And just as Nelson emphasizes the need to remain adaptable through-out every phase of an enterprise, so too can a rock climber respond cre-atively to the climb's challenges. Creativity is no more about doing whatever one wants than freedom is. Creativity and freedom both require precise navigational techniques; otherwise, both devolve into mere floun-dering and flailing. The importance of the algorithm for the hothouse effect is that it trains all members to think clearly and critically. The problem-solving sequences that Casey Powell and Arthur Nelson encourage are analogous to the grids drawn onto their canvases that guided Florentine painters in depicting perspective or the prescribed proportions of the human body that helped so many Greek sculptors achieve mastery.

Nelson views creativity as the fusion of purpose and a willingness to act in a high-risk environment. Nelson, like many other creative leaders, emphasizes that real creativity requires action. For Nelson—as for Beard, Tita, or Powell—money does not seem to drive his entrepreneurial spirit, but rather the desire to fulfill important social and community needs. His real-estate developments continue to play an important role in the region's economy, but they also fund a wide range of projects that reflect his strong community ethic and fascination with the innovation process and creativ-ity. Nelson cofounded the Technical Education Research Center (TERC), Inc., in 1965, which conducts research and curriculum development for students in kindergarten to twelfth grade in math, science, and technology. With about seventy projects going at once and funded mostly by grants from government agencies such as the Department of Education and the National Science Foundation, TERC plays an important role in improving education throughout the United States. In 1979 Nelson cofounded Cambridge Development Laboratories, Inc., to develop commercial educational software based on TERC's research. Although not the primary founder (an honor belonging to Dr. Michael Folsom of MIT), Nelson was one of ten cofounders of the Charles River Museum of Industry in Waltham. Nelson also cofounded the 128 Business Council, which, among other things, established bus routes to link Route 128 businesses with the city of Boston, benefiting both the companies of Route 128 and Boston residents who have access to a broader spectrum of jobs. The Charles River Public Internet Center (CRPIC) on Waltham's dynamic Moody Street was cofounded by Nelson as a free public-access computer center that welcomes students, the homeless, recently arrived immigrants, and anyone else who needs to develop computer skills or establish an Internet account. The CRPIC is funded by renting out four state-of-the-art computer training classrooms to corporations. Nelson also founded the American Innovation Institute to develop innovation strategies for industry.

The heart of Nelson's entrepreneurial approach resides in the values that drive him to balance business success with the establishment of services and nonprofit enterprises that promote the social good. When he moved his offices to their Prospect Hill site in 1984, his wife, Eleanor Nelson, immediately saw the need for on-site day care for employees, and immediately implemented it. The bus service that links Waltham and Boston grew out of a shuttle that Nelson initiated for his workers twenty years ago. Nelson established a mentorship program where MIT and Harvard Business School professors connected with young entrepreneurs, who received free rent and services for one year at his Route 128 entrepreneurship center.

When asked about the role of creativity within an organization, Nelson states that one must start with creative people and let them run with their projects. Nelson looks for people who get excited about the idea and the vision in part because he believes the critical moment is the launch, or the commitment to risk action. The launch, of course, while not at the very beginning of an enterprise, occurs in its early stages. The team one gathers before the launch is the best guarantee that you'll be successful. "Good people attract good people," Nelson points out, just as Richard Lazere noted that good people are the best "filters" for keeping a company on track.

Organizationally, each division of ten to twenty people at the Nelson Companies runs itself and all hold weekly meetings in which all employees participate, not just the managers. TERC, however, has 150 people, and with the jovial laugh that punctuates so much of the interview, Nelson says that "Every one of them feels they're running TERC."

Speaking with Arthur Nelson, I started thinking about establishing networks of hothouses. Nelson seems to have created, through a lifetime of experience, a formula for proliferating viable hubs of creative activity. A network of hothouses potentially increases creativity exponentially. A network of networks raises the level of complexity in both nature and human society, and bears strongly on the potential power of the hothouse effect. Whether embedded in thirty-plus framing shops that belonged to a vital creative network of their own; a global trade network whose hubs include the International Chambers of Commerce offices, the GMC's various centers, and the central hub of one entrepreneur's mind; the variety of companies started by Arthur Nelson; or Edwin Land's vision of proliferating corporate research and manufacturing centers, the hothouse effect exhibits an ability to expand into a potent network of hothouses, which in turn could produce the breakaway hothouse among them, which then serves as the core for another network, and so on.

THINKING LIKE THE MASTERS

The hothouse effect requires a rapid increase in intellectual capital throughout an organization. At the personal level, intellectual capital refers to the mental resources that each person brings to his or her job, including knowledge, ideas, creativity, emotional maturity, and leadership skills, as well as ownership of intellectual property. The intellectual capital of a group comprises all individual contributions plus the knowledge embedded in the group's institutions—that is, archives, old copyrights and patents, oral tradition, cultural norms that enhance operations, and so forth. Not all this knowledge needs to be proprietary; the flow of intellectual capital through a company, for instance, rises and falls according to the quality of new hires or departing personnel, and the level of learning that occurs on the job each day.

The hothouse develops techniques for raising the intellectual capital of as many of its members as possible as it launches and sustains the hothouse effect. When Peisistratos lured Attica's countryfolk to Athens and gave them a stake in its economy and culture, he provided thousands of people with vast amounts of information and complex ideas in a hands-on immersion experience. Is it possible to increase rapidly, efficiently, and lastingly, intellectual capital across an entire workforce in a modern-day company?

Bill Seidman, founder and CEO of Cerebyte, Inc., offers one solution, an interactive program that teaches users to think like experts in their fields.

Cerebyte not only accelerates the learning process but also identifies, encapsulates, and transmits an invaluable knowledge set usually ignored in both the educational and business worlds. Cerebyte's self-guiding and interactive programs summarize and organize the core knowledge and cognitive processes that experts employ that enable them to perform like experts. Cerebyte distinguishes itself at the development end; its models of how experts think are based on Seidman's research into the qualities that distinguish expert thinking in any field.

The company starts by identifying the experts within an organization. As Seidman states, "Organizations *always* know who the experts are." That doesn't mean they necessarily utilize experts to maximum effect, but that everybody generally knows who does the best work and has the most extensive knowledge base. Seidman points out that the top performers operate with a mental model that differs from that of their colleagues: They tend to be "more passionate, moral, and aligned with key effects." The experts' ethics and passion speak to the values component of the hothouse effect. The drive to mine the secrets embedded in the principles, materials, and technology of a discipline or industry also exemplifies one of the hothouse effect's distinguishing characteristics. Being aligned with key effects involves the ability—honed by experience, knowledge, and instinct—to achieve maximum impact by directing one's energies toward the most powerful leverage points. Levers allow us to lift heavy weights with a relatively low application of force. Similarly, experts leverage powerful results by *positioning* their knowledge to exert the greatest force on a situation. Thus it's not only *what* an expert knows but *how* she or he applies knowledge. Top performers do not always *know* more than others, but often they can concentrate their knowledge more intensively, tenaciously, and strategically than their colleagues.

Seidman found that experts construct streamlined mental models of their tasks and utilize those models as guidance systems to deliver action and knowledge in the most effective way possible. The models function as complex problem-solving algorithms, although the best performers can also improvise on top of the algorithm. *Seidman believes that an expert's success comes from how he or she conceives and manages these models.* When they construct their models, experts include a lot of data that other practitioners leave out. For example, some companies tell Cerebyte how difficult it is to establish a set of best practices in their companies because political factors play a role in deciding what and how things get done. Cerebyte responds by simply asking whether the company has any high-level performers. The answer is always yes, of course. Cerebyte then points out that the best performers have already calculated all the organizational factors, including politics, in constructing the mental models they need to achieve their objectives. This ability to input elements that others ignore or don't even grasp is one important aspect of expert behavior that Cerebyte's programs capture.

Because Cerebyte builds its programs around the experts' mental models, companies find them valuable for enhancing communication among a company's divisions or between partnering companies. When a large school-photo company decided to convert to digital cameras, the company found that its six divisions perceived themselves very differently from one another, which resulted in significant differences in regard to film choice, the nature of production facilities, the structure and focus of their business models, photographic style, and their approach to their photographic subjects. Thus the company anticipated having to adopt a complicated array of digital equipment to accomplish the transition to digital cameras. However, in constructing a program for the company, Cerebyte found that the top performers in each division all used similar structural models in determining and implementing operational strategies. Cerebyte uncovered these commonalities precisely because of its own operational model, in which its staff drills deeply into the assumptions and core principles that underlie the best practices of a company or industry and its experts.

This analysis led to the development of a program for the company's six divisions to work cooperatively with one another. Once the Cerebyte program—which was based on those interdivisional commonalities—was applied, the members of each division mentored the other five in regard to their own divisional culture. Finding this common ground resulted in the divisions aligning their practices with one another. In practical terms, the company found that it only needed two versions of a digital camera to convert all six divisions to digital photography, a more streamlined and less expensive solution than they had anticipated. When they built the cameras and created the support infrastructure, they were able to address divisional needs from a companywide perspective rather than one division at a time. The overall atmosphere among divisions shifted from prickly antagonism to trust and collaboration.

Seidman's attention to the fundamental structures of learning allows Cerebyte to get beneath deeply held assumptions that organizations have about themselves. Because several hothouse factors involve the community's ability to do this, the program has a direct impact on creativity.

The most powerful use of Cerebyte's programs, however, may lie in the company's ability to deliver high-level learning in encapsulated form to many employees at the same time. These programs are equivalent to an across-the-board upload of a value-rich database. Any business can benefit by raising the overall awareness, problem-solving abilities, analytic skills, and creativity of a large number of its members. Seidman notes that Cerebyte helped two companies prepare for a merger by creating programs that introduced internal modes of thought and operation to one another. In other words, Cerebyte's programs allow an entire population to absorb a great deal of cultural content very rapidly. The programs provide guided coaching and opportunities to put ideas into action immediately. The structure of the transmitted knowledge reflects the thinking patterns of the organization's masters, and the program itself serves as a mentor to those who use it, a relationship that can be taken over by the experts themselves.

Cerebyte provides one outstanding model for transforming organizational thinking quickly and across the board, almost as the equivalent of a powerful cultural event that shifts deep-seated assumptions and modes of thought. Interactive programs that guide users through the *experience* of thinking offer a meta-cognitive approach to learning that helps learners engage in higher level mental operations. This sudden broadly based upgrading of intellectual capital also parallels a rapid engagement with a metasystem, one of the most potent hothouse factors. As learning technologies such as Cerebyte's become more available in schools and the marketplace, the hothouse effect may be implemented on a national or even global scale.

THE ART OF THE IDEA

By sponsoring his employees' exposure to a wide range of powerful ideas through courses, salons, and various art events, and by encouraging on-the-job initiative and personal development, Terry Beard created a dynamic, idea-rich environment that thrived on the teamwork and commitment of people whose work lives had suddenly become very stimulating and enriching. Bill Tita's vision took shape over decades as an entrepreneur, ethicist, and engineer until a glimpse of the Internet in action triggered the powerful idea of a global network that could connect people throughout the developing world and promote the exchange of goods and ideas to the benefit of all. Arthur Nelson, with the wisdom of many decades and many deals, states quite simply that every company begins with an idea. His career illustrates how to amplify the impact of a successful business by proliferating hubs of creativity that are knit into a greater whole. The nonprofit, socially oriented side of the Nelson Companies benefits from the business expertise and funding of the for-profit side, while the for-profit side benefits from the inspiration and ideas generated by the nonprofit companies. As ideas circulate, they ideally pick up momentum, leading to more ideas, some of which become the first flicker of a new start-up.

Bill Seidman is in the business of ideas: analyzing them, mapping them, and reconfiguring them so that they reflect optimal patterns of use, transmitting them via Cerebyte's programs, and ultimately seeing their substantive impact in two main ways. The business benefits, of course, as in the case of the photography company. In addition, though, Cerebyte aims to enhance the ability of each individual user to utilize ideas, to "handle" them with maximum effectiveness. All four of these businessmen have found their inspiration and insight by maintaining focus on the major themes, or key ideas, that drive not only their companies but their own passion and effort to create a lasting impact on the world, their customers, and those with whom they work.

9

THE THIRD DIMENSION: PERCEPTION/LEARNING

The third realm of perception/learning delves into the processes that govern the generation and exchange of ideas. The word *perception* refers to how we take in the sense impressions and concepts from the outside world, as well as how we experience our own internal mental events. The actual mechanisms by which we attach meaning to internal and external experience remain a mystery, although neuroscience has charted many of the processes of consciousness. But wherever perception might reside, our ability to make the most of what we see, hear, feel, touch, smell, sense, think, intuit, feel, and imagine (the 10 senses?) determines personality, intelligence, talent, and our interaction with the world. Once we perceive anything, whether we see a tree, realize we're in love, or taste a peach, the perception must go somewhere. It may be stored and forgotten, reflected upon, made part of a more elaborate set of ideas, or communicated to someone else. If it is useful or interesting, the perceiver feels he or she learned something.

These explanations, however, focus solely on the *content* of the perception. Equally important is the *medium* by which something is perceived, transmitted, and processed. Our media—such as pictures, print, or television—shape our perceptions on such a profound level that the medium itself often contains the most important information about a situation, which is why the cultural historian Marshall McLuhan proclaimed that "the medium is the message" forty years ago. But this is also true at the physiological level: Our reality is beholden to the structure of body and brain, to how we experience our senses, and the dictates of gravity, inertia, friction, and electromagnetism. Every perception we have reaches us as a series of electronic messages traveling along our nerves. We are already digitized. Even the technology that presumably helps us to observe reality more accurately is constrained by the physical and mental apparatus that created them—that is, by us and our materials. That applies to math, language, telescopes and microscopes, engines of mobility and power, ballistics, and the computer. It's a commonplace that we often see or hear what we *expect* to rather than what is really there.

Therefore, uncertainty riddles all we do. Our perceptions are restricted by the media that transmit them, yet, paradoxically, we sometimes can see and feel beyond the limits imposed by our usual modes of perception; artists, inventors, shamans, scientists, and thinkers challenge the "givens" of a situation, which include the hard-wired physiological media that shape our reality. Picasso jolts our visual expectations and scientists reveal what we otherwise would never see or know. Experiencing this shift in perception can be exhilarating and enriches our own creativity as well.

Everything comes back to the electrical signals coursing along the nervous system to the processing system in the Emerald City of the brain. Our perceived reality is digital at root, but the experience of our reality—perhaps our perception of our perceptions—is sensory and narrative. We perceive and then translate our impressions into signs or code, which we can arrange into strings of meaning, that is, stories. The narrative strings, short as a grunt or long as an epic, provide frameworks for meaning and coherence; we act in response to messages that we ourselves create within our own minds. We then use language and thought to construct meaningful statements or narratives about the messages and about our own actions. These eventually provide us with a view of reality that enables our senses to navigate the world and link up with other people who ratify or challenge our version of reality. The fundamental structure of reality—within which we all generally agree on distance, the rhythms of time, the shape and solidity of things, colors, and so forth—provides a baseline of sanity and functionality that society enforces as ruthlessly as any inquisition enforces its own ideology.

In the gap between perception and the act, and the act and perception *of* the act, lies the entire history of human deception and misunderstanding, in other words, human history. Using the narrative strings that link the energy fields generated by each of our perceptions, we create the design of culture and civilization. That gap spurs forward the creation of culture and mind. The gap is also the vanishing point into which we plunge to figure out what is happening to us. But to tap into our creativity, we must seek

Exhibit 1. Panel from the East Baptistery Doors by Lorenzo Ghiberti, second quarter of the fifteenth century: *The Sacrifice of Isaac* (the angel staying Abraham's hand is in upper-right corner). The perspective carved into the bronze landscape and the realistic detail enhance the drama by transforming the pictorial space into a stage set in which figures have more freedom to move and interact. This combination of mathematics, realism, drama, invention, and detail reflected not only the elements of a new artistic style but also the cultural and mental landscapes of the Renaissance that Florence so powerfully crystallized. (Courtesy of Oberlin College Visual Resources. Photo by Giacomo Brogi [d. 1881].)

Exhibit 2. This view of the north slope of the Acropolis from across the ancient Agora (marketplace) displays the grandeur of the giant rock whether capped by shining new temples or legendary ruins. Peisistratos's temples preceded the fifth-century B.C.E. buildings seen here. This anonymous photo, circa 1900, shows the marketplace before the restorations familiar to visitors today. (Courtesy of Oberlin College Visual Resources.)

Exhibit 3. In this *kylix,* or shallow cup, painted by Exekias, the greatest of the black figure painters, 540–520 B.C.E., Dionysus, god of wine, has just turned a gang of threatening pirates into dolphins. Dionysus was a deity of intoxication and irrationality, but he is depicted as the calm at the center of the storm he so often arouses. He is also a god of creativity, as symbolized by the vine blooming along the mast. (Courtesy of Oberlin College Visual Resources.)

Exhibit 4. The *School of Athens* by Raphael. One of the most famous of all Renaissance paintings, it is an ode to the era's debt to ancient Greek learning. Plato and Aristotle share center stage. Plato, probably a portrait of Leonardo da Vinci, points his finger to the sky to indicate his celestial philosophy, while Aristotle gestures downward to demonstrate his more earthly scientific concerns. Diogenes the Cynic is sprawled on the stairs, an allusion to his crude personal habits. Raphael's self-portrait is the second figure from the lower right. (Courtesy of Oberlin College Visual Resources.)

Exhibit 5. The Bauhaus building, designed by Walter Gropius, 1925–1926, in Dessau, Germany. The geometric simplicity announced its modernist ethic and the desire to provide clean, inexpensive housing for as many people as possible. (Courtesy of Oberlin College Visual Resources.)

Exhibit 6. The Wassily Chair by Marcel Breuer, 1929–1932, named in honor of Wassily Kandinsky. It is made of bicycle tubing recycled from the German bicycle brigades of World War I and khaki recycled from military uniforms. The opportunistic and whimsical use of materials, the clean design using industrial products, and the fundamental purity and grace of geometry, demonstrate elements of Bauhaus design and postwar sensibility. (Courtesy of the Busch-Reisinger Museum, Harvard University Art Museums, anonymous gift. Photographic Services, copyright © President and Fellows of Harvard College.)

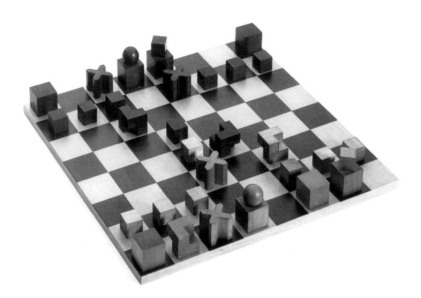

Exhibit 7. Chess set by Josef Hartwig, master craftsman, Bauhaus. The shapes of the pieces indicate how they move. Rooks are square, bishops diagonal, and knights L-shaped. The rotated square at the king's crown shows he can move one square in any direction, while the queen's spherical crown denotes her ability to move in any direction but as far as she wants. The pawns, with little square heads, move only forward but capture only diagonally; the latter trait is not indicated in the design. The set makes an elegant and explicit statement of the Bauhaus objective of integrating function and form. Cherry-wood, 1924. (Courtesy of the Bauhaus-Archiv Berlin, (c) Artists' Rights Society [ARS], NY/VG Bild-Kunst, Bonn.) Photo by Genter Lepkowski.

Exhibit 8. The renovated Federazione Italiana Consorzi Agrari tower in Castel San Pietro Terme, near Bologna, Italy, home of Loop Design Centre. (Photograph by Fabio Baraldi, reprinted with permission of Loop Design Centre.)

Exhibit 9. On this vase from Attica, painted by the Amasis Painter in the sixth century B.C.E., two predators bring down their prey, an ancient European and west Asian symbol of the wax and wane of life and time. Above them, echoing the theme, two wrestlers grapple. For the Greeks, contests always resonated with the most serious themes. Theseus, the Athenian hero, was a wrestler, representing the mind's ability to leverage energy to overthrow brute force, just as the Athenians defeated the Persians. (Courtesy of Oberlin College Visual Resources.)

Exhibit 10. Studio of Leo and Gertrude Stein, 27 rue de Fleurus, Paris, circa 1907. Some of the seminal works of modern painting hung on the walls of the apartment Gertrude shared first with her brother, Leo, and then with Alice B. Toklas. Picasso's portrait of Stein appears at the top where the walls meet. The nude is also Picasso's, and the picture below Stein's portrait is a Matisse. The works of Manet, Daumier, and Renoir also grace the wall. (Courtesy of Dr. Claribel Cone and Miss Etta Cone Papers, the Baltimore Museum of Art.)

Exhibit 11. *The Maids of Avignon* by Pablo Picasso (1907). The picture proclaimed a new era in art and can be considered a cubist manifesto. The influence of African mask sculpture on Picasso is evident in the planes of the women's faces, and the kinetic effect of the cubist style travels through the women's bodies into the space between and around them. (Photo by Edward van Altena. Courtesy of Oberlin College Visual Resources.)

Exhibit 12. The gathering of physicists in 1927 where Einstein, seated front and center, grilled Werner Karl Heisenberg (back row, third from viewer's right), Niels Bohr (middle row, far right), and Wolfgang Pauli (back row, fourth from right) about quantum theory. Max Planck is in front row, second from left; the lone woman is Marie Curie. (Credit: Photographie Benjamin Couprie, Institut International de Physique, Solvay. Courtesy of AIP Emilio Segrè Visual Archives.)

Exhibit 13. Making *Kind of Blue,* April 22, 1959. From left to right, Paul Chambers on bass, Julian "Cannonball" Adderly, pianist Bill Evans standing next to Miles Davis, who is seated at the piano, and John Coltrane. Drummer Jimmy Cobb is not in the photo. The picture speaks volumes about leadership and collaboration. (Photographer: Fred Plaut. The Fred and Rose Plaut Archives, Yale University Music Library.)

its source—the realm of perception—where the rubber of reality hits the electronic superhighway of the nervous system. *Perception* represents the underlying structure that gives birth to ideas, while *learning* is a form of exchange that involves actively reconfiguring and transforming those ideas. At its deeper levels, learning reconditions and repatterns our perceptions so we experience the world in a more satisfying and creative way. The following factors all deeply involve perception and learning, and all play an important role in generating the hothouse effect:

20. Each person is respected as a learner, producer, and potential visionary, and the organization actively promotes education for all its members.

21. Clear, simple, flexible, and effective problem-solving algorithms are taught to and used by all members of the organization.

22. People learn and use a variety of sensory and body-centered techniques to stimulate their creativity at work.

23. Analytic and experiential inquiry into fundamental principles of perception and learning plays an important role in the work of the group.

24. Members learn by immersing themselves in surroundings saturated with information and materials.

25. The community has experienced sudden and rapid engagement with a much larger and more complex meta-system early in the hothouse cycle.

26. Members utilize unorthodox structures of thought: metaphor, models, meta-cognitive thinking, meditation, thought experiments, and more.

27. Time is perceived as a palpable dimension and is harvested for its creative energy.

28. The group is open to broad external currents in art, politics, and society.

We have seen ample evidence that the mysteries of perception fascinated history's hothouses, which is natural considering their passion for art, invention, science, and thought. Perception occupies a central place in creative disciplines; it is not simply another interesting area of research. Perception shapes the values, ideas, assumptions, and operating principles that govern individuals and define the character of groups. Understanding how perception influences our thoughts, feelings, and actions enables us to do the following:

- Heighten our perceptions.
- Disturb the habits and routines that reinforce our usual modes of perception.
- Experiment with alternative ways of perceiving.
- Create new forms and ideas that follow logically from these new perceptions.

Hothouses get that way by pushing the boundaries of perception and consistently challenging the perspectives that most others accept without question.

#20. EVERYONE IS A VISIONARY

One benefit of seeing everyone as a potential visionary is that it may well be the stonemason who is the smartest guy around, as was the case in Athens during its golden age when Socrates, a mason by trade, wandered the streets. The person sweeping floors at the Rowland Institute may become a top-notch technician. Inventions and ideas come from the human mind, and perception, the ground of the mind, can be more or less acute in any individual. The mind is the ultimate democrat, which is why so many underserved students, once given a shot at education, blossom so rapidly. Education involves preparing the mind for the task of (1) visioning the world, (2) revisioning it, and (3) figuring out how to turn that new vision into reality. The greater the number of people who become educated as thinkers and creators, the more thinkers and creators we'll have, and we'll more likely achieve the critical mass of ideas and practitioners needed to launch a new level of creative and productive activity.

The Bauhaus's strikingly original approach to education, described in Chapter 10, reflected its founders' values, respect for inquiry, and challenge to traditional ways of perceiving. By virtue of being at the Bauhaus, it was assumed one was a thinker, visionary, and creator. The same held for the workshops of Florence, the performance venues of jazz, or the Parisian artists' circle to which Picasso belonged, as if some gatekeeper told you: "If you enter our orbit, let's see what you've got, and if you've got it, run with it." Both the Rowland Institute and Foster-Miller, a materials research and manufacturing company based in Waltham, Massachusetts, encourage all employees to take an interest in the scientific and technical work and to participate in a wide range of discussions. The message in this type of policy is clear: You are here to think, solve, and contribute. Right from the start, that's a strong statement that the employer expects the best from everyone on staff, and yet it communicates a high level of respect for each member of the company.

#21. ALGORITHMS

Such expectations are not met by magic. Every creative act requires tools, including tools of the mind, and one very powerful tool used by many hothouses is the clear, flexible problem-solving algorithm. These algorithms operate as intellectual can openers. Instead of wrestling with a problem and tearing at it with the wrong tools, the algorithm facilitates a more incisive, ordered approach. Algorithms function as instantly accessible action plans that free us to develop more complex, effective, or elegant sequences. The organization that bestows such a powerful, adaptable tool immediately raises the general level of performance and enriches its intellectual capital as well.

The great jazz musicians understood the basic procedures of improvisation before challenging the boundaries of musical form. Thomas Edison, Sequent, the Nelson Companies, and the Bauhaus have or had explicit algorithms for approaching major creative challenges. In Florence, Andalusia, and Athens the visual artists, architects, and poets followed canonical guidelines that, in effect, elevated competent practitioners to base camp; after that, it was up to them to scale the peaks. Greek sculpture had a set of proportions considered to be ideal for depicting the human form. A mathematical grid guided Florentine artists in constructing the perspectives for their paintings. The compelling energy of Shakespeare's plays comes in part from the tight control of fundamental principles of stagecraft and plot exposition that drives the unfolding of each scene. Virtually every creative endeavor has its rules, a fact that flies in the face of modern popular belief about creativity. Whether a sonnet or five-act Shakespearian play, a three-hour movie or five-minute jazz improvisation, clear boundaries give the work shape and meaning derived from countless experiences and experiments. When this structure is translated into algorithms and standards that artists, scientists, inventors, and managers rely on (even if they decide, for strategic, creative, or misguided reasons, to violate every one of those standards), the algorithm can be transferred to other applications and taught to other practitioners.

These algorithms grow out of long practice. As Arthur Nelson said about starting up an enterprise, "After the fourth or fifth time it gets easy." Despite the different kinds of organizations he has started, his formula remains clear and simple: "Find out what needs to be done, figure out how to get it done, select the right people, get them to buy into the mission, and then let them do it." There appears to be nothing earth-shattering there, but that's the point. Algorithms are the automatic pilots that allow us to attend to more demanding tasks.

It was, in fact, a fighter pilot named Colonel John Boyd who revolutionized fighter pilot training and battle technique by introducing a single effective algorithm that has guided the field for decades: Observe-Orient-Decide-Act (OODA).[1] What makes OODA so powerful? Like many other algorithms, it may seem simple on the surface. However, Boyd effected a deep-reaching structural reconfiguration of the entire cycle of activity experienced by combat pilots. He saw each step of the algorithm as influencing the next step's implementation. He counseled pilots to repeat the OODA loop as often as possible within the same mission, and developed training methods that enabled them to move through the entire algorithm ever more rapidly. The algorithm also served to organize complex decision-making processes as well as to analyze the tactics of enemy pilots. For example, Boyd went so far as to teach pilots how to "get inside" their opponents' OODA loops, a brilliant piece of meta-cognitive analysis and implementation in which trainees learn how to think about their thinking processes as well as their opponents', and how to use that data to operate more effectively. Boyd's algorithm demonstrates the rich, invaluable role of the algorithm in creative activity. As with any algorithm, whether a musical scale or a procedure from higher mathematics, the more one masters the algorithm, the more freedom one has to improvise when necessary.

We all have algorithms, but they suffer from disuse because we rarely subject our own procedures to the scrutiny needed to codify them, which means figuring out what has consistently worked. What are the patterns? How do we distill the lessons we've learned into a streamlined sequence of easily accessed steps? The steps may be analytic or action-oriented; they may work for the artist in her studio or the manager in the field. They are subject to the scientific method: If it didn't work, why not? What caused the deviation? Otherwise, we can never be sure whether we are transmitting an effective algorithm or just random observations that reflect what we only *believe* worked for us.

#22. HOLISTIC TECHNIQUES AND
#23. PRINCIPLES OF PERCEPTION

To teach people to fulfill their natural roles as visionaries and boundary-crossing learners, our methods must rise to the occasion. Leonardo da Vinci recommended gazing at water-stained walls and letting ideas emerge as the blots stimulate the imagination, while Gustave Flaubert was inspired to write *Madame Bovary* when he paused to stare at some moss growing on a country wall.[2] French mathematician Henri Poincaré preferred gazing at the smoke from his pipe mingling with steam from his morning coffee or lying in bed half asleep while his mind slipped into gear.[3] Napoleon Hill, the first modern self-help guru, writing early in the twentieth century, found that many of America's most successful businesspeople spent time "sitting for ideas," locking themselves away in a room for thirty minutes or a few hours and letting their thoughts wander or play with the challenges of the day.[4] Jazz musicians "go to the woodshed" to work out ideas. And during tournaments, golfer Jack Nicklaus previsualizes his stroke and the path of every shot he takes.[5]

None of these methods are aimless or equatable with simple daydreaming; they are conscious techniques designed to enrich and enhance creative thinking. Many books are available that describe these techniques. Some describe entire problem-solving systems, while others focus on brainstorming, mind-mapping, puzzle solving, group activities, releasing the right side of the brain, or stimulating visual thinking. Each sense that we use or mode of thinking or perceiving we apply "lights up" a different part of our brain. When we use more of our brain we create, in effect, a hothouse effect within our own minds. Ideas from different realms of perception or areas of knowledge inform one another. A visual image may provide the solution much as the chemist Kekule's dream of a serpent swallowing its own tail triggered his discovery of the benzene ring.[6] Einstein said that he first felt his ideas in his muscles before working them out mathematically, and he recalled starting down the road to the theory of relativity when he visualized himself riding on a light beam through the universe.[7] (Oddly enough, several ancient Greek wise men were reputed to fly through space and time on magic arrows.) And just as communities generate a tremendous creative charge by transplanting marginal cultural elements to the heart of a culture, a similar power is invoked by implanting primal, sensual brain functions at the core of abstract thinking processes.

So is the ideal workplace a New Age bazaar where the scent of incense floats in between the rippling silver chords of the sitar? No, but creativity *is* a holistic activity that requires some unorthodox tools. Raising creative capital might very well mean opening the doors of perception and expanding the dimensions of learning. These techniques cannot simply be taught; they only work if it's acceptable for individuals to "sit for ideas," or build three-dimensional models of ideas on their office floors, or work out concepts kinesthetically—that is, using movement or music. In teaching these methods, I am often pleasantly surprised by how many people actually bring these perception-based methods into their daily work lives. However, it takes organizational initiative and strategy to use them extensively enough to help generate the hothouse effect. With all methods, it is important to teach *how to apply them* as well as to *do* them. If people attend a creativity workshop where they experience visual thinking, what do they do with what they've learned once they return to the office? How does it interface with *their* jobs. If the goal is simply to expose them to interesting ideas, then it might not be necessary to develop a response to these types of questions. If the goal is to raise the general level of creativity throughout the organization, it is important to build these implementations into any training that takes place.

#24. IMMERSION AND OSMOSIS

One method of structuring learning, geared more toward the design of the work environment rather than specific training elements, is via immersion and osmosis. The most efficient learning takes place through the pores, when deadlines, creative compulsion, the promise of great rewards, warding off a threat, or fear of appearing a fool in front of a group compels us to immerse ourselves in a discipline or task. Just as repetitious drills—such as fielding hundreds of ground balls, playing and replaying musical scales, practicing the same karate forms over and over, reviewing math problems till you dream about them—liberate our creative faculties in their respective fields, so too does immersion clear the way for illumination.

In the field of creativity training, the 3 *Is*—immersion, incubation, and illumination—are a favorite way to describe one aspect of the creative process. The 3 *Is* show how breakthrough ideas are most likely to occur in the quiet, relaxing moments after one has *immersed* oneself in work. After immersion, information and ideas *incubate* in the unconscious, which turns its huge processing capacity toward developing a solution. At some point, the unconscious devises a solution and offers its *illumination* on a silver platter, usually when you're in the shower or about to fall asleep or driving in rush hour traffic. This is also known as the Eureka effect after the Greek mathematician Archimides, who received a golden illumination about one knotty problem as he lowered himself into a bath. He immediately shouted "Eureka!"—which in Greek means, "I've found it!"—and ran down the street naked to deliver his solution, demonstrating once and for all that fully implementing the Eureka effect is a good way to get arrested.

In the context of the hothouse effect, immersion goes beyond intensive individual research. Immersion environments that affect an entire group will spring up spontaneously in an already functioning hothouse because that is how these groups behave, both from the pleasure taken in creation and because they understand that immersion sustains creativity. In the earlier stages, as a force that contributes to the hothouse effect, the immersion experience needs to be consciously designed because the concentrated energy of immersion requires an investment of resources that runs counter to most ideas of efficient, effective management. The immersion environment can take several forms. As in Verrocchio's workshop, Thomas Edison's laboratory, or the Bauhaus, it meant workshops and studios filled with materials, people "mucking about," projects and prototypes in various stages of development, plans and sketches tacked to the wall, and perpetual exchange of ideas. At Beard Framing it meant the continuing presence of cultural events and in-house salons in which ideas pervaded the workplace. In Athens, the soaring Acropolis buildings and ubiquity of shrines and sculptures throughout the region created a sort of vital medium in which the psyches of the Athenians were perpetually bathed, which is the function of public art wherever it is found.

Learning by osmosis is highly efficient. In my local elementary school, Judy Shannon, a third-grade teacher with more than thirty years of experience, is a local legend for the creativity she shares with all her students. Shannon possesses the creative touch in the respect, love, and connectedness she brings to every child, but it is evidenced as well in the classroom itself. Although neat and well-organized, it is a mini-labyrinth of workstations, multiple projects in various stages, colorful art work, quirky curiosities, and everywhere, children engaged in learning independently from one another, from the teacher herself, and from the materials that surround them every day.

What works for children can also work for adults. The notion of adult learning can be reduced to one simple equation: best practices in childhood learning plus experience. Teaching children creatively boils down to using adult learning methods plus lots of play and clearly defined limits. Learning is all about the body and mind, two elements shared by every human being.

The ground of all experience is the realm of perception, and the most powerful education and training reaches past the mental models that shape our thinking, to the fundamental ways in which we perceive and construct our realities. The electric charge that this type of experience carries has the power, in and of itself, to transform our mental processes.

Dr. Harris Kagan, a professor of physics at Ohio State University, is fascinated with holography, and he also teaches students how to create holographic art in Ohio State's art department. Kagan recently received a grant that will allow him to explore immersion learning by constructing a virtual reality laboratory equipped with twenty-four cameras and a rowing machine. For six minutes (about two hundred strokes) an expert rower pulls at the oars while the laser cameras photograph him. Kagan plans to reconstruct a virtual reality image of the ideal rower based on the expert's movements, which will be used to train other rowers, from beginners to members of a rowing team. The trainee enters the room, sits in the rowing machine, and dons virtual reality goggles that generate the three-dimensional image of the expert rower. Immersed in this image, the trainee simply rows. Kagan hopes that the brain will automatically correct all movements at once, an idea in accord with experts on the use of visualization for athletic training. For instance, Dr. Charles Garfield recommends that skiers mentally rehearse "the *complete* action, rather than just the beginning, middle, end, or any other segment."[8] In Kagan's model, trainees actually *enter* the visualization and their brains adjust the body's movements according to the ideal vision in the virtual reality system.

The implications for learning are profound and applicable to an endless array of skills. Using virtual reality to create an immersion learning experience illustrates one of many ways that technology will transform learning. Already, numerous paths to this immersion experience exist, many with the help of technology. We are squandering an enormous source of educational potential by not utilizing immersion methods that both accelerate learning and enhance simultaneously a wide range of mutually reinforcing mind and body skills.

#25. META-SYSTEM

One of the most propulsive factors in the formation of an emerging hothouse occurs early in the group's history: engagement with a much vaster, more complex, and sophisticated system, which I call a *meta-system* to highlight the overarching, all-pervading quality of the larger system. We have seen how Florence's exchange with the Byzantine Empire in 1438 injected stimuli into the smaller state's cultural processes. Despite the disproportionate size and power of the two systems, the emerging hothouse manages not to be overwhelmed by the meta-system because it already possesses distinctive, deeply rooted cultural forms able to withstand a storm of stimulation from the far more powerful meta-system.

The term *rapid and sudden* is critical: The smaller community's situation contrasts sharply with the longstanding give-and-take of societies that trade with and overrun one another, share philosophical and religious ideas, share a general worldview and similar political systems, and even meld their languages into one another's. Compare ancient Greece to the Persians, Medes, Sumerians, Babylonians, Assyrians, and countless others who mingled on the plains of Mesopotamia. Intercultural influence in the Tigris and Euphrates region was rapid, continuous, and unrelenting. All these groups or their descendants wound up in the Persian Empire (559–330 B.C.E.), overseer of the entire meta-system represented by Mesopotamian civilization. While cross-fertilization between communities is intrinsically creative, in the meta-system boundaries have been breached so regularly and thoroughly that it engenders a homogeneity that defuses the shock of the strange when two communities within the meta-system interact.

In contrast, between about 1200 and 800 B.C.E., Greece was isolated from the rest of the Mediterranean world. Before that, from about 1600 to 1200 B.C.E., Greece was home to a relatively well-to-do palace culture that was a modest, marginal presence among the region's empires. Around 1200 B.C.E., however, upheavals throughout the Eastern Mediterranean shattered empires, closed shipping lanes, lowered living standards, and deprived Greece of its written alphabet. When the Phoenicians reopened the shipping lanes in the ninth century B.C.E., the Greeks had been living in remote, mountain-sheltered villages for centuries, tending their isolated local traditions to a degree unknown in the plains and foothills that midwived so many aggressive ancient empires.

The so-called Greek miracle was due largely to Greece's localized, village-based system managing to maintain its cultural integrity while suddenly coming into contact with, and learning from, a highly complex and sophisticated civilization. Greece regained literacy by adapting the Phoenician alphabet to its own language. Hellenic eyes opened wide before the science and math of Egypt and Babylon, the vast empires of the Near East and Middle East, and the ancient chronologies of the Egyptians, which, whether one chooses to believe them or not, went back far beyond those our own experts have settled upon. Business-wise, the Greeks learned about letters of credit, international trade networks, and distant ports of call. Every horizon dropped away before the newly awakened Hellenic mind. Yet, because the change was so rapid and self-driven (through Greek exploration, trade, and settlement on foreign shores rather than because they were conquered by outside invaders), and occurred after the Greeks had tended their own gardens for so long, their deeply rooted local traditions were not overwhelmed by the new stimuli. The Greeks remained grounded in ancient tradition while experimenting with fantastic new possibilities of thought and action. And the small size of Greek communities meant that cultural change reverberated throughout the entire populace rather than simply among a narrow cultural elite.

At first, the Athenians experienced this only tangentially because of their relative isolation even within Greece and the pathetic condition of their economy and social order. Before the sixth century B.C.E., Athens simply could not absorb or utilize these external energies with any efficiency or purpose. When it finally did step on board the train, so to speak, Athens was propelled even more quickly into a Greek commercial and competitive city-state system far wealthier, more sophisticated, and more extensive than it had been two centuries earlier, when cities like Corinth, Mytilene, and Sparta first ventured onto the international stage.

One odd thing about the hothouse effect is its timing, which is critical in regard to the hothouse's contact with the meta-system. Hothouses rarely make the initial creative breakthrough. Corinth was the most successful Greek commercial power on the mainland from about 750 to 600 B.C.E., and many other states ran well ahead of Athens economically, artistically, and politically. But the *relative* latecomer tends to generate the hothouse effect, and this timing is linked to dynamics that govern sudden engagement with a meta-system.

The dynamic works this way. Certain communities move to the forefront in the early stages of any major societal transition while the eventual hothouse, such as Athens, may still be a stagnant backwater. Or it could already be prosperous, as was Florence, but held back by civil strife or other factors. In Italy, in the twelfth and thirteenth centuries, cities such as Pisa and Todi hit their cultural stride before Florence, but neither sustained its creative growth. When the hothouse finally breaks out of its restrictive conditions, it benefits from its latecomer status because a lot of the hard work has already been done for it. As soon as Athens became a player in the Greek economic system during Peisistratos's rule, it rapidly achieved parity with the other city-states. Individuals learn very quickly when contending with others of similar ability but more advanced skill. For instance, a chess player who regularly plays opponents somewhat better than he or she, but not overwhelmingly so, rapidly improves; similarly, Athens improved rapidly at the political and commercial games of its time.

Because of its large, participatory citizen base, Athens possessed more intellectual capital than its rivals. Thus fueled, Athens, despite its latecomer status, moved quickly to the level that Corinth and others had achieved during two hundred years of slower cultural progress. And when it came into close contact with the twin meta-systems of Egypt and the Middle East, the shock was even greater than it had been for the Greek city-states two hundred years earlier, which were little more than glorified towns at that point. Athens was simply better prepared for the contact, which, strangely enough, meant that it could experience the full shock of what the ancient civilizations could offer it. The earlier communities simply did not have the resources to absorb the full implications of the meta-system. But after decades of living under Solon's reforms and Peisistratos's rule, and with the spark provided by Cleisthenes, Athens in the sixth century B.C.E. was far more sophisticated than its rivals had been a century or two earlier. Thus, like a more powerful computer, it could process data more efficiently and more on its own terms, and in a more uninhibited, creative fashion.

The pottery industry offers an apt illustration. Corinth was in the forefront of Greek pottery making in the eighth and seventh centuries B.C.E. Its so-called Orientalizing style depicted monstrous creatures adapted from the art of the Middle East. By the time Athens came onto the scene, however, this was becoming old hat. Athens, flush with its revitalized energy, pioneered a new style of vase painting in which human interaction was the main subject. Soon the Athenians created the innovative red-figure style that gave painters even more freedom to depict motion, biomechanics, and dramatic action. Athens's economy boomed with the success of its vase industry until it surpassed Corinth's, a bitter pill that Corinth gagged on. Athenian images, style, and products caught the market wave of a rapidly expanding economy and the Greeks' growing interest in human concerns, and it was Athens that defined this era's achievements. Corinth, in effect, rode the wave of the minicomputer; Athens went straight to the PC.

In modern terms, the race does not always belong to the first-to-market. The early entrant rarely grasps the implications of its innovative product. Nor is the market ready to absorb large volumes of whatever the early bird is selling. In fact, these first products may simply not be good enough to dominate the market for long. Also, pioneers tend to make bigger mistakes because they have fewer trail markers to follow. Where is Atari today, or Univac? The pioneers that do flourish are often primarily service providers, such as General Electric, Bell Telephone and its offspring, or J.T. Thompson advertising. The hothouse, however, tends to be a late bloomer. Oddly enough, this conclusion is born out by Network Science as well, in which the hubs that are established earliest in a network rarely become either the most active or most important hubs within the network; this pattern has the force of a mathematical law.

The high-tech industry of Silicon Valley and Massachusetts's Route 128 in the 1980s and 1990s followed the hothouse pattern. The older computer companies such as IBM and Hunnewell, along with their expertise, represented the meta-system. Digital and Wang in the Boston area played Corinth's part, emerging rapidly but still too early to capture the tsunami that would carry Intel, Microsoft, Sun, Lotus, Compaq, Dell, Apple, Oracle, and a host of others to prominence. IBM, copying the Persian Empire's underestimation of Greece, missed the point of the personal computer and signed away operating system rights to Bill Gates and Microsoft. The hothouse companies eventually became absorbed into the established meta-system in which IBM, as standard bearer for high-tech civilization, still flourishes but under very different terms than before. Perhaps the newly reconfigured meta-system awaits a new challenger.

The Greek system that Athens stepped into just after 600 B.C.E. was already linked to the era's meta-system. The abstract mind-set of theoretical and practical math; the sheer quantity of knowledge stored in Egypt and Babylon; and the cultural achievements of other Greek cities were revealed to the Athenians within just a few decades in the sixth century B.C.E. As a result of this rapid exposure, the old local culture never had time to be diluted or driven underground. Just as the magnificent art form of tragedy retained its Dionysian roots, so too did the new expansive, restless, intellectually driven culture of Athens retain a profound resonance with the fatalism and rhythms embodied in the old worldview of Hellenic village life. The rapid and sudden contact with the meta-system helps to preserve the excitement and vitality of a young, local culture in the full flush of youth.

#26. MENTAL MODES

The thinking of highly creative individuals is marked by unconventional modes of thought, at least when they're being creative. Metaphor, thought experiments, metacognitive thinking, and the like are more explicitly mental versions of the techniques found under Factor #22. Because they involve shifting one's perceptions, they can potentially transform the entire group culture if broadly applied. For instance, in my children's elementary school, the students are taught the use and function of metaphor from the earliest grades, thus enriching their use of language and appreciation of good writing. The research of Georgi Lozanov, the Bulgarian founder of accelerated learning, suggests that the optimum way to learn foreign language vocabulary is to hear the words at the rate of one every ten seconds, which best suits the brain's ability to absorb information.[9] Einstein used thought experiments to work out his theory of relativity and to test quantum theory. Nikola Tesla, perhaps the greatest inventor of all, tested his inventions by operating and fine-tuning them—visually, in his mind.[10]

Metacognitive thinking is a general term for "thinking about thinking." When we detach ourselves from our own thought processes, we can improve or fine-tune them as Tesla did his machinery. Meditation has become more and more popular worldwide over the past forty years, and many of its benefits of reducing stress, clearing the mind, and even lowering the frequency of brain waves to enter a state of heightened creativity, can be achieved through movement exercises and even via electronic means.

These techniques remind us that the mind is an athlete. It benefits from training, is stimulated by learning new tasks, and possesses natural gifts. Some people will be great natural "math-letes," or be naturally gifted in mechanics, design, business, art, or whatever. Many will be multitalented. Some might be world-class from day one and others develop their talents only after years of hard work; still others achieve a level of competence that brings them satisfaction but little fame or glory. But *everyone* can enhance their mental operations. Teaching these techniques to employees brings an array of benefits: enhanced motivation and satisfaction, increased intellectual activity, more and better ideas, highly charged exchange of ideas, challenge to accepted verities, and an increase in creative activity.

#27. TIME

The hothouse effect seems to accelerate history, as though the community discovered some secret portal into the slipstream of time. Within the hothouse, time follows the rhythm of creative work rather than drumming the beat for our daily activities, as it usually does. Time holds such power over us that it is difficult not to view it as a constant that rushes along at a regular pace, whether that pace is petty or not. Its impact on management is undeniable. As Australian futurist Richard Neville puts it, "The disappearance of time means that the shelf life of management knowledge is down to a year, and shrinking."[11] Neville's insight links management competency to the fact that the well-regulated time of the industrial era is in disarray. The accelerating pace set by technology, the synchronic effects of globalization (everything happens everywhere and it all affects each of us), and our bodies' and minds' physiological and perceptual shifts in how we experience time, are transforming knowledge and skills. Far from something we possess and know for all time, knowledge is becoming a steady stream of temporarily useful packets that we use and cast away before we're burdened by their obsolescence.

Perhaps we can cultivate time as a palpable dimension we use much as we do space. Einstein proved that time is actually the fourth dimension. But if space has three dimensions, why should time have only one? Time possesses past, present, and future, but these are really experiential indicators marking the linear time that orients us in this world. Time comes in three basic formats, however, that may in fact be dimensions: linear, cyclical, and synchronic time. *Linear* pushes steadily from the past into the future; the little arrow on the time-line denotes the present and one event follows or precedes another. *Cyclical* time constantly returns to a mythical past where things began, just as the cycle of the seasons returns to the solstices and equinoxes year after year. Life is lived in cycles that forever circle back to the time of origins. When time returns to the beginning of a cycle—for example, the vernal equinox, a birthday, or the anniversary of a great victory—it is as if one returns to the first dawn when creative energies ran rampant. At such times, time can be *renewed* by rituals that reenact the first moment of creation or channel its creative energies into the present moment. This rebirth also symbolizes the origins of human consciousness, albeit one forever bound to the cycles of nature and the need to return to the beginning. So we might say that *linear* time is grounded mostly in the future and *cyclical* time mostly in the past, although both make use of all three temporal directions.

Synchronic time expands the present. The links between events in this third temporal dimension differ from those in the other two. In linear time, *causality* is the prime agent of activity. Events follow one another in timely and orderly fashion; one event *causes* the next, and the momentum from these events causes new events. Events may split off into complex tree or web patterns, but always the movement is linear, one event triggering another. In cyclical time, the mythic time of origins pulls like a magnet on all other events. Causality is less important than *attraction*. Synchronicity, however, operates via *resonance*. And while the linear mind uses logic and analysis to establish a causal chain, the cyclical mind relies on empathy to achieve harmony with nature's rhythms, and the synchronic mind uses what is often called higher consciousness to perceive the resonance that connects phenomena in unanticipated ways.

It would be difficult to live within synchronic time in a society governed by linear time, although myth-based, cyclical-time societies tend to accord great honor to synchronic types. (Whether or not one *believes* in synchronic time, it is a descriptive model that appears in many traditions, so it is certainly worth considering as a mental construct that wields influence over human thought.) Synchronic time is associated with peak experiences, those moments when one acts at a greatly enhanced level of awareness and skill. Peak experiences produce strange temporal effects: Time seems to stand still, one anticipates everything that is about to take place an instant before it occurs, special connections spring up between people without logical cause, and so on. In synchronic time, the logic that binds events to one another in linear or mythic time is lifted, and people often feel released from the demands of life's usual structures and strictures.

The variability of time is real for many people. Athletes experience time slowing down or standing still at a clutch moment when everything comes together and they make a magnificent play. When the mind concentrates at the intensity associated with higher levels of creativity, the number of "mental events" increases dramatically. We may generate in five minutes the same number of images and thoughts we normally have in an hour. The five minutes can *seem* to expand to thirty, and we may be shocked to learn how little time has actually passed. A baseball player may concentrate so intently that the half-second it takes a pitch to cover the distance of sixty feet, six inches from pitcher to home plate seems to stretch just enough to shift the advantage to the batter. Perhaps great athletes have the ability—whether innate or self-conditioned—to slow down time in this way and in effect play at a different rate than the rest of their league. The converse is even more common: An all-consuming task tricks our normal cognitive rhythm into experiencing six hours as almost no time at all.

Creativity commonly produces both effects. When one follows the pace or rhythm of creativity, it yields more irregular yet often more efficient work patterns than the typical workday. As Andre Millard writes of Thomas Edison's disdain for regular work hours, "The eccentric hours of work at the laboratory derive from the pre-industrial tradition in which craftsmen controlled the pace and timing of their work. This tradition clashed with an industrial order that attempted to maximize investment in machines and buildings by organizing the workday of its employees."[12]

Millard points out that the crafts tradition has its own creative rhythms, which follow neither a 9 to 5 nor a 24/7 pattern.

Just as farmers cultivate fields, so too do hothouse members cultivate time. They learn how to bring themselves into an enhanced state of creativity. The memoirs of diverse masters such as Mozart, the English poet Samuel Taylor Coleridge, Einstein, Robert Louis Stevenson, and novelist Virginia Wolfe all refer to experiences of time passing in odd ways. It is possible to cultivate this perception, to bring it about or watch for its arrival, and use it for creative ends. The de Stijl group of artists and designers, who at times collaborated with the Bauhaus, expressed this alternative view of time in a 1918 Manifesto:

> There is an old and a new consciousness of time.
> The old is connected with the individual
> The new is connected with the universal . . .
> The new art has brought forward what the new consciousness
> of time contains: a balance between the universal and the
> individual.[13]

This was written two years after Einstein's second paper was published and the rest of the Manifesto contains explicit allusions to the role of World War I in shaping de Stijl's creative response to the still new century. Einstein and the war both shattered the dimension of time as it was lived in the old world that was rapidly fading.

#28. EXTERNAL CURRENTS

Let us return to space. The world outside the workplace swarms with clouds of data and ribbons of information thick as confetti during a carnival. Some pieces capture our attention, but mostly the workplace filters out the blizzard of input. Just as our brains filter the data vacuumed up by our senses so that we are capable of more than an occasional gasp of amazement at the storm of impressions breaking over us, so too without this filter no organization could accomplish anything.

Despite the benefits of this regulatory mechanism, too much regulation has drawbacks as well. Modern technological and bureaucratic society constricts our awareness in ways that have been expounded upon at length by many observers. Businesses also apply a very fine filter to what they deem relevant to their work. Yet, modern companies cannot simply shut themselves off from general social trends. Hothouses always seem to be attuned to these trends, which often provide them with their best inspirations. Could Digital, Wang, or IBM have spotted the PC trend earlier? Was IBM's view of the PC a reflection of its attitude toward the Selectric typewriter—a low end, not very glamorous product for IBM? Had IBM been closer to the youth culture and its garage tinkerers, would it have realized that PCs were a completely different creature? Were there engineers at Digital who understood the PC's challenge, but were unable to overcome the corporate commitment to the minicomputer? In its glory days, Digital hired anthropologists to study the company culture. It would have been more beneficial to direct anthropological scrutiny beyond the boundaries of the company to seek the social trends that would translate into marketplace shifts.

The fascinating book *Engineering Culture* by Gideon Kunda shows how a large high-tech company in the Route 128 area exercised control over its corporate culture even while apparently promoting an intrapreneurial, innovative work style.[14] "Tech," as Kunda calls it, engineered the supposedly open exchange of ideas and opinions so that it actually reinforced company ideology in regard to hierarchy and especially strategic direction. The implications for the hothouse effect are numerous. The dynamics of control can easily be extended to allow the *appearance* of a vital, creative system while the reality falls far short. Companies also pay a costly price for this sort of self-deception, as the history of many Tech-like companies has demonstrated. The demise of Digital and Wang owes more to a failure of business intelligence than to obvious mismanagement. The information they needed lay outside the cognitive frameworks from which they operated, and no one read the clues or, if they did so, no one utilized the messages effectively.

NOTES

1. A good Web site to visit for Boyd's writings and articles about him is "Defense and the National Interest" at http://d-n-i.net/second_level/boyd_military.htm#discourse.
2. Jean Paul Richter, *The Notebooks of Leonardo Da Vinci: Compiled and Edited from the Original Manuscripts,* vol. 1 (New York: Dover Press, 1970), p. 254.
3. Willis Harman and Howard Rheingold, *Higher Creativity: Liberating the*

Unconscious for Breakthrough Insights (Los Angeles: Jeremy Tarcher, Inc., 1984), pp. 28–30.

4. Napoleon Hill, *Think and Grow Rich* (New York: Fawcett Crest, 1960), pp. 181–182.

5. Michael Murphy and Rhea A. White, *In the Zone: Transcendent Experience in Sports* (New York: Penguin Books, 1995), p. 154.

6. Harman and Rheingold, p. 41.

7. John Briggs, *Fire in the Crucible: The Self-Creation of Creativity and Genius* (Los Angeles: Jeremy Tarcher, Inc., 1990), pp. 167, 311.

8. Charles A. Garfield with Hal Zina Bennett, *Peak Performance: Mental Training Techniques of the World's Greatest Athletes* (Los Angeles: Jeremy Tarcher, Inc., 1984), p. 145.

9. Sheila Ostrander and Lynn Schroeder, with Nancy Ostrander, *Super-Learning* (New York: Dell Publishing, 1979), p. 68.

10. Win Wenger and Richard Poe, *The Einstein Factor* (Rocklin, CA: Prima Publishing, 1996), p. 21.

11. Richard Neville, *Footprints of the Future: Handbook for the Third Millennium* (N. Sydney, Australia: Richmond Ventures, 2002), p. 18.

12. Andre Millard, *Edison and the Business of Innovation* (Baltimore: Johns Hopkins University Press, 1990), p. 33.

13. Paul Overy, *De Stijl* (London: Thames and Hudson, 1991), p. 46.

14. Gideon Kunda, *Engineering Culture: Control and Commitment in a High-Tech Corporation* (Philadelphia: Temple University Press, 1992).

10

THE BAUHAUS: LEARNING BY PERCEIVING

During the fourteen years of its existence from 1919 to 1933, the German Bauhaus blazed trails in a host of disciplines including architecture, painting, sculpture, education, and the design of just about everything, as well as pioneering methods for maximizing creative activity within a community by experimenting with and refining the very way its members perceived form, color, technology, the disciplines of art and design, and the nature of perception itself. After the Nazis closed it down in 1933, many Bauhaus members came to the United States, where they regrouped at what came to be called the Institute of Design in Chicago, exerting a powerful influence on all aspects of architecture and design down to the present day.

ORIGINS

The Bauhaus can trace its origins back to the nineteenth-century rebellion against the Industrial Revolution's impact on the countryside and its people. This was most acutely felt in England, the world's most powerful industrial power and the quickest to industrialize. The "satanic mills" that William Blake castigated in the late eighteenth century had come to be viewed as blight a century later. And the devastating effects on formerly proud countryfolk who now lived amidst toxic pools of arsenic and mercury in industrial towns, and whose children worked fourteen hours a day, never seeing the sun, roused the social conscience of influential segments of English society.

John Ruskin, an art critic and essayist, held sway over the intellectual atmosphere of late-nineteenth-century England in a way scarcely imaginable today. Ruskin's solution to industrialization and pollution lay in the medieval guilds, with their emphasis on handicraft, cooperative living, mentorship, and respect for mastery. Ruskin's ideas were adopted by William Morris, a printer and design guru, who in turn influenced the Arts and Crafts movement in the United States and a host of movements in England. Even today, the Ruskin Mill in Nailsmith, a town in the Cotswold area of Gloucestershire, retains the flavor and values of Ruskin and Morris's vision. The mill is home to various working craftspeople. It is also an educational center for troubled youths, a studio center for practitioners of traditional crafts such as felt- and wool-making, a theatre, and home to scientific and low-tech engineering initiatives in nutrition and food production. Nearby, the larger town of Stroud boasts old working mills and factories and a publishing house whose family ownership has been in the trade almost since Gutenberg invented the printing press. Stroud even uses its own currency within town limits, and has always been home to freethinkers, religious reformers, artists, craftspeople, and social activists. The values that animate Stroud and Ruskin Mill hearken directly back to Ruskin and Morris, as did the Bauhaus.

One day, in 1896, a Prussian "cultural spy" named Hermann Muthesius entered England. His mission was to discover the secrets of England's industrial success.[1] (See the discussion under Factor #28.) At the time, Germany's economy was the fastest growing in Europe. Unification had unleashed tremendous economic and cultural energies in Germany. Among the latter was a mystical nationalism that revered an allegedly unique Germanic quality bred in blood and bone, forest and bog. Many Germans professed to despise what they viewed as England's bourgeois character and France's arid intellectualism. Germany's destiny, they believed, was to reinvigorate European civilization, and Germany was rife with notions of iron will, racial purity, national destiny, the *ubermensch* (or "superman"), and images of Nordic blonds gazing possessively into the future. At this point, members of many political persuasions bought into these beliefs, which the Nazis eventually made their own.

Muthesius the spy stayed in England for six years. Upon his return, the Prussian government followed his recommendations that modern artists teach German workers to be more productive using the workshop methods championed by Ruskin and Morris. The Prussian government established workshops in all Prussian handicraft schools and installed modern artists as teachers. Soon, small workshops that produced household goods sprang up all over Germany.[2] At the same time, Germany's industrial production surpassed England's, although this cannot be attributed to the new workshops. As tensions rose as prelude to World War I, many Germans welcomed the chance to demonstrate their superiority over the French and English by defeating them in armed conflict supported by their impressive industrial base. The war didn't turn out as planned (big surprise), and the slaughter in the trenches, the pointlessness of the whole endeavor, political revolution, and the loss of faith in leadership transformed Europe. Artists responded with movements such as Dadaism, which proclaimed the absurdity of all previous social and artistic tradition, and Surrealism, which meticulously depicted distortions in the perception of space and time. It was a disturbed and disturbing time.

EUROPE AFTER THE RAIN

Yet many felt the time was ripe for society to strike off in new directions. Walter Gropius, a German architect, took over leadership of the Weimar Craft School in 1919. Gropius was deeply influenced by the workshop experience of prewar Germany. He changed the school's name to the Bauhaus because he saw the art of building—*Bau*—as all-inclusive, embracing architecture, sculpture, decoration, design, art, and, in fact, the entire cultural and physical landscape. (See Exhibit 5.) Under Gropius, the Bauhaus bridged traditional creative oppositions such as art and design, layperson and artist, and school and production center. (See Exhibit 6.) Gropius intended that studio masters practice onsite as well as teach. They would mingle with the students, all dedicated to the "oneness of a common idea" just as members of the medieval guilds were. Theory and practice would energize one another. As art historian Sigrid Weltge states, "The Bauhaus envisaged the professional of the future as a designer with aesthetic and technical skills acquired from a master capable of teaching both."[3] Students would benefit from the masters' skill, experience, and vision, while masters derived advantage from their students' fresh insight, innovative spirit, and enthusiasm.

The Bauhaus also harnessed energy from another duality that Athens missed entirely and that Renaissance Italy tapped: women and men. The postwar Roaring Twenties was a period of liberation for many women, especially in the cities. The Bauhaus welcomed women as students and teachers, first only in the weaving school, but soon in other areas as well, as Weltge notes.

> For the weaver it was no longer enough playfully to discover
> personal inclinations by chance. Instead, she began systemati-
> cally to investigate a whole range of design problems in an
> environment that resembled a laboratory more than a studio.
> In such a setting, the key to success must be co-operation and
> a common strategy.[4]

As Weltge implies, women in this "laboratory" stepped into the role of experimenter that had long been closed to them. Women in art no longer focused simply on personal inclinations discovered by chance, but they adopted *and* adapted the so-called masculine model of practice and collaboration that marks scientific inquiry.

Karla Grolsch taught physical education and coached sports at the Bauhaus from 1928 to 1930.[5] Marianne Brandt went from student in the metal shop to its acting head in 1928–1929, and "her works—above all her lamps—remained among the best of the Bauhaus products."[6] Dörte Helm, Kitty Fischer, Else Mögelin, Margarete Willers, and Ida Kerkovius "were accomplished artists by the time they arrived at the Bauhaus,"[7] and Gunta Stölzl's influence as chief luminary of the weaving workshop was felt throughout the institute.[8] Gertrud Grunow taught students that inner harmony was essential to creativity, an influential idea in the Bauhaus's early years.

> You close your eyes, and after a short period of inner reflec-
> tion, you receive an instruction, either to imagine a certain
> colour ball and to feel it by penetrating it with your hands, or
> to concentrate upon a note played at the piano. In less than
> no time almost everyone is fully in motion, each in their own
> individual way.[9]

Grunow envisioned a Platonic ideal of "universal equilibrium of color, music, perception and form anchored in each person—rediscovered through physical and mental exercises."[10] This mysticism was balanced by rigorous instruction in technique, another duality that the Bauhaus used as a source of creative energy.

The most influential master after Gropius in the early years of the Bauhaus was Johannes Itten. Like Grunow, Itten approached both art and education by emphasizing continual analysis of the themes, materials, and processes that drove the artist's work, and he urged students to internalize the principles that guided them. He devised numerous activities to sensitize students to contrasts in texture, color, light, and touch, and encouraged them to learn their own rhythms, harmonize with their inner being, and develop a well-tuned personality.[11] In short, Itten was obsessed with perception and believed that creativity required reshaping the perceptions and reprogramming the experience of one's body, the space it inhabits, and the textures and densities of the surrounding world. "A centering process of meditation and breathing exercises preceded Itten's formal class sessions. To further relax and loosen the body he asked students to draw with both hands, which often resulted in surprising calligraphic, almost oriental designs. He strove to extend the self-awareness of each young person beyond personal consciousness to a heightened sensitivity for the properties of materials."[12] Itten constantly wove opposites together: "intuition and method" and "subjective experience and objective recognition." In short, he recognized that creativity involved rigorous analysis (as Factors #4, #5, and #23 indicate). His teaching began with the body, with breathing exercises and gymnastics, and students sought the pure essence of forms and "heightened sensitivity" to the properties of materials.[13] To him, contradiction was central to creation and creativity alike. Reflecting a common Bauhaus and hothouse theme, Itten employed paradox to help students experience external objective reality from a subjective standpoint, and to expose their subjective, inner worlds to objective analysis.[14]

Itten and Grunow's ideas survived their tenure at the Bauhaus. Their holistic vision of art and design recast the image of the creator from romantic, tormented soul toward a view of the artist, inventor, and designer as part scientist, contemplative, and technician. They clearly defined creativity as a process that challenges any perceptual or canonical norm that happens to restrict the artist's exploration of reality. Both Itten and Grunow articulated a position the Florentines accepted as natural: The creator draws upon all aspects of existence. Each of us absorbs perceptions not only from the psychological and social realms but from the physical, transcendental, sensual, intuitive, and conceptual, all of which is available as the fundamental material of our creations.

Gropius proved to be an outstanding leader. He had to be. Despite Grunow and Itten's message of harmony and inner peace, the Bauhaus was not immune to conflict, which Gropius managed with a participatory leadership style. Each master could submit written statements on important questions for general distribution. Students had a strong voice on the Bauhaus Council and Gropius consulted them over important issues; he "created a strong sense of community spirit, cooperation and shared responsibility." His sole aim was "to leave everything in suspension, in flux, in order to avoid our community solidifying into a conventional academy."[15] Yet, like Grunow and Itten, he was an idealist who hoped the Bauhaus could integrate the individual with society as organically as humans had once been integrated with nature.

AFTER GROPIUS

Many members criticized this approach as being too open-ended and subjective. In 1928, Gropius decided to step down and pass the wand of leadership to Hannes Meyer. In January 1926, Gropius offered the masters a critique of the institute's leadership, which of course included himself above all. He urged strong leadership in the workshops and soon brought in Hannes Meyer as his successor as director.[16] Gropius managed the transition unselfishly and with the best interests of the school in mind. He had the Solon-like courage to hand power over to someone whose vision for the Bauhaus he did not fully accept. But he did recognize that Meyer was the best person to guide the Bauhaus's next stage of development.

Meyer led the Bauhaus through a critical shift that was to cement its lasting influence on the modern world. He turned immediately to issues of production and technology. The Bauhaus had already developed mass-producible products, but some masters considered the commitment to fine arts and spirituality distracting to the creation of innovative designs suitable for mass production and distribution. Nonetheless, this two-stage evolution of the Bauhaus—starting with a strong spiritual and artistic orientation and then shifting into an industrial mode—probably was one of the keys to its creative genius. By the time Meyer took over, the Bauhaus had so immersed itself in its visionary values and its exploration of materials and perception, and established such innovative modes of learning and creative activity, that these elements all continued to exert a powerful influence over the implementation of production-oriented goals.

Besides, the transition had been going on for a number of years anyway. Laszlo Moholy-Nagy came to the Bauhaus in 1923 and directed the preliminary courses until 1928. Moholy-Nagy had earned his law degree in the heady, creative, and unsettled atmosphere of Budapest in 1918. He was also a painter, sculptor, and theorist on art and education. In some ways, his multifaceted background and his approach to the Bauhaus mission made him the quintessential Bauhaus master. In the five years after he arrived and before Gropius stepped down, Moholy-Nagy "emphasized more than anyone at the Bauhaus had done before him the relationship between form and function."[17] He was, like others there, obsessed with questions of perception, and like Itten and Grunow, he designed courses to awaken students to the sensual properties of their materials. Many of his innovative exercises focused on sharpening the sense of touch and he also promoted "an unceasing exploration of the technical materials of the age."[18] In an approach that prefigures studios such as Loop Design Centre in Bologna, Italy (see Chapter 11), his "preliminary course teaching included the study and construction of designs, experimenting with light and its reflexes, blueprints for typography and stage-design, kinetic metal construction, and experiments in film and photography."[19] Moholy-Nagy drew international attention for his successful synthesis of functionality and technology on the one hand, and his uncanny ability to train students as creative innovators on the other. As head of the metal shop, he established "the link between craftsmanship being practiced in the workshops, the education of the students, and their inclination towards industrial design."[20] The fusion of the elements of art, technology, education, and practice in any form tends to kindle the hothouse effect.

Conflict over the Bauhaus's direction continued in the Moholy-Nagy years, during the second half of Gropius's leadership. In 1926, in a Bauhaus publication, the painter Georg Muche argued that "the creative artist was superfluous when it came to designing forms for industry. The form process started not from the elementary forms and primary colours investigated by the artists, but from the working of the machine."[21] Muche not only objected to the emphasis on Grunow and Itten's self-focused approach to artistic training but also to the influence of theoretical artists such as Kandinsky and Klee. However, as Magdalena Droste notes, "It was a development to which the Bauhaus had in fact already responded."[22] The roles of the world-renowned Klee and Kandinsky had been reduced, and painting itself was yielding pride of place to industry and technology. This conflict over political direction was fueled in part by a salary dispute: Younger masters wanted to know why they were paid so much less than the painters. The struggle reveals the difficulty in balancing creative activity and business concerns. Those devoted to the latter were as passionate and artistically ambitious as anyone at the Bauhaus, but their mission focused on the mass production they hoped would improve life for the masses. This demanded a more function-, technology-, and production-oriented approach than the painting workshops taught. By 1930, the mural workshop had contracted with the Rasch Company to market the workshop's wallpaper and this success was viewed as a model for other workshops as well.

The transition to Meyer's leadership was fairly smooth, with Gropius recommending his appointment even though he knew Meyer would steer the Bauhaus toward the industrial studio mode that Gropius did not particularly favor. In fact, the two soon realized they were not compatible and so they had little to do with one another. Meyer, however, was a very effective leader. He expanded production operations, reorganized many workshops at considerable cost savings without cutting back on staff, and clarified the relationship of theory and practice in the important architectural department. Just as Moholy-Nagy intended his emphasis on the balance between form and function to raise the status of the "function" half of the equation, so too did Meyer seek to raise the status of "practice" by establishing its importance apart from theory. Meyer was also a smart businessperson, replac[ing] an excessively wide, varied range of products with a small number of standardized models.[23] The push to standardize had a compelling logic in terms of the Bauhaus mission. The institute always focused on the elemental and essential nature of form and material. Thus, even though standardization is often viewed as the enemy of creativity, at the Bauhaus it reinforced the creative impulse because it grew out of deeply held convictions about the functionality of art, form, and essential character of design. (See Exhibit 7.)

When Meyer set about reconceiving the Bauhaus's function, he conducted numerous meetings with faculty and students for several weeks; only then did he frame recommendations. He also wanted to raise awareness of the social and biological sciences, and to that end he brought in various lecturers. Nor did he neglect the painters. He retained the free painting classes that Klee and Kandinsky had instituted, but urged them to strike "a sort of balance which, together with increased science teaching, was to nourish workshop activities. The existence of these classes provoked countless discussion at the Bauhaus itself upon the role of art in the design process."[24] Meyer saw to it that "[w]orkshop activities were no longer based on primary colours and elementary forms, but on questions of utility, economy, and social target groups."[25]

In his vision for the institute and his strategies for advancing it, Meyer proved to be an outstanding manager of creativity, responsible for much of the Bauhaus legacy. Under Meyer, the Bauhaus fulfilled its vision of integrating dynamic opposing forces. This would have been impossible without the first stage of Bauhaus development (a stage with two major phases demarcated by Moholy-Nagy's arrival). Meyer did not come in wielding a

sword meant to excise all that went before him. He accomplished the transition to a more socially, industrially, production-oriented institution gracefully and graciously, maintaining the Bauhaus's traditions while updating
them for the challenges of the industrial age.

Gropius and Meyer were not the only leaders at the Bauhaus, although
they were the first two of the three directors. Moholy-Nagy, Itten, Grunow, Otti Berger, Marianne Brandt, Klee, Kandinsky, and others provided
leadership, many in more than one context. Even conflicts and transitions
were handled respectfully, without damage to the Bauhaus at least until the
political turmoil of the final years that were marked by the rise of Nazism
in Germany. The openness to creative trends, debate, and communication
enabled the Bauhaus to live up to its lofty ambitions. Despite Meyer's success, however, he was forced to resign by Dessau's city government in 1930
for political reasons. Mies van der Rohe, the architect who spearheaded
the so-called international style of skyscrapers, took over as director. In
1932, the local government, urged on by regional Nazi leadership, closed
the Bauhaus down. Mies and a couple of other teachers lobbied Nazi cultural officials on the school's behalf, claiming it represented a distinctive
German art form, but the effort failed. The school survived under Mies in
Berlin for a few more months until finally closing in 1933. In 1934, the
Nazis declared all modern art to be "un-German," "alien," and "Bolshe-
vist." The Bauhaus moved to Chicago where it flourished as The New
Bauhaus and then the Institute of Design, where the Bauhaus precepts
survived:

> The intent of the New Bauhaus to bring students into direct
> and constant contact with current scientific thought is of great
> educational significance. For if the artist is really to function
> in the modern world, he [sic] must feel himself a part of it,
> and to have this sense of social integration he must command
> the instruments and materials of that world.[26]

THE ULTIMATE HOTHOUSE

The Bauhaus exhibited every one of the thirty-six hothouse factors. When
the institute was founded, there was no guarantee that it would succeed,
much less become the twentieth century's most important center of design,
and that by a long shot. It overshot its original ambitious goals by building

its creative vision into every organizational structure, procedure, and process. The creativity exercises of Itten or Grunow, multisensory approach of Klee, workshop-based pedagogy, cosmic visions of Kandinsky and Itten, role of mentorship and mastery, provisions for conflict management, almost unlimited exchange of ideas, respect accorded those at the lower end of the hierarchy, imaginative celebrations, fusion of art and design, and utilization of technology in both areas, helped the place bloom with incredible innovation. In other respects, such as the spirit of regeneration current after the crisis of World War I or the cosmopolitanism of postwar Germany, which exposed the artists to a flood of ideas akin to a meta-system, historical processes lent a hand. In some areas, such as exceptional leadership, the Bauhaus may seem simply lucky, which in no way diminishes the importance of that factor. However, the leadership was so strong because it adhered closely to essential values. The Bauhaus's values embraced a spiritual belief, expressed differently by different masters, that their work had cosmic implications, not in an egocentric way, but through its sources in the deepest laws of perception and harmony. Its explicit mission was to change the world. Organizationally, it was designed so that everyone's concerns would be given a hearing. Bauhaus leadership established frameworks for resolving conflict that actually worked and the Institute drew together an incredible array of artists from an equally incredible array of disciplines: painting, architecture, weaving, metallurgy, wallpaper design, furniture making, theater, physical training, sculpture, lighting, industrial processes, print making, and more. The Bauhaus pioneered applying whole-mind techniques to artists' training, and the staff unabashedly integrated the visionary with the pragmatic. In the beginning, teachers were designated as "masters" as a sign of respect not only for individual achievements but also for the discipline in which they had achieved such lofty esteem. The social atmosphere was intellectual, playful, theatrical, and festive, and rather than proving a distraction, it animated and focused the intense creative work that was the Bauhaus's hallmark, exemplifying the important role of the Social/Play dimension in the hothouse effect.

The Bauhaus's impact has been so pervasive and enduring precisely because it integrated elements that seemed so disparate and unconnected to everyone else. To do this, it devised innovative ways to communicate, practice, teach, think, perceive, organize, and produce. It also proves to organizations submerged in practical realities that one can fuse creativity and pragmatism, art and industry, and spirit and technology. In many respects the ultimate hothouse, the Bauhaus stands as a model for any organization on a quest for the ultimate energy resource—creativity.

NOTES

1. Magdalena Droste and bauhaus archiv, *Bauhaus: 1919–1933*, translated by Karen Williams (Cologne: Taschen Verlag, 1990), p. 10.
2. Ibid., 10–11.
3. Sigrid Wortmann Weltge, *Women's Work: Textile Art from the Bauhaus* (San Francisco: Chronicle Books, 1993), p. 41.
4. Ibid., p. 97.
5. Westphal, p. 503.
6. Droste, p. 243.
7. Ibid., p. 47.
8. Weltge, p. 46.
9. Droste, p. 33.
10. Ibid.
11. Ibid., p. 31.
12. Weltge, p. 55.
13. Ibid.
14. Droste, pp. 25–26.
15. Ibid., p. 50.
16. Ibid., p. 161.
17. Westphal, p. 46.
18. Ibid., p. 49.
19. Ibid.
20. Ibid., p. 50.
21. Droste, p. 161.
22. Ibid.
23. Ibid., p. 176.
24. Ibid., p. 188.
25. Ibid., p. 196.
26. Charles W. Morris, 1938, in Hans M. Wingler, *The Bauhaus: Weimar, Dessau, Berlin, Chicago*, translated by Wolfgang Jabs and Basil Gilvert, edited by Joseph Stein (Cambridge, MA: MIT Press, 1962, 1980), p. 195.

11

A CONTEMPORARY BAUHAUS
IN BOLOGNA

The train stops at Castel San Pietro Terme, sixteen minutes from Bologna's main station. You get out and wait for the train to move on before crossing the tracks. For a moment, you feel like the Sundance Kid after the train deposits Butch, Katharine Ross, and the Kid in Bolivia: "*This* is Bolivia?" However, once past the train station, the bell tower of the ancient fortress town rises over the shoulders of newer construction that is "only" several hundred years old. Just across the road another tower, more modern than Castel San Pietro's but no less striking, dominates the fields in which cabbages grow and across which kings have marched.

You are met by a woman who gracefully combines charm and efficiency, Maria Rossi-Thiébaud, manager of business development for Loop Design Centre (LDC). Maria explains that the newer tower, LDC's headquarters, is still undergoing renovation (since completed). It used to be an agricultural center and its old title will remain emblazoned on an outside wall: Federazione Italiana Consorzi Agrari (see Exhibit 8).

It is difficult to spend time at Loop Design Centre without thinking of the Bauhaus. A few years ago, Francesco Coppola, an architect and the founder of Loop Design Centre, decided he wanted to change his role within the structure of his company, pulling himself out of daily marketing and administrative tasks so that he and other key staff could focus on the creative work that is the heart and soul of the company. This occasioned a subtle but definite shift in the business model, too. Being a creative sort, Coppola was not content to shift around a few organizational pieces. Instead, he took a risk and, with his staff of about thirty employees, consolidated the company into a single site that most resembles a contemporary Bauhaus.

Like the Bauhaus, LDC is dedicated to a multidisciplinary vision of modern design. Coppola specializes in architecture, design, and major ceramics projects. Under the name Navalia Design & Creative Consultants, the company also specializes in communications and public relations projects aimed at helping clients develop, enhance, and refine their public image. It also works with corporate partners in devising creative solutions for lighting systems, mosaics, cladding systems, specialized construction solutions, raised access floors, bathroom design, and landscaping. The workspace itself still contains many operational elements of the ancient barn and silo. The air-conditioning system is incorporated into the walkways suspended throughout the old silo, and the pipes have been lit from within, their surfaces scraped into designs that glow when the lights are switched on. But the integration of the old granary with modern technology brims over from the decorative and functional to the creative work of the building itself. Lighting in the exhibition spaces comprises large industrial metal disks hanging from the ceiling with four smaller disks suspended from each. The smaller disks provide a variety of light colors; each one is governed by its own computer and the entire array is connected to a central computer, offering endless possibilities for using light in exhibitions, classes, institutes, and commercial events.

Color makes a bold statement on the outside as well. The building includes an amphitheater that gives access to the basement floor, four additional stories, and above that a sort of half-floor open loft that serves as Coppola's studio. The exterior walls are painted a bright orangey ochre and cool gray Italian wash. The two transparent elevator shafts become great rectangular tubes of light at night and the rooms are all painted different colors. LDC's central workspace exudes a similar liveliness; it's basically an open space in which people, suggestions, and ideas circulate freely, cultivating the synergy Coppola sought when consolidating design operations in one place.

Coppola envisions LDC as a hub for producing and promoting its own products, but also as an all-purpose design center that influences how design is viewed and marketed throughout Europe. He created the center because he was seeking a new way to market his products. For example, laying out newly designed tiles as if they are merely one more set of samples, in the traditional manner, does not do justice to the product's quality and possibilities. Working with customers in a direct sales environment also took Coppola and key staff away from the creative process, the engine driving the company and its products. This is a common dilemma for creative people whose work becomes the core of a successful enterprise. Coppola decided to do something about it.

The new model is based on the company's partners using LDC products *and* marketing and selling them. Being freed from marketing and sales responsibilities gives LDC the ability to offer an integrated array of services for its clients. The ground level of the headquarters houses the Royal Institute of British Architects' bookstore, reinforcing the company's close ties with partners in the British design industry. The bookstore also contributes to Coppola's vision of LDC as a multidisciplinary center that enriches the general understanding of design even as it provides a full range of services—such as research, design, manufacturing, and marketing—for various markets, much as the Bauhaus did.

The landscaped garden leads into a theater that is fully equipped for video conferencing and electronic and live performances; a restaurant on the subfloor; and laboratories for producing molds, plastics, mosaics, and architectural models. Coppola also anticipates that a new department of the University of Bologna that will be sited at Castel San Pietro Terme will further energize the local scene. With all this activity, says Rossi-Thiébaud, the people in the immediate area are excited and curious about the center. There's an interesting reversal of history at work here. Castel San Pietro was built in the Middle Ages as a southern bulwark for Bologna. From its tower, named Il Cassero, the San Pietrans would light fires to signal the great towers of Bologna; the two tallest surviving towers are visible from LDC's rooftop balcony on a clear day. Now, instead of defending Bologna against the outside world, Castel San Pietro Terme houses an organization whose goal is to draw ideas from all over the world and propel them into the city's orbit.

LDC's partnerships enable it to work closely with companies that already have an extensive sales network and for whom it can provide a variety of services, which represents a more flexible organizational structure than vertically integrating research, design, production, marketing, and sales. For one mosaics customer, LDC designed, wrote, and produced a coffee-table quality book highlighting the company's striking mosaic work on building projects worldwide. The synergy between the mosaic and communications businesses is one sign that consolidating into the granary has worked. Similarly, LDC's communications branch, called Navalia, designed the corporate image for a major Italian merchandiser, the image for the company's international cycling team, and the layout of its stores. In short, LDC's creative environment encourages a multiconceptual approach to its client relationships. This close association with partners can be structured in a variety of ways. Basically, LDC is saying to partner/clients: "Tell us what you need. We'll make it for you." The company then does just that, which is why traditional sales models do not work. It's not about the product per se, but about the collaboration among all members of the creative team, both at LDC and within the client's organization. One customer, for instance, came looking for ceramics for a mosque, and in the course of discussions, LDC also developed a lighting solution for the project.

While the Bauhaus was founded with explicit visionary goals, LDC looks first to continue its success as a company. As Coppola points out with an amused smile, you can't do anything without being financially viable. But the company is also clearly set on becoming, in effect, a hothouse that influences European design. Coppola is aware of the analogy to the Bauhaus, although he seems reluctant to claim too exact a parallel with the legendary group. Nonetheless, parallels do suggest themselves. The "utopia," as Coppola calls it, of the ideal creative environment lay behind the foundation of the Bauhaus, as we've seen. Gropius, also an architect, could have opted for an architecture studio with some associated research facilities. Instead, he took a brilliant creative leap that was the key to the Bauhaus's success. In gathering together so many visionary practitioners, Gropius clearly intended the Bauhaus to transcend usual categories of business or studio and this is paralleled in the agricultural center housing LDC's headquarters, laboratory, bookstore, theater, and exhibition and educational space.

Coppola believes that the current creative environment needs this multifaceted, multidisciplinary hub of activity. "What is lacking today is the exchange of ideas," he says. As were the Bauhaus masters, Coppola is concerned about the widening gap between theory in design and architecture and the way products and buildings interface with people in the real world. He also agrees with the assertion that we are currently in an exciting golden age of materials development and experimentation. And while Coppola refers to other spaces in Europe where architectural design, exhibition space, and galleries coexist, LDC would be one of the rare places where people are actually working in an atelier/laboratory setting as well. And, Coppola emphasizes, all aspects of the company operate from an effective business model.

The Bauhaus was a laboratory for experimenting with materials and form, but it was also a highly innovative educational institution. LDC, although not a school, has many points of contact with the Bauhaus's approach to creativity.

■ *LDC hopes to shape the pedagogy of design via its courses, workshops, institutes, and influence of its specialized bookstore.* Coppola also strongly believes that the architecture and design professions have to address how people perceive, think, communicate, and work within and around their products. Implicit in his approach is an awareness of the perceptual and sensory realms and the mutual impact they have on design products. (See Factors #3, #19, #23, and #28.)

■ *Like Athens and Florence, both the Bauhaus and LDC reinvented figurative wheels at every turn.* What is a chair? What is the relationship of the chair to the biomechanics of the human body? How will the design of the chair affect the way people feel when sitting in it? What qualities of steel make it a perfect material for designing and manufacturing a chair? Paul Klee applied his theories linking color and musical scales to his painting, while Bauhaus designers and architects investigated color from scientific and psychological perspectives, and applied it in strikingly original ways to products and buildings.

Coppola has a similar analytic, exploratory, and imagination-driven approach. He speaks passionately about finding new uses for traditional materials. For example, the resins used to cover floors can be impressed with patterns using one of LDC's techniques. Whether imparting a special metallic gleam to wall tiles or refining a client's product presentation, the emphasis is always on rethinking the basic media in which the artists and designers work. (See Factors #4, #5, and #24.)

■ *Coppola speaks of a "play sensibility," a "candy store" of ideas and materials both for LDC's designers and customers.* The exhibition spaces are viewed as theaters for presenting each product's "story" rather than as empty rooms to fill with saleable objects. (See Factors #33 and #34.)

■ *Coppola promotes a creative approach among his staff as well.* As is true of many members of hothouses, the staff seeks solutions from a variety of sources, many of them unconventional. For instance, perhaps a client wants a new stuffing. Coppola will encourage people to start looking at fabrics from the 1960s, 1970s, and 1980s, seeking inspiration in ideas from the past. This is akin to a creativity technique known as "scanning" in which we browse through—or scan—a wide range of diverse inputs in order to jog the mind into fresh and original perspectives. Thus a book on textiles that one art director is using for his research has sprouted a forest of stick-on notes referencing colors, forms, materials, sizes, and measures.

As in every hothouse, LDC's creative teams have full latitude to conduct their own research and seek their own directions for product development. As did Dr. Land, Coppola provides input and defines the broad objectives. There is a great deal of discussion among the teams about ideas, designs, materials, and other project elements. Coppola tends to draw together small teams or even just the best person for a particular job and works directly with them, although that person or persons will also touch base with whoever can help. Eventually, one of the designers will simulate a design on the computer and then the actual samples will be created at LDC. The creative team knows exactly where a product will be used before they begin work, but that sort of intrinsic limitation tends to stimulate creative, adaptive solutions. (Factors #2, #11, #15, and #20.)

■ *In managing intellectual capital, LDC also seems to be ahead of the curve.* As Coppola describes it, companies like the fact that LDC does the research for them. Meanwhile, the research for one product is kept accessible and used to build a pool of ideas and stimuli for work on future products. This is critical to the hothouse effect. Companies constantly toss aside some of their most valuable assets because once a particular solution works in a given product, all the information learned while arriving at that solution, as well as rejected prototypes, is ignored. Yet, if Edison failed 99 percent of the time, as he liked to say, do we actually believe that he discarded 99 percent of the data he accumulated while achieving his solution? The millions of pages of documentation at the Edison National Site in West Orange, New Jersey, attest otherwise. At Loop Design Centre, the creative reserve of ideas is actively managed. With open spaces, music, high ceilings, a young staff, and a light, airy atmosphere, the space seems well suited to keeping ideas in constant circulation. (See Factors #9, #10, and #12.)

Coppola calls LDC a place "where people meet and things happen," which is really a bare-bones definition of a hothouse. Coppola wants the old agricultural center to welcome the people of the region, students of craft and design, professional designers and architects from around the world, LDC's business partners, and its own staff. There are many outstanding creative design companies in the world whose mode of operation is unconventional from a typical business perspective. But that alone is not the definition of a hothouse. Loop Design Centre is one of those companies that captures the hothouse spirit because of the following:

- The range and depth of the functions that the organization embraces
- Enrichment of the mental environment
- Its educational mission
- The intensive interface among a number of core disciplines
- The constant challenge to the basic assumptions governing core disciplines
- A leader more focused on creative work and the company's mission as a transformative force than on simply "expanding," and with a relaxed, inclusive leadership style
- An innovative business model integrated with the company's creative mission
- A view of the past as a source of inspiration while recognizing, as Rossi-Thiébaud pointed out, how Italy's rich artistic traditions also inhibit innovation
- A working environment that seeks to maximize creative and investigative activities

LDC goes beyond managing the creative process as it pertains to business. Instead, it seeks to spark the equivalent of a hothouse effect by enriching the entire environment in which it operates, from Castel San Pietro Terme to Bologna, the European design scene, and the global marketplace. LDC is consciously setting out to become a hub of activity, not only a place in which ideas circulate but from which they are pumped into the world at large. The business model is designed to augment this effort via partnerships, a focus on core strengths, and a dissolving of the boundaries between research and development, on the one hand, and presentation and marketing on the other.

Loop Design Centre provides a working model for other companies with lofty creative ambitions. It is not, of course, organized identically to the Bauhaus nor would anyone at LDC make extravagant comparisons to the legendary institute. But Loop Design Centre is an extraordinary place and can lay claim to upholding the Bauhaus legacy of aesthetics, vision, values, and initiative. And like the Bauhaus, LDC draws its creative vitality from an active engagement with the deepest perceptions and assumptions of the various disciplines to which it is devoted. Along with other dynamic, innovative companies and educational institutions, LDC can perhaps one day become part of a network of highly creative hubs whose concerted energies can have a profoundly positive effect on the way we live.

12

THE FOURTH DIMENSION: SOCIAL/PLAY

While a group's internal dynamics can be analyzed from many perspectives, the hothouse effect draws heavily on areas of social activity for which less creative groups are not generally distinguished. The social dimension comprises several fundamental categories of human life, including crisis, leadership, language, beauty, and play. Crisis and leadership have a universal symbiotic relationship. No matter how effective leaders are in good times, they are only truly tested in a crisis. Language knits a society together. In the hothouse, language takes on a highly charged aspect that fuels creativity. Play's role in creativity is well documented, but though championed in business-related creativity literature, play tends to be minimized in business. The playful and festive spirit is, however, so central to creativity that finding a place for it in organizational life is imperative if creativity is on the agenda. Beauty, meanwhile, exerts a power beyond the ability to delight; as we'll see, it is a prime moving force in inspiring all productive work. These elements of human experience manifest as the following factors in the emergence of the hothouse effect:

29. A highly charged vocabulary emerges to describe the group's distinctive creative processes.
30. A strong business model provides the resources and structure that support creative activity.
31. The community continually produces highly effective leaders.
32. Crisis draws the community together and releases hidden reserves of creative energy.

33. "Playing" with ideas and possibilities pervades many group processes.

34. Social occasions are planned imaginatively, express organizational creativity, and promote social rapport.

35. The community creates beauty in one form or another.

36. The culture of the organization discourages assertions of power based on an individual's position within the hierarchy.

#29. HIGHLY CHARGED VOCABULARY

Creative communities generate new words, symbols, visual images, concepts, and even sounds to communicate more fully and precisely newly emergent ideas, conceptual frameworks, products, and environments. This new vocabulary stimulates creativity and fuels the hothouse effect, functioning as a hyperoxygenated language parallel to the speech of everyday life or work. It is not a language of jargon and cryptic acronyms but comes out of the spontaneous expression of people engaged in stimulating work. In turn, the new terms can profoundly affect society at large. We "read" sculpture the way we do because of the vocabulary of forms and words bequeathed to us by the world's sculptural traditions (that vocabulary includes the sculptures themselves); from sculpture, the language of form influences how we envision and talk about space and design. Eventually, the ongoing repetition of the language changes our perception of space and form.

The impact of this type of vocabulary goes beyond the descriptive power of the terms. It reinforces cultural bonds and its descriptive potency stimulates creativity, as does any enrichment of language, whether it be visual, verbal, musical, or even tactile and olfactory (as in the creation of fine wines). Athenian vase paintings used the hero Theseus as a symbol of intelligence capable of overcoming brute force. Several dramas portrayed him as having a special ability to resolve deep psychological and social rifts. Theseus became part of the symbolic vocabulary of a city that prided itself on a rational approach to problem solving and public policy, and its ability to balance the polarized forces of creation and destruction (see Exhibit 9).

Francesco Coppola of Loop Design Centre speaks directly about the company's aims and projects, but he rarely talks about one medium at once. In a conversation with Coppola, light can be many things: decorative and industrial, a product and a way to make a corporate statement, an exhibition resource and an element in mosaic design. Corporate communications, visual design, and materials are inextricably linked in Loop's vocabulary, in large part because the founder speaks and thinks that way and encourages staff to use the same sweep of expression.

Jazz, of course, produced a vocabulary so compelling and alive that it is impossible to imagine American English without it. The word *jazz* itself was an invented word and caught on because it so well expressed the spirit of the new music and the 1920s in general. Modern poetry owes much of its rhythmic freedom to jazz. Dante's supple use of Italian in *The Divine Comedy,* Shakespeare's extraordinarily rich and multitudinous vocabulary, and the twentieth-century Greek poet Seferis's reclamation of demotic Greek as a language of beauty, power, and subtle expression, all demonstrate how an entire language can be transformed in one giant gamma burst of creativity.

It is not just that we express ideas with language; rather, language operates deep within our brains and our use of it actually restructures and stimulates our cognitive processes. The more alive and supple the language, the more impact it has on our thought processes. Compare the phrasing of "To be or not to be, that is the question" with "Sometimes I ask myself if it's really worth going on with my life." Pianist Jonny King compares jazz to a language: "When I sit down at the piano and improvise, I am speaking a language I have developed over the course of decades of playing and listening, a language I have inherited from the likes of Louis Armstrong, Charlie Parker, Miles Davis, and countless others."[1] Many hothouses possessed several such sets of terms; and like any common language, they forge bonds among those who use them. In a hothouse, the terms are so laden with meaning and possibility, they raise the creative level of the entire community, much as mineral-rich underground streams raise the water table and fertility of an entire region.

#30. BUSINESS MODEL

Everyone interviewed for this book alluded to the critical role played by a strong business model in sustaining creativity. While this may seem at first an obvious injunction akin to "buy low and sell high," the connection is both subtle and strong. A good business model means that an organization pursues primary objectives while earning a good return on investment. In a hothouse, a natural synergy between creative and financial elements often emerges early, and the hothouse effect is likely to take off when this synergy takes hold.

Francesco Coppola consolidated Loop's operations in the old agricultural building at Castello San Pietro to free up his creative staff from administrative tasks and to foster collaboration among Loop's departments. However, he also was quite clear that the shift was part of an improved business model in which Loop's partners market Loop products in a more sophisticated and effective way than previously possible. Mike Jahnke, describing Sequent's extraordinary efforts in the interests of customer service, commented that it was a good business model precisely because Sequent's customer orientation led to better products and closer ties to its customer base. Arthur Nelson's business model includes establishing nonprofit institutions aimed at promoting innovation through industry partnerships, improving U.S. education, closing the digital gap in U.S. society, and proliferating creative hubs in the form of museums and conferences. His passion for creativity infuses his business decisions as well, and he notes that without the business model to support it, no creative initiative can survive. At Foster-Miller, President Bill Ribich and scientist Jay Boyce describe their business model largely in terms of managing the prolific outpouring of creative ideas generated by their staff. And scientist Jim Foley, who worked closely with Edwin Land, frequently alludes to the latter's skills as a manager and businessperson who thought deeply about the exact business model most likely to produce a high level of technological innovation at Polaroid and the Rowland Institute.

The successful business model is somewhat analogous to the ancient cults that guaranteed a successful hunt or harvest. Periodic festivals and rituals tuned up the cosmic gears, just as a good business model keeps the organization's wheels humming smoothly along. The leisure time of the festivals also provided the freedom to play, or to create and re-create. Creativity depends on a business model that enables people to focus on creative work with few distractions. What an audience's applause is to a performer, the willingness of customers to pay for a product is to a business. Applause validates the performance, and a good business model uses creativity to build profit, and profit to validate and thus increase investment in creativity.

The business model refers to the core business practices that guarantee consistent, high-quality delivery of goods and services. It is, in effect, a giant algorithm. More focused on tasks and operations than on the business culture, but far more encompassing than a business plan, the model keeps strategy on track. Like the algorithm, it relieves an organization from having to reinvent its *modus operandi* for every new project or initiative. In terms of the hothouse effect, the business model frees up energy that can then be applied to creative ends. Thus Sequent's business model guided employees through a best-practices approach to customer service, freeing them to put all their energy into solving the often taxing dilemmas inherent in high-tech systems.

#31. LEADERSHIP

Leadership matters to the hothouse effect. While many hothouse leaders were strong and even ruthless in countering attempts on their power or lives, they basically established a supportive environment for ideas, self-expression, and creativity. Pericles of Athens counted as his closest friends philosophers, astronomers, and artists, most notably the sculptor Pheidias, responsible for the masterworks on the Acropolis and at the Temple of Zeus at Olympia, site of the Olympic games. Aspasia, Pericles's sophisticated partner, hosted gatherings that regularly discussed the treasury of new ideas sweeping across the region. In a city oppressive to women and in which romantic love was rare in marriage, she and Pericles created a stir by passionately kissing good-bye each morning. Although as a politician Pericles evinced the typical Athenian view of women, he clearly had a different personal relationship to the main woman in his life—which perhaps had a judicious effect on his leadership.

For more than 150 years (594–430 B.C.E.), Athens produced one exceptional leader after the next. Every one of these dozen or so men—despite political differences—basically supported broad political and cultural participation by the citizenry. The Medici, a powerful, immensely wealthy banking family, emerged from the hurly-burly of Florentine life to become great patrons of art and scholarship and relatively tolerant rulers during the height of the Renaissance. Several Medici were talented poets, especially Lorenzo the Magnificent. In medieval Andalusia, the caliphs and princes who ruled cities such as Cordoba, Granada, and Toledo, may have been autocrats by our standards, but most were highly cultured and tolerant of their Jewish and Christian minorities. In fact, many prominent ministers throughout Andalusia's history were members of the minority religions. Leadership sponsored—and were numbered among—the poets, philosophers, and architects who adorned Andalusia.[2] We've observed the Bauhaus's smooth leadership transition from Gropius to Meyers in 1928, and even though the institute's orientation changed then, the fundamental hothouse principles remained in place.

Many jazz musicians displayed striking leadership qualities of an expansive, generous, and strategic nature. Niels Bohr and Albert Einstein were openly supportive of, albeit challenging to, their colleagues' ideas and served as informal leaders to a large band of outstanding scientists. In Paris, where no formal hierarchy existed among the artists, Gertrude Stein was the magnet who functioned as leader within that talented circle, while both Picasso and Guillaume Apollinaire led by dint of personality and talent—and by being connected to virtually everyone in the city. Despite dramatic stylistic variations among all these leaders—compare Duke Ellington, Louis Armstrong, Stein, and Lorenzo de Medici to one another!—all actively oversaw a tolerant atmosphere in which creativity and the play of ideas received support and encouragement. Edwin Land was a master at this, while Arthur Nelson, Bill Ribitch, Francesco Coppola, Casey Powell, Bill Tita, and Terry Beard view the role of CEO as providing the freedom for employees to operate as creatively as possible. Yet, every hothouse leader possesses a large measure of steel in his or her resolve, although frequently (although not in Lorenzo the Magnificent's case) tempered by humility in the face of his or her gift or mission.

The obvious question is whether such leadership produces the hothouse effect or whether the hothouse naturally produces great leaders. It is a question similar to whether geniuses generate a hothouse or vice versa. The answer is complicated, of course, but, ultimately the greater weight falls to the hothouse effect itself. The string of highly effective Athenian leaders cannot be ascribed simply to the fortunes of birth, any more than the number of great jazz musicians, Florentine geniuses, or Parisian-based artists can. Rather, the hothouse effect creates a *platform of performance* that provides a far higher starting point for hothouse members than is available for members of other communities (although individuals in the latter might perform at any level).

The selection of leaders in a hothouse parallels the process that leads to the emergence of top artists; it is governed by a populace more aware and creative than their fellows in neighboring communities or rival organizations. This more discerning public taste produces a stronger value chain of decisions that results in the selection of talented leaders. The astonishing succession of popularly supported and, for the most part, popularly chosen leaders across 160 years of Athenian history *was the result* of the stunningly rapid empowerment and growing sophistication of the Athenian populace. Athens's sixth-century leaders prepared the way for the hothouse effect; the exceptional leaders of the fifth century B.C.E. reflected and focused the energy released in the populace. And because they were well-prepared by their own culture to assume leadership, they were able to guide that energy as well. But the extent to which leaders "lead" is purely a function of the extent to which they resonate with and give definitive form to the energies of those they are leading. In effect, a leader must learn to follow on a deeper resonant level while showing the way at the more apparent level of public action.

#32. CRISIS

One odd correlation among history's hothouses is the number that underwent significant crises in the early stages of their creative florescence. These crises come in many distinct forms. Athens's crisis—and that of Greece itself in 480 B.C.E.—was the attack of an empire so vast that Athens would have been an insignificant town, and mainland Greece only one minor province, within it. Florence dealt with an avalanche of problems: intensive civil war in the thirteenth and fourteenth centuries, the Black Death of 1348, financial upheaval, and occasional threats from powerful enemies such as the Holy Roman Empire, France, the papacy, and Milan. The Bauhaus and the related Dutch art group de Stijl rose out of the ashes of World War I and the disillusion and disruption that followed, while jazz reflected the ongoing crisis of African Americans living in a virulently racist society.

Elizabethan London triumphed in 1588 over the Spanish Armada that Philip II sent to dethrone England's Elizabeth I. Shakespeare was twenty-four at the time, the same age as Plato when Athens finally lost the Peloponnesian War to Sparta and her allies in 404 B.C.E. Plato actually started his career as a dramatist. However, the effects of the war that began three years before he was even born, combined with the execution of Socrates, his teacher, in 399 B.C.E. (a direct outgrowth of the postwar atmosphere), tinged Plato's philosophy with a melancholy rejection of both democracy and the material world in general. Shakespeare, on the other hand, would have celebrated the one startling triumphant event of the Armada's defeat. Indeed, his career as actor and playwright may well have ended had Philip won and Elizabeth been deposed. Instead, Shakespeare is the "anti-Plato" whose work embraces every passion, intrigue, betrayal, act of nobility, and confusion that flesh is heir to. Perhaps there we have the difference between victory and defeat. Or perhaps the gulf is between a hothouse that has lost its bloom and begun to decline (Athens) versus the vitality and confidence of one that has just shifted into hyperdrive (Elizabethan London).

Obviously no organization should generate a crisis just so it can benefit from resolving it. Nonetheless, the benefits that hothouses achieve by surmounting crises can translate into everyday business practice. The popularity of terms such as *crisis management* and *change management,* and the ongoing difficulties in the American and global economies, indicate that many organizations actually do manage from crisis to crisis anyway.

Once the hothouse weathers a crisis, it tends to feel it is starting afresh. As Arnold Hauser wrote of Florence, "After the shocks of the great financial crisis, the plague, and the *ciompi* revolt, this generation had to start almost from the beginning again."[3] The crisis usually occurs after a significant cultural shift has already begun, a shift that often triggers the crisis. Thus, Persia attacked Athens because, flushed with confidence after Cleisthenes's reforms, the bold young democracy aided the Greek cities of Asia Minor in their rebellion against Persia. Jazz was energized by the increasing assertiveness of African Americans in regard to the crisis of U.S. race relations. Florence's conflicts were rooted in the great economic and social revolution sweeping across Europe at the end of the Middle Ages.

It is not the old order that responds successfully to the challenge, but *the newly emerging order gestating within the old.* This tells us something about who can best handle crises, or rather, whose input and commitment is vital to success. While leadership may belong to the old guard, those who implement the response, and who expect to shape the new post-crisis world, will be *those people most committed to the newer models.* A large proportion of this younger, more innovative generation will be engaged in meeting the crisis. This will not be a small cadre of leaders itching to join the inner circle, but everyone who knows in their gut that something new is at work. The citizens of Athens's new democracy won the battle of Marathon in 490 B.C.E. although outmanned by the Persians, and then, fully armed, ran a real marathon back to the city to prevent its betrayal to the Persians by Athenian opponents of the democracy. That's commitment.

A successful outcome, then, does not just alleviate the threat, but sweeps away the stifling effect of the old order and its rules, values, and objectives. The group that led the organization *into* crisis, or those who share that group's values, cannot supply the energy to break the cycle that led to the crisis. Thus, the hothouse effect is launched by a double-release mechanism—*internally,* the old order is cleared away just as the *external* enemy is defeated or crisis met. Successfully meeting the crisis validates not only the community but also the vision of its younger members; the entire experience matures and energizes them. None of the hothouses paused for breath after resolving the crisis or lapsed into self-satisfaction. Rather, the new class quickly expressed its values through bold action. The Bauhaus founders understood that World War I had swept aside the legitimacy of older forms of expression. Through public statements and manifestos, innovative design, and a bold concept for the school itself, they quickly made their values and intentions known. After Greece defeated Persia in 479 B.C.E., almost all the Greek city-states hurried back to business as usual. Athens, however, at once asserted itself as leader of the city-states newly liberated from Persia. This astonished and outraged the other victorious city-states, but Athens left them flat-footed; none had the cultural preparation provided by its great leaders or the entrepreneurial spirit of its people.

#33. PLAY

In Verrocchio's workshop, a festive and playful atmosphere often prevailed, with Verrocchio playing music, Botticelli playing jokes, and da Vinci playing with strange robotic toys he invented. Jazz musicians "play" music, and improvisation is the ultimate form of play, because it is spontaneous, whimsical, and liberated and yet behind it lays endless practice and devotion to perfecting technique. Perhaps our notion of the word *play* needs retooling before we can confidently inject it into business.

Johan Huizinga, the great theorist of play, states that play is taken very seriously within the boundaries of space and time that define the game itself.[4] Inside the white lines, on the court, or on city streets, the game is serious business. Once over, however, the game recedes into the realm of make-believe and whether a player loses or wins should not decide his or her intrinsic personal worth. The space in which the game is conducted is sacred, in a sense: One doesn't violate it by bringing in rules from outside the game. Players often put on a so-called game face and don uniforms to transform themselves from individual into team, from a civilian into a hard-driving, hard-hitting athlete. Teamwork draws individuals closer to one another, but remarkable individual feats also earn great acclaim; despite clear rules and boundaries, the game reveres individual flare.

Thus, the play spirit at work doesn't really mean that employees take twenty minutes to solve puzzles, dart around the halls on that late 1990s icon the silver scooter, or entertain one another with forced camaraderie. Instead, people have the leeway to reflect, improvise, tinker, rearrange, brainstorm, juggle, and in general, play with ideas, materials, language, and whatever else is available. Jazz improvisation takes place within the context of a musical score—one usually starts with a song or at least a riff or sometimes just a key or chord and then moves out from there. The song may prove unrecognizable for much of a performance, but without some boundaries, notes would have no rhyme, reason, or musical significance. Playfulness in the workplace means that people can experiment and fail without fear of being labeled poor workers, losers, or wastes of time and money. Thomas Edison expected a failure rate of over 99 percent, but he also had more successful inventions than anyone else and grew wealthy despite his high failure rate. Managing failure is not quite the same as managing risk and would be a useful skill to teach in settings, like Edison's, where a high failure rate actually can facilitate a large *number* (as opposed to a high *rate*) of successes.

An office in which the boss jokes around with staff and conducts Friday afternoon golf outings may be playful and light-hearted, but not necessarily creative or effective. Managing playfulness effectively means entering "the game" (the meeting, project, discussion, or task) seriously, making sure everyone is engaged in the core activity, but giving staff the freedom to fully explore and improvise with ideas. A sense of play gives ideas a chance to develop that our usual methods of tearing at and trimming them does not. In turn, group members carry this spirit into all their interactions, thus benefiting the entire atmosphere of the workplace.

#34. FESTIVAL

In primitive and ancient society, festivals were celebrated when life felt secure, such as after the harvest or at the onset of winter, when labor was done, the tools put away, and days started lengthening. Just as algorithms provide us with an automatic pilot for some tasks so we can concentrate on more challenging ones, so too do times of plenty and stability allow us to coast through life for a while and tinker or reflect on the extraneous and the luxurious—that is, on improving things. Huizinga asserted that all human culture developed from play and celebration, when people are liberated from the daily demands of survival and thoughts wander in all sorts of odd directions. Informal play seems to be part of our nature, something puppies and lion cubs do, while actual games and sports are descended from the festival-related contests that celebrated the harvest or honored a slain hero. Games are a perfect laboratory for testing rules and strategies without the constraints and demands of self-defense or the need for shelter and food. The festivals themselves produce an exalted sense of well-being and group synergy that renews creative energy. In fact, from a religious perspective, that was precisely the purpose of festivals and ritual—to renew the cycle of time and life's fecundity. The theater performances of the Bauhaus; the Panathenaic procession and Dionysia of ancient Athens; and the endless succession of celebrations and festivals of Renaissance Italy all renewed creative energy. And while the company picnic might have a positive, albeit passing, effect on morale, a truly creative celebration can heighten a community's creativity in a more enduring way. But can we realistically cultivate the festive spirit of play within a business?

Even in business, creativity *is* play. We play with materials, ideas, images, alternatives, and possibilities. Necessity is not really the mother of invention except in the most dire of circumstances. Necessity actually tends to constrict invention. Under the harsh whip of necessity, most societies simply buckle down, avoid risk, and continue on with business as usual. Electric lights were not necessary, but they happened as part of the centuries-old fascination with nature's unseen forces, which finally got turned to practical ends. Once electric lights are installed in one neighborhood, though, it becomes "necessary" for everyone to have them. Desire is the mother of necessity. Creativity happens in the festive moment, when we apply our surplus energies to those questions that intrigue or bother us. A new creation—such as art, an invention, or an idea—tends to pop into our heads when doing work that we love, and then we begin to literally play with the idea, run through variations, and mentally experiment with courses of action. Before we ever take up pen or brush or chisel, set up a laboratory, or call a meeting to discuss a new strategy, we have already played around with our new creation—rehearsed it, as we would in preparation for a performance or festival—in our minds. If we did not, we could not proceed.

One needn't be overly ambitious. Staff can mark monthly birthday celebrations with informal performances. Group art projects that express a mission or community cohesion, visits to community centers or nursing homes, group theater projects, regular outings such as occurred at Beard Framing, and lunchtime poetry readings all contribute to a tradition of ritual or celebration in the workplace. As people become comfortable with the idea, you may become more ambitious. The Bauhaus staged parties that each person attended dressed in highly decorative costume. Such events lend themselves to a theme, for instance, each person attends as a piece of equipment or a procedure. At retreats, performance or art can be used to explore workplace issues. The play and festive elements encourage teamwork, group rapport, and a spirit of freewheeling creativity.

#35. BEAUTY

Beauty has a profound physiological impact on how we perceive and respond to the world—it is a powerful *social* event. Theories of beauty abound, but for now, let's just acknowledge that our perception of beauty, albeit somewhat subjective, is nonetheless fairly consistent. Most people agree on what is beautiful, whether it is a landscape, painting, animal, or human being. To loosely paraphrase U.S. President Abraham Lincoln, "Some people won't agree on what's beautiful all the time and all people won't agree any of the time, but lots of people will agree on what's beautiful most of the time." Second, whether or not truth and beauty always coexist, beauty and delight certainly do, although the delight may be tinged with darker sentiments. Third, delight is a powerful, uplifting emotion that affects us physiologically. Fourth, as Plato pointed out, beauty seems enhanced rather than diminished when we apprehend the principles that lead us to consider something beautiful. And fifth, beauty is a high-resolution phenomenon. A thing of beauty is a highly compressed program packed with data in concentrated form because beauty is determined by a balanced expression of life's fundamental conditions: form, perception, space, time, knowledge, desire, kinetics, and so on.

Beauty's role in the hothouse effect is more obvious in the output, for instance, as a work of art. But does it really function on the input end, as a factor that contributes to the hothouse effect? Absolutely. Whether it is in the form of a painting, building, invention, manufactured or crafted object, cockroach-free apartment, or seamlessly running organization, beauty is the final goal of service and production in most industries. The shape of a tool that achieves its purpose with ease and efficiency is intrinsically beautiful based on function alone, whatever it may look like. Function and design operate in tandem most of the time: A tool (whether knife, baseball bat, computer, or power plant) that performs well often is distinctively pleasing to sight and touch.

Thus, an awareness of beauty and how to achieve it can be crucial to refining and perfecting a product. Beauty motivates in and of itself: We want beautiful things and the thrill of creating beauty is one of life's great joys and satisfactions. Similarly, we all enjoy being in a beautiful place and beauty in the work environment inspires us. The physiological effects of beauty will one day be fully recognized and we'll realize that beauty is a necessity. Beauty establishes benchmarks of achievement that enable us to set goals and standards in any area of activity. The first well-honed spear whose maker demonstrated that it worked better than poorly worked weapons established a benchmark not only for hunters and warriors but for the actual idea of craft itself and, with it, an aesthetic that could be applied to human-made objects. The spear and the idea of the spear, and the idea of quality as a key test to impose on other aspects of life, all become markers defining a new cultural order different from the one that simply saw spears as sharpened and otherwise unmodified sticks.

Beauty clearly transmits powerful positive messages throughout any environment, messages that affect the behavior of virtually everyone there. Beauty is intimately linked with creativity and stimulates it in every aspect of life. Bringing beauty into the workplace cultivates strong intergroup connections and enhances organizational credibility. Beauty is one of the most powerful socializing forces and its influence, except in certain cases in which beauty and appetite become confused, is invariably beneficial.

#36. HIERARCHICAL BEHAVIOR DISCOURAGED

We have already noted that, from the perspective of network science, the hothouse effect is an anomaly. That is, one way of describing a hothouse is by considering it as a network with a high proportion of highly successful and active hubs, which in purely mathematical terms means hubs with a lot of links that play a vital role in the network. If we recall the formula from Chapter 5, in which Value (V) = *Number of Sources of input (S)* + *Average Flow per source (F)* + *Links (L)*/TIME (T), disregarding qualitative assessments for the moment, we can say that the hothouse effect occurs when network activity reaches a critical threshold and the entire system shifts into a high-performance mode of creative activity, in whatever manner that is understood in a given field. Because the hothouse effect calls on the efforts of as many members of a community as possible, and because, as we see from Factor #20, that each person is viewed as a potential creative hub, the hothouse tends to promote an egalitarian ethic among its members. This was true of the democratic Athenians and proud Florentines, but it was and is equally evident at each of the companies that appear in this book.

This is not a case of too many cooks spoiling the broth. A bunch of cooks gathered around a kettle of soup does not a network make; it is a misapplication of creative energy because the potential contributors are clustered into one single hub. For a system to work, tasks need to be specialized. The CEO is the CEO and has certain responsibilities; as history has shown, this may include occasional ruthlessness. The same holds for every job. In a hothouse, however, the position that a given person has within the operational hierarchy does not allow him or her to disregard or disrespect other people or their opinions. To borrow an idea from the philosopher Immanuel Kant, each person must be treated as an *end* in themselves, as if their place in the world has as much dignity and respect as anyone else's, including our own. They cannot be treated as *means* to *our* ends. This is, in effect, a more stringent version of the Golden Rule. Again, that is not to say that performance reviews will all be positive, or that people can't be fired. Nor does it mean that every idea is treated equally, by any means. But all such assessments and responses are based on qualitative criteria rather than the results of political infighting and the self-indulgence of position power.

It may be objected that such behaviors are inescapably human. Certainly we can't expect to eradicate any given behavior because the steps it takes to "purify" a social group lead to even worse problems. But the respect, encouragement, and tolerance that mark the environments of Sequent, Rowland, Foster-Miller, Beard Framing, or Nelson Companies stem from the beliefs of their leaders and clearly defined policies. The emphasis here is not on the assertion of equality, but on clearing away negative power-based behaviors that inhibit full creative expression.

NOTES

1. Jonny King, *What Jazz Is: An Insider's Guide to Understanding and Listening to Jazz* (New York: Walker and Company, 1997), p. 10.
2. María Rosa Menocal, *The Ornament of the World* (Boston: Little, Brown and Company, 2002), p. 211.
3. Arnold Hauser, *The Social History of Art,* vol. 2, translated by Stanley Goodman with Arnold Hauser (New York: Vintage Books, 1951), p. 32.
4. Johan Huizinga, *Homo Ludens: A Study of the Play Element in Culture* (Boston: Beacon Press, 1944, 1955), p. 18.

13

RE-CREATING THE UNIVERSE

At the end of the nineteenth century, Europe and the United States felt a rising sense of anticipation. The wonders of technology, celebrated in expositions such as the Paris World Fair of 1900, and almost a century of relative peace, had imbued the industrialized world with optimism, confidence, and an almost religious belief in human progress. The last century of the millennium—the *twentieth century*—was on its way and signs of modernism were everywhere: the new horseless carriages, the grand Eiffel Tower in Paris, the wireless radio and telephone, the inventions of Edison including the electric lights being installed everywhere, and a tremendous industrial boom led by Germany, England, and the United States. The *Titanic* was built as an ode to this new century, and its sinking was thunderously echoed in the demise of Europe's dreams during the bloody Great War of 1914–1918 that ended not only the nineteenth-century fantasy of what the twentieth century would be like, but laid to rest a centuries-old notion that civilization's rules and certainties raised humanity far above the savage conditions of our ancestors.

The bold, confident pre–World War I energy was reflected in the art of the time. It was in Paris that Pablo Picasso and Georges Braque created the painting style known as Cubism that captured the kinetic, revolutionary quality of the new century. At the same time, in 1905, Albert Einstein published his first paper outlining the Theory of Relativity, which basically transformed humanity's view of the universe. Yet Einstein, Picasso, and Braque were only the most celebrated of many who changed the way we experience the universe. After the disillusionment and numerous crises of

World War I and its aftermath, this creative energy continued unabated, but art now seemed marked by a profound pessimism, alienation, and turning inward. In physics, Einstein's relativity continued to evolve, and it was joined by the rapidly developing field of quantum mechanics, the exploration of the subatomic realm. Both the Paris of the pre- and postwar periods, and the loosely knit community of physicists, reflect the incredible energy of the hothouse effect in unique, noteworthy, and illuminating ways.

"EVERYBODY BROUGHT SOMEBODY . . ."

> This was the year 1907. . . . Picasso had just finished his portrait of her [Gertrude Stein] which nobody at that time liked except the painter and the painted and which is now so famous, and he had just begun his strange complicated picture of three women. . . . Little by little people began to come to the rue de Fleurus to see the Matisses and the Cezannes, Matisse brought people, everybody brought somebody, and they came at any time and it began to be a nuisance, and it was in this way that Saturday evenings began.[1]

"Everybody brought somebody," and Gertrude Stein's apartment in Paris on rue de Fleurus became the central hub of a creative outpouring already well under way. Stein played a special role in the Paris community and the energy concentrated at her apartment triggered a hothouse effect that lasted for decades and profoundly influenced painting, literature, politics, and even our very image of what it means to be an artist and live a creative life (see Exhibit 10).

Paris's artists, like the jazz musicians, were not connected by formal organizational links. And neither were the bonds between them simply the result of the randomly distributed affections of friendship. Rather they were cultivated, in the hothouse manner, in large part due to their shared objective of achieving revolutionary results in their respective pursuits.

"If you are lucky enough to have lived in Paris as a young man, then wherever you go for the rest of your life, it stays with you, for Paris is a movable feast."[2] Thus wrote Ernest Hemingway, a chief figure in the post–World War I wave of Paris writers and artists, expressing the feeling akin to being in love that the hothouse effect arouses in those fortunate enough to be swept up by its wavelike energy, much less those who actually participate in galvanizing the hothouse effect. Paris, like any other city, can be cold, lonely, and heartless. Hemingway's emotional transport comes from his immersion in a time of creative ferment, an emotional rush that youth and beautiful surroundings amplify, but whose heat is provided by the fires of creation.

Parisian art historian Pierre Courthion captured the difference between Paris as a friendly haunt for artists and intellectuals, which it had been since the twelfth century, and Paris as a hothouse swarming with all manner of creative people in possession of all levels of talent, as it was in the pre–World War I era, when he wrote:

> True, since the days of the Romantic movement Paris had been a lodestone for aspiring artists but never before to this extent. You now could see men and women from all countries of the world rubbing shoulders around the marble-topped tables of the Montparnasse cafe's and it was when the new-comers were thronging to this part of Paris and our young "Montparnos" making history that Apollinaire published his famous work The Cubist Painters.[3]

The cafés were social hubs fueled by coffee, wine, youth, and passion—creative and otherwise—where the playful atmosphere so conducive to creativity flourished. Ideas circulated with abandon, friendships were forged on the basis of mutual interest in the arts with whoever happened to be sitting at the table. But Paris's hothouse effect was fueled by other social hubs as well. Gertrude Stein's apartment, with its Saturday night gatherings and its role as destination for visitors throughout the week, was one such hub. Stein collected the paintings of Cezanne, Picasso, Matisse, Braque, and others before they gained acceptance, and her walls were covered with their work. Thus, quite unintentionally, Stein constructed an immersion experience for herself and her visitors, a gallery where the era's creative vision entered each visitor's consciousness via the powerful process of osmosis.

Saturday night at Gertrude's was not the only salon that played an important role in the Parisian hothouse. The magazine *La Plume* began its Saturday soirées in 1889 in a café cellar. The soirée was still a regular event when Apollinaire's name shows up on the attendance sheet in 1903.[4] Apollinaire biographer Francis Steegmuller quoted participant Ernest Ray-

naud—poet and police official who became a good friend of Apollinaire's—to capture the excitement of these meetings:

> It is nine P.M. Streams of students, poets, and artists . . . keep
> coming from Montparnasse, Montmartre, and Batignolles
> and flowing into the café . . . a long narrow cellar is filled to
> overflowing with a wildly gesticulating crowd. . . . Everywhere,
> in every corner, were the faces of people one knew, friends
> who had come with the sole intention of listening to poetry.
> . . . But what is happening now? Why the commotion, the
> jostling? Why is everyone standing? A police raid? No! It is the
> great Verlaine who is coming in. "His felt hat is his halo."[5]

Not exactly a corporate atmosphere, but the hothouse elements are
universal: the excitement, the wild exchange of ideas and products (poetry)
among a diverse group of practitioners, the sense of *play* that infuses the
entire event, the values of integrity ("No attitudinizing") and commitment
to the work deriving from the innate authority of the discipline itself, and
the role of the master (the poet Verlaine) whose presence, like that of
masters in any context, raises the entire tone and sustains the event's values
and standards of quality.

Within a few years after 1903, Apollinaire was to befriend the most
important painters in Paris, including Pablo Picasso. Apollinaire's description of Picasso's studio reinforces the impression that creativity in Paris was
driven by the constant weaving of links among people and the ideas that
drove them:

> His studio, cluttered with canvases, representing mystical har-
> lequins and drawings on which people walked and which
> everyone was allowed to carry off with him, was the meeting
> place of all the young artists, all the young poets. That year
> André Derain met Henri Matisse, and the meeting gave birth
> to that famous school of the Fauves to which belonged a
> large number of young artists who were later to become
> Cubists.[6]

And Steegmuller adds, "Apollinaire felt he had moved into a world
that was the best possible world for his own creation."[7]

The alliance of writers and painters in Paris sparked the cross-disciplinary fertilization of ideas that marks many hothouses. When Cubism, which Picasso and Braque had invented around 1907, began to garner some critical notice by 1912, it was Apollinaire who wrote the article in the newspaper *Le Temps* that gave Cubism and the theories of "an entirely new art" its most prominent exposure to that point. Apollinaire also sought to achieve a new kind of poetry, in part through the use of industrial imagery, so that his art could express the implications of living in the era of the machine. He turned out to be a prophet, for World War I, which ended up killing him, introducing the modern technology of mass destruction to European audiences. The Eiffel Tower, completed in 1889, had by this pre–World War I era "become a familiar feature of the landscape," according to Pierre Courthion. "[T]he Tower played the part for painters of a gigantic still life set up in the very heart of Paris."[8] Painters were fascinated by this raw assertion of the power of steel, industrial design, and human aspiration; at the equivalent of 98 stories, the tower was by far the tallest human-made structure on earth until surpassed by New York's Empire State Building in 1931.

Stein, as well as championing the new painters, wrote lengthy novels and memoirs with a specific mission: to transform the English language. Stein sought to undermine the dominance of the subject–verb–object structure of sentences that so deeply influences our thought processes. Meanwhile, the Cubists, led by Picasso and Braque, established the direction of modern art and transformed their audience's view of the world by breaking down the traditional relationships among viewer, object, and the plane of vision.

Paul Cezanne, who died in 1906, was the Cubists' great inspiration. In his work he sought the basic forms that govern our visual environment, a goal of many abstractionist painters who came later. Like Stein, Picasso, Apollinaire, Braque, and others of their time, he sought to revitalize our perceptions. Cezanne reconceived the figure–ground relationship—the way a figure stands out from the background of a scene—so that a village melts into its landscape while the form of the landscape seems to surge through the structure of the village houses. Picasso and Braque extended this vision, destroying the separation of figure and ground and capturing the way perception tries to come to terms with movement and shifting perspective. In that self-reflexive way that great art often has, their work also comments on the psychology of a world in which Cubism actually makes sense—that is, their world, that of the new twentieth century, which they in part created. Picasso painted "The Maids of Avignon," the watershed work of modern art, in 1907 (see Exhibit 11), two years after Einstein announced his theory of relativity. And while the new physics directly influenced another great innovator, Vassily Kandinsky, who served as a Bauhaus master, no such direct link connects Einstein and Picasso. What does connect them, however, and which draws in Stein, Apollinaire, and others as well, is their revamping of a paradigm of human consciousness that had reigned for centuries by shifting notions of space, time, language, and more.

The new modernist direction was different from anything that had gone before, and the Cubists knew this intuitively. The best artists often possess an uncanny ability to sense major shifts in the cultural climate before they've manifested anywhere else and to express these shifts through their art. That is a thrilling moment, when one imbibes the energy of the cutting edge of change but still operates from a mixture of devotion and antagonism to tradition. It is precisely that balance that accelerates the creative cycle and propels a group into the hothouse effect. Cubism actually can serve as a study in the theory of relativity. An object in a Cubist painting is seen from multiple angles or as if it's in several places at once. In a sense, it is painted as if it is moving *or* as if the observer is moving, or as if the object, painter, and observer of the painter are all moving at once, relative to one another. The mysterious sympathy that resonates between two sets of artists and scientists working at the same time is not uncommon and hints at important things about both art and science. In Leonardo da Vinci, of course, both roles appeared unified, but the artists of Athens, Florence, the Bauhaus, and jazz all combined their intuitive creativity with rigorous research and analytic thought. This was no less true in Paris. As Courthion points out,

> So it is not surprising that a new generation of painters aimed at painting more deliberately [than their immediate predecessors]—and at a distance from the motif—objects quite simple in themselves and almost geometrical in form, which . . . did not "tell a story" and even had no obvious subject . . . this then so novel form of art, *at once revolutionary and Cartesian* [that is, highly logical]. . . . The Cubist's aim, in short, was to record not the facts of visual experience, but the system of ideas they generated.[9]

"We'll always have Paris" Bogart reassures Bergman in *Casablanca,* perhaps the most romantic movie ever made. Paris had always been a destination for Europeans because of its sexual mores, which were more permissive than most anywhere else on the Continent. But the *romance* of Paris stems for the most part from the hothouse effect that flourished there through the first four decades of the twentieth century. This is the Paris that beckoned expatriates seeking art, adventure, freedom, and the seductive atmosphere of the Left Bank, the subject of countless books, memoirs, films, and daydreams. Paris's intellectual energy has never quite let up for the past eight hundred years, which makes it well-suited to produce, periodically, a particularly buoyant creative atmosphere. Even after World War II, the city did its part in spinning off various philosophical schools, political manifestos, and excellent writers.

Although the leading edge of the hothouse days has been dulled, Paris itself is still a creative center. But it is the early part of the twentieth century that for millions of people stamps Paris as the ultimate magical blend of romance, creativity, and passion. The melancholy note so often attached to this chord sounds largely from the echo of World War II and the sense of impending loss as the war swept closer and closer and the German occupation proved far worse than anyone had anticipated. But the period during which a community experiences the hothouse effect leaves behind more than memories. Parisian art dominated the century and provided a vision of beauty, inspiration, and community that grant solace and sense to an increasingly relativistic, uncertain world. And as for dreamers and lovers, well, we too will always have Paris.

EINSTEIN, BOHR, HEISENBERG, AND FRIENDS

A report recently hit the Internet that claims researchers have found that the speed of gravity is approximately the same as the speed of light. The findings proved one more prediction made by Albert Einstein. In 1905 and 1916 Einstein wrote a couple of scientific papers that reformatted the universe: His theory of relativity included very strange ideas such as space is curved, time slows down as one travels faster, and energy and matter are interchangeable. Einstein's equation, $E = mc^2$, indicated that a little bit of matter could produce a huge explosive burst of energy under the right conditions. At the same time, the world's leading physicists were redefining the nature of matter. The subatomic environment, it turned out, is ruled by an entirely unsuspected set of laws belonging to a field dubbed quantum (tiny bits of energy or matter) mechanics. Inside each of the almost infinite number of atoms in the universe and throughout all its radiant energy—light, radio waves, X-rays, gamma rays, and so forth—the laws of quantum mechanics hold sway. Quantum mechanics and Einstein's theory of relativity together demonstrate that the vast distances and mass of outer space and the subatomic realm both operate according to laws fantastically different from the standard Newtonian mechanics that govern the world we see and touch every day. The two systems—quantum mechanics and relativity—together explain the behavior of electromagnetic energy, light, and extreme atomic effects, such as occur in black holes, in which the atoms of certain collapsed stars are so crushed together they can no longer be classified as atoms.

The point of immediate interest, however, is that the physicists of that heroic era worked together in ways that reflect the dynamics of the hothouse effect. The new cosmos did not simply depend on a few dispersed innovators. As Werner Heisenberg, one of the discoverers of quantum mechanics, explains: "[I]t is important to emphasize the very great role of personal relations in the development of science or art."[10] To illustrate how a strong social component and intensive circulation of ideas led to scientific discovery, Heisenberg cites Einstein's acquaintance with Max Planck, one of the leading lights of the era, and Einstein's close friendship with Max Born, conversations with Niels Bohr, and correspondence with Arnold Sommerfeld about relativity and quantum theory. (Sommerfeld's birth city of Königsberg produced more great mathematicians from the seventeenth to the nineteenth centuries than any city in Europe, including several close in age to Sommerfeld, raising another tantalizing hothouse mystery.)

Heisenberg observes that "A large part of the scientific analysis of those extremely difficult problems . . . was actually carried out in conversations between those who took an active part in the research." In early 1920s Munich, Heisenberg, and many other physicists "discussed almost daily the difficulties and paradoxes in the interpretation of recent experiments."[11] A network of letter-writing connected Einstein, Bohr, the Munich group, and others, and these were read aloud in seminars and discussed. Heisenberg relates about Bohr, "The enormous influence of Niels Bohr on the development of physics in his time was not primarily due to his papers, but to his way of discussing again and again with his partners the fundamental difficulties of quantum theory."[12] Formal social occasions such as the Bohr Festival in 1922 propelled the development of quantum mechanics. Heisenberg attributes some of the festival's success, in which Bohr lectured on his ideas, to the glorious springtime weather and the same spirit that animated the Bauhaus: the feeling that the Great War was over, which gave the gathering "the marks of a joyous new beginning . . . in the international relations of science . . . in the tasks of the newborn atomic physics."[13] Visiting Bohr in Copenhagen often entailed a long walk through the wild meadows along the sea while discussing one's latest work and its implications.

This solidarity was particularly important because time has obscured an odd fact about the emergence of these two momentous areas of knowledge: For several years, they were so far ahead of scientific thinking that Einstein's papers originally generated very little interest in the scientific community and, as Heisenberg puts it, "Planck's quantum theory in those days [1920s] was really not a theory, but an embarrassment . . . it brought ideas that led, on many points, to difficulties and contradictions, and hence there were not many universities where there was any desire to tackle these problems seriously"; nor were Bohr's theories widely taught.[14] Einstein's theory of relativity was accepted earlier, in 1919, when it was verified experimentally and Einstein became a celebrity overnight—fourteen years after his original paper.

Heisenberg, writing in the 1970s, hearkens back to the sheer romance of the golden early days of quantum physics. An avid outdoorsman, he recalls the outdoor activity that punctuated the research sessions. Balloon experiments "started from a beautiful island in the Mediterranean. . . . Certainly the warm sun of the Mediterranean has contributed to the scientific success of the experiments. But this gay time had now gone, and particle research had to be done in the 'matter of fact' atmosphere of huge accelerator establishments."[15]

In addition to factors such as the challenge to the perception of the universe, matter, space, time, energy, and science itself; the active integrated exchange of ideas that marked the early romantic era of twentieth-century physics; the strong social camaraderie that marked relations among the leading innovators; the feeling of release after surviving a major crisis (World War I); and even the sensual qualities of the festival and outdoor experiments, Heisenberg notes another hothouse theme: the importance of the discipline's origins and traditions. Heisenberg had no doubt that the problems he and his colleagues addressed continued the tradition of Copernicus, Galileo, Kepler, and Newton even while overturning the universality of their findings.[16]

In 1927, at the Solvay Congress in Brussels (see Exhibit 12), Einstein kept posing "thought experiments" to Heisenberg that challenged the quantum theory, which he couldn't bring himself to accept. Heisenberg, Bohr, and Wolfgang Pauli worked on an answer to Einstein's daily thought experiment until evening. By dinnertime, Heisenberg writes, they were able to negate Einstein's objection. This game of intellectual tennis went on for several days, at the end of which the trio had returned all of Einstein's volleys. One can almost read the relief in Heisenberg's line, "In the end we . . . knew that we could now be sure of our ground."[17]

Mastery and mentorship supported the intensive, in-depth exploration of the very core of the discipline—and the core of reality in general—that triggered the hothouse effect among this generation of sensational thinkers. Yet Heisenberg offers an interesting postscript to what he referred to as a fruitful period. He believed that the history of any field shows that "We apparently have little freedom in the selection of our problems. We are bound up with the historical process." In fact, one of the characteristics of a so-called fruitful period is precisely the fact that "the problems are given, we don't have to invent them. This seems to be true in science as well as in art. . . . If Einstein had lived in the twelfth century, he would have had very little chance to become a good scientist."[18]

Thus, the hothouse effect owes something to the problems that a long, sporadically progressive tradition places before us: no big problems, no creative response. Yet we might question this conclusion. The evolution of society shows periods of little cultural change punctuated with intense periods of creativity. While Heisenberg attributes this unevenness to the emergence of key problems at different times, we might argue the problems are always there and that it takes a certain kind of society or group to recognize and respond to them. In any case, why did one Greek city respond differently from dozens of others? Did Athenians uncover a set of problems that stimulated them to these efforts, problems unrecognized by or irrelevant to the other Greeks? Or were these problems only defined *after* the Athenians forged ahead with their own unique creative vision?

NOTES

1. Gertrude Stein, *The Autobiography of Alice B. Toklas* (New York: Vintage Books, 1933, 1990), pp. 6, 41.
2. Ernest Hemingway, to A.E. Hotchner, 1950, epigraph for *A Moveable Feast* (New York: Simon and Schuster, 1964, 1992).
3. Pierre Courthion, *Paris in Our Time,* translated by Stuart Gilbert (Paris: Skira Press, 1957), p. 105.
4. Francis Steegmuller, *Apollinaire: Poet Among the Painters* (New York: Farrar, Straus and Co., 1963), p. 85.

5. Ibid., pp. 81–83.
6. Ibid., p. 136.
7. Ibid.
8. Courthion, p. 108.
9. Ibid., p. 99.
10. Werner Heisenberg, *Encounters with Einstein* (Princeton, NJ: Princeton University Press, 1983), p. 4.
11. Ibid., p. 5.
12. Ibid.
13. Ibid., p. 39.
14. Ibid., pp. 37–38.
15. Ibid., p. 62.
16. Ibid., p. 3.
17. Ibid., pp. 115–116.
18. Ibid., p. 3.

14

"IT'S ALL IN THERE"

Perhaps no major art form has produced as many master practitioners in so short a time as jazz in the fifty years extending roughly from 1920 to 1970. One reason is mathematics: With nearly twenty instruments in common use in a variety of formats (such as big band, innumerable small group variations, or solos) and an emphasis on both solo flights of individual creativity and tightly knit collaboration, there is plenty of room for a large number of top performers to shine. Jazz's popularity and its numerous performance venues provided plenty of room as well.

VALUES

The jazz world is a consummate expression of the hothouse effect. Certain deeply held values were central to jazz. As the contemporary drummer, band leader, and music educator Winard Harper said one night at Manhattan's Jazz Standard, "There ain't nothing better than this old art form. Whatever you want, it's got. Democracy, love, respect—it's all in there." The artists knew, from the beginning, that jazz was a crucial expression of the artistic and intellectual visions of African Americans. Later, the bebop style pioneered by Charlie Parker, Dizzy Gillespie, and Thelonius Monk right after World War II was both meant and understood as a bold assertion of African American pride and autonomy.[1] When Miles Davis literally turned his back to audiences rather than trying to ingratiate himself with them, young black musicians saw it as a statement that their art and dignity as artists were paramount in the room, as opposed to their traditionally perceived roles as entertainers. Jazz was fueled by values imbued with a moral stance against the racism that threatened the musicians' lives and aspirations. The music was one arena where racism could not call the shots, even if it did assert itself in financial matters or in the old taboo against blacks and whites playing together on stage. As the civil rights movement transformed race relations in America, jazz drew more and more explicitly on the African side of its ancestry, and many musicians used the music to express their identities as blacks. At the same time, major performers such as Sun Ra, Roland Kirk, John Coltrane, Miles Davis, and Eric Dolphy explored the broader cosmic and spiritual aspects of their art just as Kandinsky and Itten did at the Bauhaus.

Commitment to social transformation seems to come naturally to hothouses and the effect is more likely to occur when individuals with this grander perspective work together. This fervent commitment was evident on the part of the Athenians at the Battle of Marathon in 490 B.C.E. and in the art of the Parthenon more than fifty years later. These values do not always take political form: Picasso, Stein, and Apollinaire viewed their revolution in art and perception in largely apolitical terms. Among jazz musicians, drummer Art Taylor explained that:

> [A]ll jazz musicians were part of a tight brotherhood (which included several women, too). They worked together, hung out together, shared many of the same social values and experiences. . . . But it was mainly the music, and the knowledge of how powerful this music was, how deep was its potential as a spiritual and consciousness-raising force, that held the brotherhood together.[2]

Jazz writer Eric Nisenson links shared social values to the musical quest even more closely:

> At heart was the belief that the music they played had frontiers to be explored, and that jazz had a future that seemed as unlimited as the reaches of the stars or the depths of the oceans. It was a future that was keyed to the potential future of its home country . . . jazz was a powerfully progressive

force in American life because it was a music based on the deepest kind of hope.³

INTO THE CORE

Confidence that reaches beyond mastery of craft and aims at profound social change and even spiritual awakening can only be based on rare levels of achievement. Values derive strength and integrity from commitment to a discipline's core principles. The value we assign to work depends, in large part, on the skill, insight, information, intellect, and emotion that goes into every discipline, craft, and industry. Values come from the legacy of sacrifice, contribution, passion, risk, and effort that each discipline demands. It is hard to imagine a master machinist who doesn't have a passion for tools or for taking on complex projects at home. No decent jazz musician ignores the great stylists who came before, not just out of respect, but because their work is what creates jazz—that is, the theories, lessons, music, and spirit. Legendary saxophonist John Coltrane observed, "I have listened to about all the good tenor men, beginning with Lester [Young], and believe me, I've picked up something from them all, including several who never recorded."⁴

We live in a results-oriented society. Yet, to cite Immanuel Kant again, the moral worth of an activity resides not in our interest in it or its alleged purpose *but in the act and activity itself.* This may seem closer to Zen than the thinking of an eighteenth-century German philosopher, but the logic is compelling. We might say that even the *existence* of an end result is questionable. Any culmination is the razor's edge of an entire legacy of events. So, then, why would we think that our entire moral purpose lies in that thin edge of culminating activity? One can engage great ambitions and fail by most standards, but inspire the world in the conduct of its affairs. "It's not whether you win or lose . . ." actually has a rich philosophical legacy. In *doing*, one finds the enduring results. Each action is its own end, and only human delusion raises to the highest level of achievement the arbitrarily chosen final event of a richly layered sequence of acts.

Jazz's excitement comes in part from the fact that a fragment of a given performance—such as a solo, phrase, introduction, or instrumental exchange—may prove to be its highlight or even account for that piece's immortality. Of course the overall integrity of a performance or piece is important, but the culmination of the piece—unlike the denouement of a play or the final effect of a poem—is less important in jazz than in virtually any other art form. A performance is as likely to be remembered for one or two great solos as for the overall effect of the evening. The challenge to explore, transcend, and redefine assumptions, whether they concern the way a song is performed, how instruments blend or duel with one another, harmonic or modal theory, or the very nature of jazz and even music itself, is central to jazz's existence and mission. The values that jazz inspires are inseparable from the frameworks that shape the work itself, including the improvisational artistry that defines jazz. More than any other creative form other than some performance art, jazz incorporates unpredictability.

Nonetheless, unpredictability is based on an intensive study of music theory, as the great innovative pianist Thelonius Monk fully understood:

> As a teacher . . . Monk kept insisting that musicians must keep working at stretching themselves, at going beyond their limitations, which really were artificial limitations that came from their having absorbed conventional . . . standards of what can and what cannot be done on an instrument.[5]

As music journalist Ashley Kahn writes, "The genius of Charlie Parker and Dizzy Gillespie was to reinvent jazz's harmonic and rhythmic possibilities. Their solos broke through to new territory in jazz harmony, locating new notes to play in the chordal structure."[6] Miles Davis recalled in an interview with Nat Hentoff in 1958,

> When Gil [Evans] wrote the arrangement of "I Loves You, Porgy," he only wrote a scale for me. No chords. And that . . . gives you a lot more freedom and space to hear things. When you go this way, you can go on forever. You don't have to worry about [chord] changes and you can do more with the [melody] line. It becomes a challenge to see how melodically inventive you can be.[7]

During the intensive creative period from 1945 to 1959, musicians redefined the nature of jazz, challenging traditional reliance on chord structure and shifting into a modal form that provided new challenges to their improvisatory genius. Miles Davis and composer George Russell combed libraries for sheet music by innovative composers such as Alban Berg, Bela Bartok, Igor Stravinsky, and Sergei Prokoviev,[8] while Coltrane studied Ni-

colas Slonimsky's *Thesaurus of Scales and Melodic Patterns.*[9] The quest to create deep structural change in the music has persisted throughout the history
of jazz, and that process seemed unrelenting from 1920 to 1970.

It is difficult to imagine a more intense process than endless nights of
performance, jam sessions, and discussions carried out among hundreds,
even thousands, of practitioners. Bands met one another crossing the country from club to club and exchanged ideas. Musicians moved easily from
one band to the next or formed their own groups to articulate their ideas.
The circulation of people assured the circulation of ideas. Carl Woideck
quotes novelist Ralph Ellison on this process:

> More often than not . . . jazz's heroes remain local figures
> known only to small-town dance halls, and whose reputations
> are limited to the radius of a few hundred miles. . . . Being
> devoted to an art which traditionally thrives on improvisation,
> these unrecorded artists very often have *their most original
> ideas enter the public domain almost as rapidly as they are
> conceived, to be quickly absorbed into the thought and tech-
> nique of their fellows* (emphasis by author).[10]

The hothouse criterion that the pyramid of performance widens out at the
top achieves almost surreal dimensions in jazz. The local favorite may well
have been one of the greatest trumpet players ever, but no one outside a
restricted geographical circle would ever know it. Many of us have experienced this. In a Virginia bar I watched a seventy-year-old bluegrass banjo
musician, known only to other musicians, leave his superb picking behind
and shift into wild chord changes that seemed to fuse bluegrass and jazz
into one single style. When Miles Davis played in Los Angeles with his
quintet in 1956, the West Coast musicians who played "cool style" jazz
were blown away by the group's innovations and the pure cool style instantly became obsolete. The great irony here is that it was Miles himself
who created the cool style in 1951, playing with some of these same musicians; he just dropped in to let them know something else was going on.

Jazz illustrates why values are inseparable from work itself. The commitment to a community beyond oneself builds a value system that is not
based solely on primary needs such as food, shelter, sex, money, status, and
acquisition. The jazz community was as loosely knit, in a formal sense, as
we can imagine. It was bound together by commitment and even surrender
to the music and the percolating process of interaction that Ralph Ellison's

quote captures so well. Or, to stir Immanuel Kant awake once more, to a devotion to the tone, the phrasing, the moment of creation rather than some abstract purpose. That requires discipline, sacrifice, integrity, and love, precisely the qualities that forge moral purpose and values. What drove musicians to the heights of creativity was neither the cool scene, nor the competition to be best or most innovative, nor a desire to be rich and famous, nor the intoxicated nights—it was the passion and the music, the thrill of the chase for the notes, the riff, the extended solo that felt like

> just another way of saying this is a big, beautiful universe we live in, that's been given to us, and here's an example of just how magnificent and encompassing it is. That's what I [John Coltrane] would like to do. I think that's one of the greatest things you can do in life, and we all try to do it in some way.[11]

MASTERS AND MENTORS

The masters of jazz wrestled with the giants of the past much as Jacob wrestled with the angel. But they sought not to overcome those giants, but to learn from them and earn their visas to previously unexplored territory. We have already noted the profound respect, even reverence, accorded the masters of jazz by those who followed them. This is a bottom-line aspect of the jazz community. Like baseball players, sailors, and golfers and their fans, jazz musicians and fans stay connected through a rich store of anecdotes and remembrances in which a ten-, fifty-, or one-hundred-year-old event is retold as if it happened yesterday. "Zimmer told me how he ran into Carl Hubbell at a dinner one night. . . . We looked up and out of the fog the Nimitz [a U.S. aircraft carrier] was bearing right down on us. . . . I was there when Miles played his first gig with Bird." The lesson is underlined in story after story: This is how you learn, this is how Miles played one night, you've got to put in time "conversin' with the elders." Saxophonist and composer Steve Coleman explained:

> When I listen to Charlie Parker, I imagine there's a lot that I miss—messages they were throwing back to each other across the stage, all kinds of things that we just hear as music today. . . . At one point, Bird couldn't play shit. And then he became this great master. What happened in between? What were

the steps? I don't care if it was Bird, Einstein, or whoever.
What were the steps that took them from where we all come
from to that point?[12]

That question goes to the heart of creativity: How do we get there? How
did *they* get there? Every young musician ponders those questions, just as
rookie athletes observe the demeanor and practice of veterans, and smart
young business managers watch and learn from those whose positions
they'd like to have some day.

Mentorship relationships were especially powerful in jazz because musicians traveled together and constantly helped one another out. Of course,
there was plenty of destructive and hostile behavior, as there would be in
any group constantly on the go and that worked until dawn, but the overall
impression is of a community in which teaching and encouragement were
central. Miles Davis recalls how in his first gigs with Charlie Parker's group,
Parker would turn the solo over to him and leave him hanging—either to
play or leave the stage. He played. John Coltrane would drop in on Thelonius Monk early in the morning. Monk, the mentor, would go to the
piano, start playing, and look expectantly at Coltrane until he took out his
horn and joined in. But these are only highlights of a nightly process of
teaching, sharing, exchanging, mentoring, and challenging that enriched
the infinite fertility of the jazz medium.

Mentorship was built into the structure of the music. The big bands
had a hierarchy of veterans and newcomers, of proven and untested talent,
but everyone needed one another to sound as strong as possible. In small
groups, the leader often took younger musicians under his wing and introduced them to the intricacies of improvisation. Suggestions from talented
youngsters were also generally accepted, as at the Bauhaus, the Florentine
studios, or the exchanges among physicists. In jazz, younger players had to
be heard from, because if you let someone into your band, you were near-
equals anyway: He or she is going to play and success depends on youngsters as well leaders. Kahn cites pianist Bill Evans's observation that, "I
don't think we would've had Coltrane's great contributions without
Miles's belief in his potential. Because at the beginning, most people won-
dered why Miles had Coltrane in the group . . . But Miles really knew,
somehow, the development that Coltrane had coming"[13] (see Exhibit 13).

TRANE, BIRD, AND THE NETWORK

Despite the great success of albums such as the Davis-led *Kind of Blue*,
Coltrane, nicknamed "Trane," had to move beyond even where he could

go with Miles. As their colleague on *Kind of Blue*, alto saxophonist Nat "Cannonball" Adderly said, "You've got to hand it to him, you know. In the middle of a successful career, Coltrane decided he wasn't playing anything and made up his mind to go ahead and develop something that had been in the back of his mind all along."[14] As Coltrane expert Carl Woideck notes, "There was no outside influence demanding that Coltrane move on from his comfortable accepted position as a rising young tenor man in the pattern of [Dexter] Gordon, [Wardell] Gray, and [Sonny] Stitt. He was being accepted, even welcomed, on this basis."[15] Coltrane fit no pattern, not that of "Gordon, Gray, and Stitt," or any other jazz great.

This inner drive of the high-powered creative person needs to be respected not just because it comes from within but because it simply cannot be managed. Lewis Hyde, in his classic study of creativity, *The Gift*, provides numerous examples of highly creative people who viewed their creations as a gift from some "higher" source.[16] It has been countered that manuscripts that Mozart supposedly wrote when in an inspired trancelike state show heavy editing, but anyone who has done creative work knows that such objections only beg the question. Sometimes it is the germ of an idea that occurs in the moment of inspiration, or a musical passage that provides the core of one's work—these processes do not by any means negate the need for revision, reworking, rethinking, or painstaking development of an idea. The twentieth-century sculptor Louise Bourgeois stated, "There is a long lapse between the first creative vision and the final result; often it is a matter of years."[17] But the initial inspiration is of paramount importance and often occurs in a dreamlike, trancelike, or meditative state.

Jazz is the only art in which improvisation is the central creative activity. The continual emphasis on improvisation, on individual creativity, drives jazz's creative growth. Combine this with the fact that jazz represents perhaps the purest example of ideas circulating throughout an intensively active network and we see that the synergy of these two factors elevated jazz's achievement to astonishing heights. Here was one way it worked: In New Orleans, a new music is born from an almost untraceable mingling of musical lineages both venerable and modern. As musicians travel up the Mississippi River and rail lines to other cities, they inspire a growing network of practitioners. The links between members of this network are not static; they are actually *feedback loops* in which one person's innovation links up with scores of musicians and thousands of fans who transmit their verdicts, or feedback, along the channels linking the cities, musicians, and fans. Some loops are more direct than others, such as "cutting sessions" in which the loser leaves the stage, battles of the bands, and mentorship. The musicians cycle the feedback through their own creative processes and send out the results as new links that generate new hubs for the jazz network. As the positive feedback loops become more powerful and links and hubs proliferate, more and more energy is concentrated in the hubs until the system seems to take on a mind of its own and great players seemingly come out of nowhere in a sustained burst of creative energy. In this regard, the jazz system operated with incredible efficiency.

One night, a young alto saxophonist steps to the stage. Data has already been transmitted about this musician: His playing is so off-base, a noted drummer dropped his sticks during the alto's solo, cutting him down in mid-note. This night, however, something else happens. The musician plays complex chord changes, notes spin off his fingers and out of the horn faster than anyone thought possible, and his tone is confident and firm. The solos soar like a bird in flight. The band members perhaps exchange startled glances. The audience heats up. At this hub, this core event, the message is being formulated that will be transmitted throughout the world of jazz. More and more people come to see him play. Critics rave. Because his charisma is dazzling and his mind brilliant, and because he plays like no one had ever imagined, he becomes a legend, with other musicians trying to emulate him. His personal style becomes *the* style, a way of playing disseminated by the formal and informal mentorship that he dispenses. Overlaying the global network of jazz, a new network emerges, the Charlie Parker-bebop network, blazing new pathways for creative growth. As more and more fans flock to his gigs and those of his fellow stylists, the new network's energy builds. The music brings people to clubs where they buy alcohol, which makes the club owners richer so they can pay the musicians more. Profit, as well as love of the music, fuels demand among club owners, recording executives, and booking agents. More musicians enter the jazz world, absorbing the alto player's lessons quickly because they are nurtured on his music. Other hubs of musical activity arise, and more money is spent. Charlie Parker's chief collaborators generate their own fields of activity. Bird, as he is known, becomes a monumentally generative hub in the jazz network.

If Charlie Parker was—and still is—a hub, does that mean the musicians are jazz's hubs? To an extent, but the hubs are also the bands, the clubs, the studios, and any city or town where jazz is played. According to the science of networks, any network will be dominated by a few powerful hubs, and then a significantly larger number of medium-size hubs, and finally, many smaller hubs, all according to mathematical formulas that show a rapid increase in the number of hubs as the hubs decrease in importance. But just as the hothouse effect has an extraordinarily high number of practitioners at the highest levels—that is, dozens of superb artists in Florence compared with a few in Perugia or Sienna—so too does the hothouse network have a disproportionately high number of active and important hubs.

Jazz was exceptional for its large number of important hubs with many links, as though ten major cities lay between New York and Boston, or St. Louis and Chicago, a situation that defies the logic governing the formation of networks or the growth of cities. Creative work is different, however, because while Parker, Gillespie, Monk, Max Roach, Bud Powell, and Miles Davis were inventing bebop, Count Basie, Louis Armstrong, Benny Goodman, Artie Shaw, Duke Ellington, and a host of others were producing absolute masterpieces in their own styles. In addition, each of those bands featured extraordinarily innovative musicians such as Lionel Hampton, Johnny Hodges, Teddy Wilson, Lawrence Brown, Paul Goncalves, and dozens of others. Furthermore, pre-bebop greats such as Coleman Hawkins, Lester Young, Billie Holiday, Frank Sinatra, and Ella Fitzgerald energized jazz either through bebop and/or continued adherence to their basic styles, while younger *post*-bebop players emerged with *their* new ideas. We can go on; the point is, jazz from its beginnings consisted of layer upon layer of creative activity that produced a creative network of unprecedented density.

Whatever their individual personalities, virtually every jazz musician felt humble in one respect: their relationship to musical tradition as embodied by the masters who preceded them. Jazz was imbued with a tremendous creative generosity that may have reflected the African American community's close bonds, a generosity that extended to the musicians of earlier generations who operated in an America where Jim Crow ruled the south and prejudice ran wide and deep in the rest of the land. And generosity requires humility, in the best sense of the word.

Paired with this humility, however, many jazz greats possessed a will to create and express their gifts as tough as the steel of a samurai's sword. This tends to be true of all great "creatives." Thomas Edison simply could not give up until he found what he wanted; the drive was knit into the fabric of his being. What else would sustain a hypochondriacal Marcel Proust through endless volumes of an autobiographical novel that maintains its brilliance throughout? We feel most free when in the throes of creative passion, yet that is precisely when we have absolutely no choice: We *have* to follow this singular path and yet we feel free!

Although many believe that the golden "age of giants" of jazz innovators has passed, jazz remains startlingly original and vibrantly alive with brilliant practitioners who—somewhere each night—make beautiful, innovative music. The music is forging new alliances with different styles from around the world, and the seeds nurtured via jazz's hothouse effect have spread across the waters. One way or another, creativity finds its way. As Cannonball Adderly observed about Coltrane, he didn't have to set off on his musical quest. Creativity is internally driven and always seeks its highest level. Conditions, however, do not always cooperate, and the hothouse effect is fairly uncommon. It is perhaps the managerial challenge of the century to find a way to tap into that creative drive, for surely it runs, however silent and deep, through the hearts and minds of every human being.

NOTES

1. Scott DeVeaux, *The Birth of Bebop: A Social and Musical History* (Berkeley: University of California Press, 1997), p. 22.
2. Eric Nisenson, *Blue: The Murder of Jazz* (New York: St. Martin's Press, 1997), pp. 24–25.
3. Ibid., p. 25.
4. Carl Woideck, *The John Coltrane Companion: Five Decades of Commentary* (London: Schirmer Books, 1998), p. 27.
5. Ibid., p. 51.
6. Ashley Kahn, *Kind of Blue: The Making of the Miles Davis Masterpiece* (New York: DaCapo Press, 2000), p. 67.
7. Ibid.
8. Ibid., p. 27.
9. Ibid. p. 71; Woideck, p. 172.
10. Woideck, p. 27.
11. Ibid., p. 114, from an interview with Coltrane by Don DeMicheal in *Down Beat,* April 12, 1962.
12. Larry Blumenfeld, interview with Steve Coleman, "Unshrouding the Mysteries of Steve Coleman, in *Jazziz,* June 1998, p. 45.
13. Kahn, p. 49.
14. Woideck, p. 17.
15. Ibid.
16. Lewis Hyde, *Imagination and the Erotic Life of Property* (New York: Vintage Books, 1979).
17. Christiane Meyer-Thoss, *Louise Bourgeois: Designing for Free Fall,* translated by Catherine Schelbert, Jorg Trobitius, and Friederike Mayrocker (Zurich: Ammann Verlag, 1992), p. 180.

15

CREATIVE VISIONS IN RESEARCH AND MANUFACTURING

Manufacturing uses machinery to extend the process of inventing and crafting objects into the realm of mass production and standardization, which enables us to produce immense quantities of surplus goods. This surplus, in turn, fuels the expansion of economic activity as well as the increasing complexity of the social and economic systems dependent on manufacturing. Since the onset of the Industrial Revolution in the eighteenth century, manufacturing has been popularly associated with images of power, progress, pollution, wealth, and exploitation. Its association with creativity has been tangential, usually centering on the many outstanding inventors who devised the core machinery of the industrial and postindustrial eras, such as James Watt and the steam engine, Robert Fulton and his steamboat, Thomas Edison, Alan Turing and his contributions to the computer age, and a host of others. However, once the big wheels start turning, the marriage of manufacturing and creativity seems to devolve into separate living arrangements.

This perception, however, is highly distorted. Despite the dehumanizing aspect of the factory assembly line and the sweatshop, and the sheer inhuman power of machinery, creativity is knit into the very fabric of manufacturing, even when one looks past the innovative and entrepreneurial energy inherent in the invention process. This is truer today than ever before for a number of reasons:

■ The materials available for use in any given industrial procedure and any product have grown exponentially with advances in chemistry and materials science.

191

■ Computerization offers a myriad of possible pathways to increasing efficiency, quality, support, and distribution of all products.

■ Globalization also generates an equal number of alternatives in the organization of resources and productive capacity, the marketing and distribution of goods, and corporate oversight.

■ A host of social, legal, and environmental considerations make the management of a manufacturing operation more complicated than it has ever been.

■ The recognition that many line workers can contribute to the success of an enterprise when given the opportunity to be creative and innovative means that stimulating creativity throughout a manufacturing organization may be an inexpensive way to achieve outstanding returns.

This chapter shows how two exceptional organizations infuse creativity into every aspect of the manufacturing process. Foster-Miller, which we will consider first, is a research and manufacturing company in Waltham, Massachusetts. The second, the Rowland Institute for Science in Cambridge, Massachusetts, was founded by one of the legends of American business, Dr. Edwin Land, who combined a brilliant scientific mind with a superb practical and theoretical approach to both invention and industry. Both demonstrate the possibility of extending the hothouse effect to the factory floor.

A GOLDEN AGE OF MATERIALS

Foster-Miller's laboratories, production facilities, and offices stand across Route 128 from the Nelson Companies headquarters. Clear a few trees and you've got a perfect line of sight between them. Sitting at lunch with Dr. Bill Ribich, president of Foster-Miller (F-M), and Jay Boyce, one of F-M's chief research scientists, I am once again struck by the commonalities among enterprises that share an overriding creative orientation. Employee-owned F-M was named one of the fifty most innovative small businesses in America by *Inc.* magazine in 2002. It was founded in 1957 by Dr. Eugene Foster of MIT from a classic creative insight that involved unifying two opposing forces. Foster had worked on many design problems with designers who didn't know science and scientists who didn't know design. He knew there was a need for a corporation that combined the best of both. Today, F-M is a leader in developing custom-engineered polymers. Ribich and Boyce agree emphatically that we are in a golden age of materials development. They did, however, provide a glimpse into why even golden ages have their daunting challenges.

Boyce notes that F-M can produce two or three new compounds a month. The company uses sophisticated computer models to design a molecule and obtain a predictive picture of what the molecule can do. After that, F-M needs to make the new material and then bring it to market. The cycle to take a new material from the onset of research to profitability was traditionally twenty years. Today, development of new materials goes much faster, but successful marketing still demands the following:

- The material be applicable to a real-world problem
- The technology required to mass produce it be available or at least possible to develop
- The product be manufactured at a cost that allows a profit
- A marketing and distribution infrastructure exists that can actually sell the product

I found Ribich and Boyce's view of the problem fascinating: Foster-Miller can create materials worthy of a golden age, but there simply aren't enough users in the value chain to utilize these materials. Sometimes the material itself poses too many challenges, but sometimes the problem is much simpler: not enough companies with enough research facilities and staff to transform materials into successful products. Add in all the existing materials and the option of simply modifying materials rather than inventing new ones, and the backlog of untapped potential applications becomes mind-boggling. Imagine a great storeroom of angels whose wings have been folded up simply because the skies are too crowded for them. Many of these angels have superpowers that they would love to use benevolently, but the marketplace can't figure out how to handle so many benefits at once. In many ways, materials are the angels of civilization: friable stone that can be chipped into tools, copper, tin, bronze, and iron; textiles, wood, paper, and brick; tempered steel, industrial diamonds, magnetic coils, silicon, light itself—all contain atomic secrets that human beings have uncoiled and applied as if those materials were our personal angels whose only desire is to serve humanity. Now we can create our own materials but, in something out of Alvin Toffler's book *Future Shock,* we haven't begun to grasp their potential.

Foster-Miller balances cornucopia-like creativity with a strong business model. Half the company is devoted to research and development (R&D) and, as Boyce notes, hundreds of ideas emerge from the labs. Their materials are used in the most advanced robotic, defense, and microprocessor systems. Products include cooling systems for the NASA space station, aircraft-protecting armor, underground air-conditioning of gold mines, solar photovoltaic-assisted electric heat pumps, solar thermal-powered desalination plants, cool suits for airmen and soldiers, and wind-powered turbines that produce ice. Foster-Miller personnel operated F-M robotics systems for search and rescue at Ground Zero immediately following the World Trade Center attacks.

F-M is into textiles, which is like saying that Beethoven was into tunes. The company designed its own three-dimensional braiding machine to weave ceramic fibers. F-M cures its resin fibers by exposing them to an electron beam, which makes the fibers incredibly strong. The textiles are interlocking grids of composite resins, polymers, and ceramics whose superconductivity make them perfect for transmitting energy and data; correcting for disorientation in space; providing silent communication, navigation, and orientation in military operations; and integrating virtual reality and medical sensing in the field of health.

Organizationally, Foster-Miller is well primed to cultivate creativity. Both Ribich and Boyce seem to be constantly weaving together the "woof" of creativity's exhilaration with the "warp" of market exigencies. As Boyce, who is quite verbally expressive himself, states, "We don't hire many wallflowers. We get top-of-the-line people. The real challenge of managing them is on the 'no' end because they are so creative and talented." But while F-M people are experts—most of F-M's marketing people hold a doctorate in engineering or other scientific field—they are never boxed in as *the* experts. Boyce notes that experts tend to know everything about what *didn't* work years ago, which can discourage the search for solutions. F-M encourages researchers to cross over into other disciplines and operations to share ideas and find out how to make something work. Both Ribich and Boyce affirm the importance of maintaining records of past attempts, because archiving intellectual capital keeps ideas in circulation. After all, the innovative programming language Linux is based on was an old Unix program, and the silicon chip was the result of Bell Lab scientist Russell Ohl's interest in "the crystal receiver, an antiquated radio device from the 1920s."[1]

Among the materials, processing, and design people, the original integrative vision of Dr. Foster remains vital: Members of each group interact frequently, thereby providing input that shapes the objectives and solutions of the others. The hydraulic circulation of ideas through which everyone, including administrators and staff, contributes at meetings, is encouraged by actively soliciting those ideas and by making this participation a consistent theme in job reviews. And Ribich and Boyce firmly adhere to the philosophy of getting the best people on a project and giving them free rein.

Boyce points out that "creatives" tend to go straight to the *d* in research and design. It is important to slow them down and make sure the research gets done as well. With three to four programs a month starting up, those in R&D must know all the reasons why previous solutions did not work. The Internet, however, has made research faster and more productive and accelerated the pace of innovation. It takes mere seconds to find out what a researcher in New Mexico is doing where once it took days. Oddly enough, Boyce recalls, for the first seven or eight years after its arrival, the desktop computer was used almost as a toy. People rearranged proposals over and over again until Boyce reminded them that endless cutting and pasting wasn't really the same as working. Finally, computers and software caught up with the complexity of the work, so to speak, and productivity started rising. Boyce's anecdote reminds us that product development depends on a range of systems. Information systems can be utilized anywhere from 0 percent to 100 percent effectively, which is why hothouses implement an ongoing critical and even contemplative review of the role technology plays in their operations.

In discussing innovation, Boyce observes that the old proverb of "build a better mousetrap and the world will beat a path to your door" isn't entirely accurate. Bringing the product to market is too exacting and expensive to trust to the product's merit alone. That is one reason the marketing team has such exceptional credentials and a great deal of input throughout the entire development process. "You need people to look ten years into the future and figure out what the next killer 'app' is going to be," says Boyce. Developing a new product is by no means simply a matter of pure science or a pure application of the scientific method. As Mike Jahnke said about Sequent's product development, an approach based on finding an ideal solution simply ties up too much of the budget. Boyce believes that gut instinct and intuition guide scientists, engineers, and staff at key moments, which is another reason to cultivate creativity in the environment: the step-at-a-time methodology works in an ideal laboratory situation in which time and cost are not factors, but even then, experimentation itself only carries one part of the way to discovery. All great scientists

have been strongly intuitional, and whether the outcome is the Great Pyramid, Brooklyn Bridge, instamatic camera, or 2.4 gigahertz PC, it took
many "Eureka!" moments before those achievements became viable.

Foster-Miller also provides solutions to manufacturing problems. The
company literature provides the following four-step algorithm that guides
it in designing processes that save money and reduce risk:

1. Brainstorm innovative yet practical solutions.
2. Use bench scale tests to determine the top two or three solutions.
3. Develop a prototype of the best solution and refine it.
4. Complete the design, and manufacture, test, and deliver it.

Like other powerful algorithms, this one came not only from experience
but from the inquisitive, analytic, and creative mind-set that drives innovation in every field.

"HE'S IN THE SHOWER . . ."

Dr. Edwin Land, founder of Polaroid Corporation and, in 1980, the Rowland Institute for Science in Cambridge, Massachusetts, often became so
enthused about an idea he would call his scientists at all hours, especially
just before dawn. After being woken up many times, the scientists' spouses
simply told Land, "He's in the shower." Each scientist believed it was only
his or her spouse using the excuse until one day Land remarked with a big
grin, "I've got the cleanest crew in town." Only then did they realize that
either (a) the spouses had worked out their solution together, or (b) human
ingenuity runs along predetermined paths.

Not that Land's crew ever tired of working with him. When speaking
about Land with Jim Foley, a chemist who worked closely with him at the
Rowland Institute, it is clear that Foley still misses Land, eleven years after
his boss's death. "Everyone just respected him as somebody who cared
about people . . . Land showed what we can aspire to. He put so many
things together in the right way. He was a philanthropist, a gentle person."
Once, as Land and several employees ate a late meal together at the famed
Boston seafood restaurant Legal Seafoods, Land realized that the bluefish
paté might be suitable for one of the employees' wives who, Land remembered, had a serious food allergy. Land asked to speak with the chef. The
latter, normally reticent about his recipes, nonetheless gave Land a list of

every ingredient (although the recipe now graces Legal's tablecloths). The paté was indeed suitable and Land ordered up a batch of it for the scientist to bring home for his wife. Almost twenty years later, Foley still shakes his head that someone that busy and renowned not only remembered the specific allergy but also arranged a special treat for a person not even present at the time. "That's leadership," Foley says. "You'd follow somebody like that into hell. That's why I came [to Rowland]. I would've done very well at Polaroid. But this has been the most incredible experience of my whole life."

In the annals of invention, Thomas Edison holds the most patents with 1,093. Edwin Land is second with 533, while many of the scientists who worked at Polaroid and Rowland, Foley included, hold numerous patents as well. According to Foley, Land was unrelenting in his quest for solutions, which Foley calls "one of his really, really special traits," and one Land shared with Edison. Foley believes that Land's approach to research was innately strategic, and Foley describes Land's approach as including a reconnaissance stage during which one sought the broadest perspective. Once Land found the weak spot, the entry point, he quickly converged on the solution. In a sense, Foley described a basic but useful behavioral algorithm. Any problem, Foley noted in a statement that recalls Casey Powell's approach, has many solutions. One needs to find the most achievable, "the non–Rube Goldberg solution," in Foley's words.

The problem-solving algorithm Foley described was reflected in Land's business acumen. "When it came to business, everything was simple, elegant, and concise. He directed all resources towards one thing, a practical and robust solution. Land was one of those remarkable people—there are only a few around at one time. He was brilliant, hardworking, innovative, a good businessman." And always Foley remarks on Land's consideration for everyone who worked for and with him.

Land gave his people great latitude in pursuing their research interests and solutions. Land's view was "simply to advance science and try to do things that are really important, not just because of the money, but because it's an importance scientific problem to solve," according to Foley. Foley, whose mother died of cancer when he was a child, recounts that when Land recruited him for Rowland, he told him, "Do anything you want. Just make it important. Find a problem that you think is important and put your heart into it." Foley immediately began to work on devising drugs needed for a new cancer treatment based on photodynamic therapy involving drugs that go straight to the tumor and only became toxic when illuminated with light, thus destroying only the tumor rather than healthy cells.

One could even deliver the light via thin fiber optics. Foley's goal was to design a drug that left the body as quickly as possible because the main drug then in use stayed in the body for three months, during which time the patient had to be cautious about going outside during the day.

Foley tested the treatment on mice injected with cancer drugs, but critics of the treatment pointed out that a treatment that works on artificially induced cancer has only one type of cell to defeat, while naturally occurring tumors comprise numerous phenotypes. So Foley approached Tufts School of Veterinary Medicine, which agreed to use the treatment on afflicted family pets whose owners were willing to try it. The treatment had no secondary toxic effects and it proved successful on several cats and one dog. The work has since been licensed to a biotech company with the goal of extending the treatment to humans. Dr. Land championed the process and Foley speaks movingly of the importance of having his work appreciated by a man of Land's caliber.

Foley describes how Land was deeply involved in designing the Rowland Institute's building. He organized the institute's library so that the information possessed its own dynamic flow. As Foley walked me through the library, he brought me to an open, sun-lit space with a view across the Charles River to Boston's Back Bay. Large tables, comfortable chairs, and couches make this area perfect for relaxation and reflection. In fact, that was precisely its purpose, for within this space, according to Land's edict, no one could be disturbed. Anyone could retreat there to think, brainstorm, sketch, or just sit back. Foley tells a story from Polaroid that illustrates Land's respect both for his staff and the power of reflection. Howard Rogers, one of Polaroid's top scientists, was asked by Land "to work on color." Rogers spent two years sitting quietly, often opposite Land in the black-and-white lab. After two years, he stood up and announced, "I've got it." Land replied, "Now go do it." Land's faith in his people was such that he had no doubt they would make use of any sanctuary provided for the pursuit of quietude and reflection.

Adjacent to the Rowland library's reflection area a similar space with bookshelves was reserved for lounging. When any journal, book, document, or article entered the library, it spent its first day on the coffee table. The next day, the librarian moved it to a nearby shelf, where it stayed for a week. After the week was up, the text moved to the six-month shelves along the wall opposite the bank of windows along the river side. Finally, after six months, one week, and one day, the volume took its place among the stacks, where it was still easily accessible. Land wanted information to have its own vital life within the institute. Anyone could visit the library and instantly reference work according to its currency, a time-sensitive model of information management that reflected Land's view of information as essentially dynamic.

The atrium in the Rowland building had been originally designed as an open space. One day, Land asked Foley and the architects to meet him at the Gardner Museum on Boston's Fenway on a Sunday morning at nine, before the museum opened. The group had been granted access to the museum's stunning courtyard garden. With Foley and the architects gathered around, Land simply announced, "This is what I want for the atrium." Today, Rowland's atrium garden still flourishes and pathways still wind through it, fulfilling Land's desire to embed beauty in his employees' surroundings and to offer them a place to reflect and relax.

Rowland, like other hothouses, was an intellectually active place. Land brought in guest lecturers from various scientific fields to talk about their work. Land's own mind was incredibly penetrating, according to Foley.

> He was able to see something differently. We see a chair, he sees a new way to focus a camera. We can't know what his mind was like. He always asked the key penetrating question at the end of other scientists' lectures. "That's right! That's the key!" they would say.

Foley recalls that Land was entranced with color and light. He was an avid fan of Boston's annual flower show and he viewed Rowland as a place to pursue pure science that would also benefit people's lives. Foley's description of Land reminds us that creativity ultimately resides in the individual's ability to see into the core of a problem or discipline and reconfigure its most basic assumptions. At the end of our interview, Foley paused a moment. "You know," he said, "we never had a mission statement. It was just, 'Do good science.'"

Land's entire approach to both science and business reflected a compelling vision of creativity. In his own speeches and writings, Land showed the public application of the qualities that Foley, as a friend and fellow scientist, appreciated so much. In a 1944 paper, Land set forth key principles that governed his approach to innovation, principles as far-reaching and visionary today as they were back then.[2] To start, Land recommended that:

■ Research businesses employ no more than two thousand people, including fifty scientists.

■ The company be "vigorously creative in pure science."

■ Everyone view themselves as *labor* [emphasis Land's] and "The machinist will be proud of and informed about the company's scientific advances; the scientist will enjoy the reduction to practice of his basic perceptions."

■ "The business of the future will be a scientific, social and economic unit."[3]

Land presented a utopian but pragmatic vision of how the founding of at least one thousand of these companies would change the United States: Each individual will be a member of a group small enough for him to feel a full participant in the purpose and activity of the group. "His voice will be heard and his individuality recognized." Land expressed a devout faith that the meaning each person derives from his or her contribution will create a more stable, happy society.

Land, in effect, described a hothouse network based on establishing thousands of highly creative companies. These companies would liberate individual creativity and promote innovation in large part because of a relatively egalitarian ethic, concern for the personal and intellectual development of all employees, dedication to extending core knowledge in each discipline, and a strong sense of social responsibility. Land's own vocabulary seems animated by his passion for creation. He envisions each new company "contemplating all of the recent advances in pure science and in engineering [and] its staff will be alive to the significance" of this new knowledge. Land also states his faith in one of the prime tenets of creative activity: "A group of fifty good scientists [with staff] contemplating one of these fields and inspired by curiosity about them and a determination to make something new and useful, can invent and develop an important new field in about two years."[4] Determine to do something important and new, and you will achieve momentous results.

Land was alert to the nimble, responsive qualities of relatively small companies, elusive qualities still sought by corporations both large and small. He suggested that when a small company grew too large, it should split off into another company of several thousand employees. He also had a clear vision of the critical importance of intellectual capital: "A research program is never a failure. Every incident in its history will prove to be an educational factor in the next investigation undertaken." He stressed a high standard of ethical behavior on the part of scientists, and advocated a synergy "between pure science in the university and pure science in industry [that] should stimulate and enrich our social system."[5]

Land's core vision of scientific inquiry and technological innovation was summed up in a speech he made in 1959: "We all know of the flowering of the human mind that followed from Bacon's teaching of the techniques of freedom, openness, and communication, in *pure* [emphasis Land's] science."[6] It is characteristic that his allusion to three timeless qualities that support creative activity should be framed in terms of the all-purpose visionary of the English Renaissance, Francis Bacon (1561–1626), virtually an exact contemporary of Shakespeare, Galileo, and Monteverdi, the brilliant musical innovator who invented opera. Bacon's advocacy of experimentation as the essential scientific activity and his dismissal of Aristotle's mode of inquiry had a profound influence on none other than Isaac Newton. One of Bacon's more innovative ideas was to establish new types of educational and research institutions as hubs of inquiry, which Land's notion of a network of research centers recalls.

Land had a profound respect, even reverence, for the glories of the human mind, which he felt were accessible to almost anyone. He considered the way industry treats "these human minds [who] walk through the personnel door" as equivalent to IBM dropping its computers from its highest windows just to test Galileo's law of falling objects." Land observed that "These people coming in at random are carrying in them the greatest marvel of all times—the human mind that took hundreds of millions of years to make. We as technologists in industry do not use these minds at all." He urged developing "a new art and a new science . . . which, without involving emotion, examines the question of 'How do you use human minds?'"[7] (The phrase "without involving emotion" did not imply for Land a lack of passion, compassion, or any other authentic human feeling, but rather a caution against letting sentiment or politics interfere with the most effective educational design.) In a speech given upon receiving an award in 1965, Land again expressed his concern for developing suitable environments for education and research. Referring to Howie Rogers's two years of mentally working out a major research challenge, Land said:

> My point is that we created an environment, in which a man was *expected* to sit and think for two years. . . . But our universities do not train for patient and extended thought, and those few areas in government which have provided thoughtful environments are in certain danger of being swamped by the great mass undertakings.[8]

Land's scientific vision was inseparable from his ideas on how best to pursue science and technological innovation. He understood that the passion for knowledge and discovery, appreciation for beauty and elegance, and adherence to highly ethical positions, whether in regard to employees or the social impact of scientific research, depended in large part on creating the right conditions in which they might flourish and bloom. In Dr. Land's hothouses, as in the botanical variety, light and heat combined to produce miracles.

NOTES

1. Lisa Scanlon, "No P-N Intended: A Cracked Crystal Launched the Silicon Revolution," in *Technology Review,* February 2003, p. 88.
2. Edwin Land, "Research by the Business Itself," in *The Future of Industrial Research: Papers and Discussion* (New York: Standard Oil Development Company) from a paper presented at the Standard Oil Development Company Forum in New York, October 5, 1944.
3. Ibid.
4. Ibid.
5. Ibid.
6. Ibid.
7. Edwin Land, "The Second Great Product of Industry: The Rewarding Working Life," in *Science and Human Progress* (Pittsburgh: Mellon Institute, 1963), pp. 14–15.
8. Edwin Land, "Some Conditions for Scientific Profundity in Industrial Research," the Charles F. Kettering Award address, Washington, DC, June 17, 1965.

16

CHAI-T: THE "CREATIVE" HOTHOUSE ASSESSMENT INSTRUMENT TABLET

The ability to assess creativity's role within a company and to leverage strategies that shift a company's culture and resources are critical to cultivating organizational creativity. The "Creative" Hothouse Assessment Instrument Tablet (CHAI-T) provides a framework for assessing and strategizing around group creativity. It also charts the position that creativity occupies within an organization, and provides a reasonably precise vocabulary to facilitate discussion of creativity-related issues. The CHAI-T survey comprises forty questions based on the four dimensions of creativity and the thirty-six hothouse effect factors. After listing the questions, this chapter explains CHAI-T and how to calculate results, and interprets a sample chart as a means of demonstrating some ways to apply CHAI-T.

SURVEY

The survey's forty statements address values, perceptual frameworks, social dynamics, action orientation, and hierarchy—that is, issues covered by the thirty-six hothouse effect factors. It can be used to generate a profile of a department or organization, or even by an individual looking to clarify issues in his or her mind. "We/us" refers to the respondent and his or her coworkers. Responses should be based on an overall sense of a situation even if indications seem contradictory. For example, if a company handles toxic waste responsibly but keeps wages artificially low, a person may be of two minds about a statement about its ethics; ultimately, it's a matter of how one weighs the factors and applies standards in these matters. For the self-employed, responses can address the industry or organization on which the respondee wishes to focus. A consultant to biotech will consider either biotech or consulting, but the focus should be consistent throughout. Terms within the survey such as "wisdom" or "changing the world" can be interpreted according to individual judgment. Everyone understands these ideas in his or her own way, and for the purposes of CHAI-T, each interpretation is valid. Responses are based on the following scale:

5 Strongly agree

4 Agree somewhat

3 Neither here nor there

2 Disagree somewhat

1 Strongly disagree

Axis V-1: Values

1. Our work can change the world. _____

2. The organization actively promotes a positive quality of life in our surrounding communities. _____

3. Our products and services are vital to people's lives and well-being. _____

4. Virtually everyone who works here frequently studies and questions the essential nature of their jobs and the technologies—human, organizational, technical—they work with. _____

5. Working here fills me with a sense of personal and emotional well-being and commitment to higher values. _____

Axis H-1: Mission

6. Principles of justice and compassion directly and significantly influence strategy, design, and development. _____

7. Examining the fundamental practices and principles of our industry and its core disciplines serves as a source of creativity, values, and purpose. _____

8. We can try and fail without fear for our jobs. _____

9. My organization budgets significant time and money to support and encourage creative expression among all its members. _____

10. Employees are free to develop their own vision of what their jobs entail. _____

Axis V-2: Ideas

11. This organization cultivates the shift of knowledge into wisdom, and views wisdom as a guide to action. _____

12. Organizational structure grows out of innovative, idea-driven approaches to our challenges and tasks. _____

13. Organizational responses to conflict are thoughtful and imaginative rather than reactive and typical. _____

14. The organization respects thinkers. _____

15. I am respected for all my talents, whether or not they contribute to the bottom line. _____

Axis H-2: Exchange

16. My organization rewards those who display mastery at their jobs and seeks their advice, whatever their formal title or position. _____

17. Institutionalized procedures enable anyone to make suggestions or raise objections. _____

18. Intellectually exciting and stimulating conversation directly influences product development and delivery. _____

19. "Idea people" share their vision with other employees and invite feedback. _____

20. We're good at balancing opposing points of view until we produce a creative synthesis of both. _____

Axis V-3: Perception

21. How we perceive our tasks, our expertise, and the group itself are all legitimate objects of inquiry. _____

22. The organization encourages and teaches whole mind and mind/body methods for enhancing creativity and solving problems. _____

23. Our organization has benefited from contact with much more sophisticated institutions from time to time. _____

24. Sometimes time seems to help us complete a project by literally seeming to slow down or speed up. _____

25. Clear problem-solving algorithms are taught, developed, and applied wherever there's a need without regard to tradition or company politics. _____

Axis H-3: Learning

26. To be viewed as a continuous learner benefits one's career here. _____

27. People here think visually and nonlinearly. _____

28. My organization is constantly learning about itself and the environments in which it operates. _____

29. The organization pays for employees to become involved in cultural events as attendees or participants. _____

30. This is a knowledge-rich environment in which you learn just by being here. _____

Axis V-4: Social

31. This is an exhilarating place to work. _____

32. We have a strong group vocabulary of terms and symbols that promotes communication, community, and creativity. _____

33. Meetings become exciting conversations that generate action and new ideas. _____

34. My organization always seems to have its antennae out in regard to developments in art, science, and society. _____

35. We always produce effective leadership when we need it. _____

Axis H-4: Play

36. Celebrations are planned and designed in highly creative ways. _____

37. The line between work and play is virtually nonexistent. _____

38. Beauty matters greatly in regard to our products and our environment, and as an integrated objective in project management. _____

39. Frequent social occasions promote rapport among all group members. _____

40. Playing whimsically with ideas, materials, objects, and new ways of doing things is accepted practice here. _____

PLOTTING THE POINTS

The four thematic dimensions of creativity that generate the hothouse effect are the basis of the coordinate system on which survey responses are plotted. The vertical axis measures the internal factors while the horizontal axis measures the actualized factors. The forty survey questions are divided into eight groups of five questions, each of which group establishes one of the eight coordinates used to plot the graph.

To graph a response to each of the eight groups, total the scores for the five statements in that group. Total all the responses in a given group, divide by 5, and then divide by the number of persons to find the average score. (Round off to the nearest tenth.) This average yields the coordinates (2.4, 3.3, etc.). Thus, if responses to the five questions on Axis V-1 (the vertical [V] values axis, the first dimension measured) are moderately agree, neutral, strongly agree, strongly disagree, and moderately agree, the scores for those five questions will be, respectively: 4-3-5-1-4. The total is 17 and the average 3.4 (17 ÷ 5). (If 17 is the average for ten people, the total will be 170, which is then divided by 10 and then 5.) Thus, values will be plotted at 3.4 of the vertical axis. If responses to H-1 (the horizontal [H] mission axis) average out to 2.6, the point measuring the values/mission dimension will be (3.4, 2.6). *Note that unlike the usual notation for coordinate systems, the vertical (usually the "y") axis is listed first and the horizontal (usually the "x") axis is listed second.* Also, the two axes intersect at point (3, 3), not the usual (0, 0). Thus (3.4, 2.6) is plotted on the vertical axis *above* the horizontal and its position on the horizontal will be *to the left* of the vertical axis. There are no negative numbers in the system.

THE FOUR QUADRANTS

The four quadrants all have distinct characteristics. Unlike other instruments in which quadrants indicate four equally effective and legitimate learning styles or personality types, CHAI-T contains one quadrant better than the rest, one worse, and two that are mixed. Because a score of 5 is exceptional and 1 very poor, the upper right quadrant, which represents a score of above 3 for both coordinates, signifies the most creative orientation. The lower left, which represents a score of less than 3 on both axes, is least creative.

The upper right quadrant is Quadrant I and moving clockwise we find Quadrant II (lower right), Quadrant III (lower left), and Quadrant IV (upper left). Quadrant I is the most desirable result and Quadrant III least desirable, with II and IV in between. (See Figure 16-1.)

Quadrant I

Quadrant I indicates a strong creative orientation. If most of the graph lies here, the organization should be quite creative and key characteristics will include:

- Action aligned with well-articulated ideals
- Open exchange across hierarchical and functional boundaries
- Organizational structure and development heavily influenced by the creative process
- Integration of learning and operations
- Bold, innovative educational and training opportunities
- Self-critiques and periodic intensive review of strategy, programs, and operations
- A wide range of personal learning and development programs for employees
- A playful, interactive, socially vital environment

Quadrant II

Quadrant II is home to an action-oriented, less-reflective organization, a somewhat typical corporate mentality. Key characteristics are:

- A strong work ethic
- A problem-solving, as opposed to creative, orientation
- A tendency to favor short-term solutions
- Narrowly focused R&D

Figure 16-1. The four quadrants.

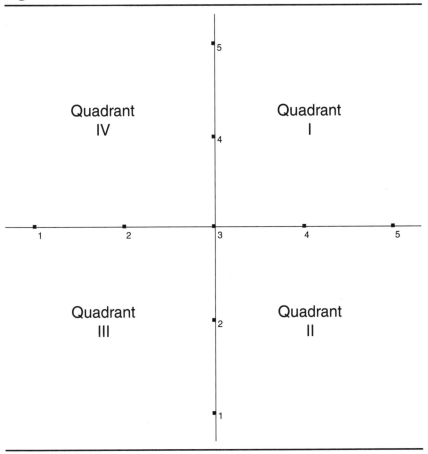

- Communication task-based with sports talk and bantering; uncomfortable across boundaries
- Organizational development focused on moving pieces around
- Learning focused on training for specific, work-related tasks; may have degree programs, but little cultivation of new skills in work context
- Social life dominated by executive junkets; possibly home to a golf, racquetball, or other sports-oriented upper management culture
- High-stress culture with values focused on completion, closure, quick decision-making

Quadrant III

Quadrant III identifies a culture that stifles creativity, initiative, motivation, and morale, such as traditional organizations more suited to the era of typing pools, assembly lines, and remote executives, or start-ups whose founder(s) view the company as a projection of their own personalities and desires. It is characterized by:

- An ethic of profit-at-all-costs
- Rigid organizational hierarchies
- Low employee participation in planning, strategy, or problem solving
- Low level of social interaction
- Behavior that nervously reflects the cues from upper management
- Difficulty in processing moral or interpersonal dilemmas
- Low toleration of conflict
- Little staff development

Quadrant IV

Quadrant IV indicates a split between ideas and reality, ideals and implementation. Often the domain of academic institutions, corporations and nonprofits frequently plant themselves firmly here as well. Some chief characteristics include:

- Strong vision statements with ineffective management
- A pleasant but inefficient work environment
- Lip service to ideals or creativity without making them part of daily work life
- Loss of intellectual capital through seepage—that is, plenty of ideas with nowhere to go
- Positive public image due to publicity value of an apparently ideal-driven institution
- Gap between ideals and reality, espoused and actual values, especially among leaders

GRAPHING THE DIMENSIONS

The position of the coordinate pairs for each of the four dimensions determines how that dimension influences the organization's creativity.

Axis (Vertical) V-1: Values

Axis V-1 measures organizational commitment to values that foster creativity. The top end of the scale, 5 on Axis V-1, indicates that employees reference their work in terms of values generally aligned with a benevolent spirit, such as justice, compassion, and tolerance. They feel their work is vital to the community, the world, and even the cosmos itself. Employees are motivated and committed because of their work's impact, and clearly articulated values drive work, strategy, and planning, even taking precedence when values and profit clash. At the low end of the scale we find a culture with little trust, in which self-aggrandizement, betrayal, and cynicism are rife, and moral dilemmas resolved in the most opportunistic and cynical manner.

Axis (Horizontal) H-1: Mission

Axis H-1 measures whether an organization lives its values and whether employees have the creative freedom to turn vision into reality. The far right or higher end of the scale denotes an active application of high ideals. Strategy, structure, and operations are shaped by each person's drive to actualize a vision for their work. At the far left, organizations are driven by short-term criteria and have low expectations for ethical behavior. Employees use the company for what it offers them because that is how they are used by the company. Work is "just work" and if the company succeeds, it does so by efficiently delivering products to meet demand and because employment factors enable it to find enough workers to neutralize high turnover rates.

Coordinate Pair 1: Anomalies

The term *anomalies* refers to a high score in one element of a dimension accompanied by a low score in the other. These are not rare because human behavior is complex, but they do contradict expectations in perplexing ways.

An organization with a high score on V-1 (values) accompanied by a low score on H-1 (mission) proclaims its ideals and may even believe it is living by them. However, because of business pressures, cynicism, or lack of concern, it does not integrate them into its day-to-day operations. We may also find here idealistic groups that cannot figure out how to bring their vision into the real world.

A high score on H-1 accompanied by a low score on V-1 reflects the open, tolerant values of leaders and other group members, but also shows that the organization has not put in place a "meta-narrative" that expresses the sustaining role these values play in the organization. The danger here is that the values are driven by individuals while the organization has no way of transmitting these values to new members or sustaining them in a crisis. These organizations may drift and lose focus after a run of successes. This anomaly is less common than its reverse—that is, scoring high on V-1 and low on H-1. See Figure 16-2 for descriptions of the values/mission dimension as manifested in each of the four quadrants.

Axis (Vertical) V-2: Ideas

At the upper end of this axis the organization draws in ideas from numerous outside sources, devises channels for transmitting and developing new ideas, and manages information and ideas creatively and proactively. Its structure encourages the free circulation of ideas and contributions are welcomed from all levels of the hierarchy. At the lower end, discussion is stifled and behavior reactive and contingency-based; innovation means throwing money at a problem or adopting a quick-fix template to jump-start a project. The company never recognizes that a consistent record of innovation requires deep-level engagement with the theories, principles, and free-floating ideas that compose the structure and determine the direction of any field.

Axis (Horizontal) H-2: Exchange

A high score reflects a free and open exchange of ideas across all boundaries—discipline, function, department—as well as throughout the hierarchy. The organization has well-defined procedures to promote this type of discourse, recognizes the value of ideas, and rewards the people who develop them, whatever their position, thereby producing a dynamic, stimulating work environment in which disagreement and competition send off

Figure 16-2. Characteristics of dimension I in each of the four quadrants.

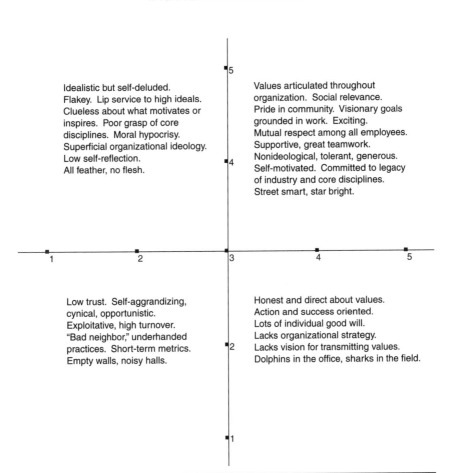

I. Values/Mission Dimension

Idealistic but self-deluded. Flakey. Lip service to high ideals. Clueless about what motivates or inspires. Poor grasp of core disciplines. Moral hypocrisy. Superficial organizational ideology. Low self-reflection. All feather, no flesh.

Values articulated throughout organization. Social relevance. Pride in community. Visionary goals grounded in work. Exciting. Mutual respect among all employees. Supportive, great teamwork. Nonideological, tolerant, generous. Self-motivated. Committed to legacy of industry and core disciplines. Street smart, star bright.

Low trust. Self-aggrandizing, cynical, opportunistic. Exploitative, high turnover. "Bad neighbor," underhanded practices. Short-term metrics. Empty walls, noisy halls.

Honest and direct about values. Action and success oriented. Lots of individual good will. Lacks organizational strategy. Lacks vision for transmitting values. Dolphins in the office, sharks in the field.

creative sparks rather than emotional fireworks. A low score describes a closed, often fear-driven, authoritarian orientation. When exchange is suppressed, very little grows. A more moderate score of 2.0 to 3.0 might describe a culture in which leaders "listen" and take ideas under advisement, but proceed as previously planned. Or leadership may generate ideas with no input from below and few feedback mechanisms, but that are nonetheless reasonably acceptable to employees.

Coordinate Pair 2: Anomalies

A high score on V-2 (ideas) with a low score on H-2 (exchange) produces good ideas with little to show. Employees become frustrated because the atmosphere is *too* heady. Even with plenty of intellectual inspiration, the organization lacks the formal structure or business model to capture and direct ideas in a purposeful, profitable manner. The company squanders its intellectual capital and the business side rarely benefits from the creative end. Upper level managers' ideas are likely implemented with little feedback from customers or those involved with production, while the ideas of lower level employees are rarely enacted.

A high H-2 score accompanied by a low V-2 indicates a group too quick to act on ideas, rarely testing them before leaping into action. People become excited about the wrong ideas, and managers are in love with the idea of being idea people, with little notion of what that entails. Too much exchange over too few ideas leads to ill-considered actions, the sort of dynamic where people can convince themselves of anything if they talk about it long enough. See Figure 16-3 for descriptions of the exchange/ideas dimension as manifested in each of the four quadrants.

Axis (Vertical) V-3: Perception

At the upper end of the scale, organizations actively promote innovative thinking and self-reflection. Nothing is sacred and whole-mind thinking is simply a part of doing business. Staff members are constantly encouraged to find new ways to solve problems, think about goals and procedures, and expand themselves as human beings. This organization will likely have a strong research component. Training uses movement, visually complex materials, visualization, and other creativity techniques. At the low end, business proceeds as usual, with individual initiative constricted in the name of tried and true company or industry procedures. Creativity is not valued, while planning and strategy reflect a pedestrian view of the business environment.

Axis (Horizontal) H-3: Learning

A high score on H-3 shows that the organization values continuous learning and promotes employees' efforts to that end. No field of knowledge is considered irrelevant to organizational goals. We would likely find a free-wheeling, egalitarian atmosphere in which organizational development, operations, strategy, and projects are directly influenced by insight into the

Figure 16-3. Characteristics of dimension II in each of the four quadrants.

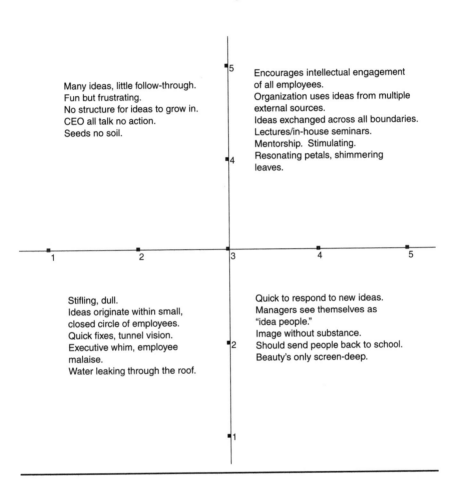

II. Ideas/Exchange Dimension

Many ideas, little follow-through.
Fun but frustrating.
No structure for ideas to grow in.
CEO all talk no action.
Seeds no soil.

Encourages intellectual engagement
of all employees.
Organization uses ideas from multiple
external sources.
Ideas exchanged across all boundaries.
Lectures/in-house seminars.
Mentorship. Stimulating.
Resonating petals, shimmering
leaves.

Stifling, dull.
Ideas originate within small,
closed circle of employees.
Quick fixes, tunnel vision.
Executive whim, employee
malaise.
Water leaking through the roof.

Quick to respond to new ideas.
Managers see themselves as
"idea people."
Image without substance.
Should send people back to school.
Beauty's only screen-deep.

cultures of the company, industry, and outside world. Support is forthcoming for employee sabbaticals, expansion of cultural horizons, and activities such as yoga or Outward Bound courses. Acquiring knowledge in and of itself benefits employees' careers.

At the low end of H-3, companies only pay or grant release time for task-based learning. Training sessions focus narrowly on people's immediate jobs. There is little incentive to question norms, and few self-correcting mechanisms built into organizational behavior. Communication is top-down because leadership doesn't believe it has much to learn from those below. There is probably a high turnover rate as bright and ambitious employees despair of ever acquiring the skills or recognition needed to advance their careers.

Coordinate Pair 3: Anomalies

A high score on V-3 (perception) accompanied by a low score on H-3 (learning) reveals a split between the thrill of challenging basic assumptions and an ability to conduct the challenge effectively. There is little relation between the goals of anointed visionaries on the one hand, and corporate learning policies, the realities of line workers' jobs, or dilemmas faced by lower and middle management, on the other. The opposite, high on H-3 and low on V-3, means the company is quick to buy consulting or training programs without considering how to internalize the resulting experience. Leadership looks to the quick-hit seminar when the company really needs in-depth work. Training that doesn't push the learning experience into challenging areas leads to the outlook one training director once expressed to me: "I don't care what they learn, I just want them to get together and meet people from other departments and have some fun." That is a worthy goal, but it does confuse sociability with learning and hence short-changes both. See Figure 16-4 for descriptions of the perception/learning dimension as manifested in each of the four quadrants.

Axis (Vertical) V-4: Social

The top of the scale implies an open, egalitarian workplace in which teamwork is based on amicability and mutual trust, and in which neither hierarchical nor functional boundaries inhibit cooperation or are used for the purposes of intimidation. Frequent social events build rapport among group members. Leadership establishes rituals to bring people together. The organization produces outstanding leaders whenever necessary, and the culture is enriched by a common language of precision and subtlety. Lower scores indicate a hierarchically dominated culture of isolation in which people fear for their jobs if they speak out, and in which ideas travel from top down, if they travel at all. Somewhat farther up the scale, around a score of 3, we find an amiable place in which people talk about sports or the kids in a superficial way, but in which the sociability does not transmit energy into the business operations.

Figure 16-4. Characteristics of dimension III in each of the four quadrants.

III. Perception/Learning Dimension

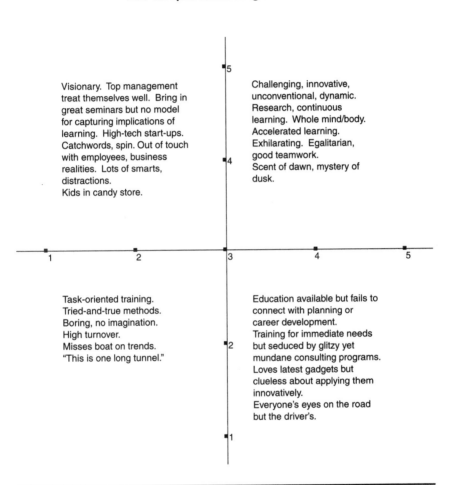

Visionary. Top management treat themselves well. Bring in great seminars but no model for capturing implications of learning. High-tech start-ups. Catchwords, spin. Out of touch with employees, business realities. Lots of smarts, distractions.
Kids in candy store.

Challenging, innovative, unconventional, dynamic. Research, continuous learning. Whole mind/body. Accelerated learning. Exhilarating. Egalitarian, good teamwork.
Scent of dawn, mystery of dusk.

Task-oriented training. Tried-and-true methods. Boring, no imagination. High turnover. Misses boat on trends. "This is one long tunnel."

Education available but fails to connect with planning or career development. Training for immediate needs but seduced by glitzy yet mundane consulting programs. Loves latest gadgets but clueless about applying them innovatively.
Everyone's eyes on the road but the driver's.

Axis (Horizontal) H-4: Play

A high score indicates a creative atmosphere in which play, whimsy, and imagination are vital to generating and implementing ideas. Social events stretch organizational perceptions of cultural norms. For instance, a party can employ, in an off-beat or challenging way, visual or verbal themes that play an important role in the culture. Retreats are particularly creative and the planning of these events is participatory. Because serious playfulness encourages unexpected links between ideas, many innovations come into being as surprises resulting from tinkering, doodling, or mucking about. As baseball innovator Branch Rickey used to say, "Luck is the residue of design." Hence the cultural design of a hothouse produces frequent "lucky" hits, or surprises. In fact, the laws of probability complement luck, because surprises can be anticipated: The more often that an organization builds creativity into its fundamental processes, the more likely it is to produce successful "surprises."

A low score reveals an organization in which everyone takes themselves too seriously, and in which creativity is viewed as a so-called soft skill. This might be the realm of the Type A manager focused solely on work. Or it could be a hard-working, successful company in which burnout flourishes and creativity is the purview of individuals or small groups. However successful, it will lose the benefits of many employees' insights and energy. Farther up the scale, around 3, the company picnic or executive golf outing prevails as the dominant expression of play.

Coordinate Pair 4: Anomalies

A high score on V-4 (social) and a low score on H-4 (play) points to a pleasant social environment with largely unimaginative celebrations, and where the line between socializing and work is clearly drawn. Socialization tends to be stratified, with lower degrees of formality among peers and a higher degree among those at different levels. The hothouse factors relating to beauty, time, and vocabulary play little or no role in the culture. A company with a high score on H-4 and low score on V-4 eschews formal social occasions but nonetheless encourages independence and creativity in its employees. The problem lies in failing to transmit creative techniques and establish an enduring commitment to creativity, and a tendency for creativity to be somewhat unfocused, since there is a degree of social isolation or fragmentation. This company may possess creative talent but have little direction from leadership and weak organizational cohesion. See Figure 16-5 for descriptions of the social/play dimension as manifested in each of the four quadrants.

CALCULATING THE RESULTS

Each of the four points is mapped onto a single graph. The points may be color-coded or numbered one to four. Once plotted, they are linked by

Figure 16-5. Characteristics of dimension IV in each of the four quadrants.

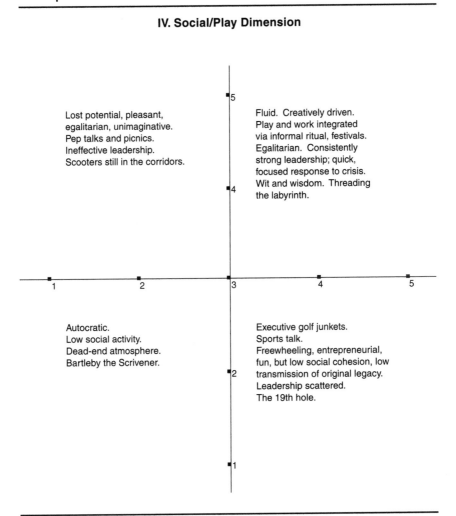

IV. Social/Play Dimension

Lost potential, pleasant, egalitarian, unimaginative. Pep talks and picnics. Ineffective leadership. Scooters still in the corridors.

Fluid. Creatively driven. Play and work integrated via informal ritual, festivals. Egalitarian. Consistently strong leadership; quick, focused response to crisis. Wit and wisdom. Threading the labyrinth.

Autocratic. Low social activity. Dead-end atmosphere. Bartleby the Scrivener.

Executive golf junkets. Sports talk. Freewheeling, entrepreneurial, fun, but low social cohesion, low transmission of original legacy. Leadership scattered. The 19th hole.

straight lines. One of the following shapes will result: a quadrilateral, a concave quadrilateral, a triangle, a straight line, or a point (see Figure 16-6). The first two shapes occur when all four points have different coordinates, and the triangle when any two points are mapped onto the same coordinates. A straight line results when either three points share a coordinate pair, or two points share one coordinate and two points another. The entire graph devolves to a single point if all four coordinate pairs are identi-

Figure 16-6. Possible shapes of dimension IV in each of the four quadrants.

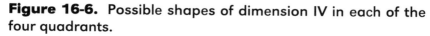

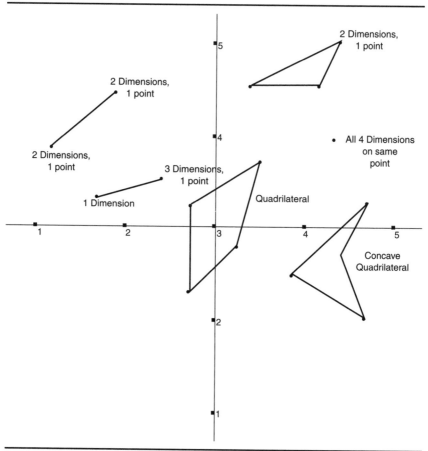

cal. Interpretation is based on (1) the shape's placement in relation to the four quadrants, (2) the position of individual points, and (3) responses to specific questions. A graph clustered around the center, but lying mostly in Quadrants II and III, will be interpreted largely in terms of the qualities belonging to those two quadrants. Graphs represented by a line or point are interpreted essentially the same as triangles or quadrilaterals. If all four points are plotted at (2.8, 2.6) in Quadrant III, that single point becomes heavily weighted. Yet, because each dimension's characteristics at (2.8, 2.6) has its own story, each point is interpreted differently. In a triangle- or line-shaped graph, the impact of a point with two or three identical coordinates won't be reflected in the graph's shape; we can only tell which coordinates have two or three points if indicated by some notation. The position of points indicates the role of each dimension in the organization. If values/mission is solidly in Quadrant III and perception/learning in Quadrant IV, the difference itself highlights a disjunction of group energies.

CHAI-T is not intended as a prescriptive template for change. It is the lens, not the picture. The initial interpretation can be valuable in identifying group tendencies, but is probably more valuable as a springboard for more precise assessment and discussion of relationships among the four dimensions and four quadrants. One can also focus on low-scoring responses. Which low-scoring areas can be addressed most quickly and effectively, and which would shift the graph closer to Quadrant I, the most creative area? Differences in responses across departments or a split in perspective between managers and other employees can also be revealing.

CHAI-T also provides points of contact between the graph and workplace situations and conditions. Why in *this* organization does the social/play dimension lie in Quadrant II, with a high score on the play and a low score on the social coordinates? What is the impact in real terms? What response does this data call for from specific individuals, specific managers? Interpretations need to be handled cautiously; they should not be used to assign blame. They profile a general set of circumstances that other modes of evaluation cannot capture, and lack of creativity in a given group can be due to circumstances prior to any given employee's tenure. This is a constructive and dynamic process, with a focus on how to energize the group, whether the initial conditions for creativity are favorable or dismal.

THE FOUR ZONES

The extreme score for each quadrant lies in the quadrant's outer quarter. Each of these four regions represents the purest expression of that quadrant's character, influenced least by the other three quadrants. These are the four zones (see Figure 16-7).

The Hot Zone

The Hot Zone, in Quadrant I, is defined by a score of 4 or above on both axes (4, 4)—that is, the far upper right of the chart. This is the dwelling place of the hothouse effect, whose outstanding qualities result from a strongly defined orientation toward creative, innovative work. If one point, or pair of coordinates, is situated in this area, the organization is

Figure 16-7. The four zones.

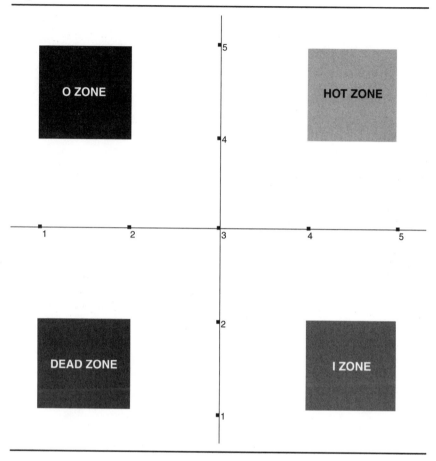

highly creative in that dimension. If most of the graph is in the Hot Zone, the organization or group is likely to be a hothouse.

The I Zone

The I Zone, in Quadrant II, is defined by coordinates (2, 4) and beyond, the far lower right of the chart. It is called the I Zone because it exemplifies the hard-driving, individualistic orientation of a high-achieving organization, but one limited by inattention to the internal qualities defined by the vertical axis. Success here is likely to be cyclical, and planning short- or medium-term at best.

The Dead Zone

The Dead Zone, in Quadrant III, is found at (2, 2) and below, or the extreme lower left. This is a quagmire marked by low motivation and low creativity. If it is profitable, it is due to a market position established long ago or by lucky accident. It is susceptible to competition, high employee turnover, cynical practices such as plant-milking, and so forth.

The O Zone

The O Zone, in Quadrant IV, is found at (4, 2) and beyond, in the far upper left. It is the realm of the abstract, idealistic, and inept. Organizations in the O Zone often believe they accomplish much more than they do, and tend to have an inflated self-image. They survive by lower-level people performing heroically to keep the basic business on track.

SAMPLE INTERPRETATION

The chart in Figure 16-8 is based on six responses from a high-tech electronics company in the Boston area. The surveys were distributed and interpreted to demonstrate the utility of CHAI-T in providing a framework and a vocabulary for analyzing the role creativity plays within an organization, and the steps one might take to enhance that role. The graph falls entirely in Quadrant III, although sufficiently far away from the Dead Zone and close to the center to imply that the problem is due to a stagnant approach to creativity rather than mismanagement. The values/mission dimension at (3.0, 2.7) indicates an essentially fair environment without a broader social mission. A closer look at the individual surveys shows that employees see any social impact coming from the importance of the product rather than from the company's relationship with the outside community.

The ideas/exchange dimension at (2.6, 2.6) describes a task- and product-oriented approach to generating new ideas. There is, however, a fair amount of disagreement in regard to this area, and while no one considered the company a hothouse, it is clear some people see their jobs as fairly creative. This probably demonstrates a split between employees, most likely based on job function, a circumstance that would contribute to the creative lag because of the failure to engage a good portion of the employees. However, even employees who rated the company positively consider it only moderately creative.

Figure 16-8. Sample chart interpretation.

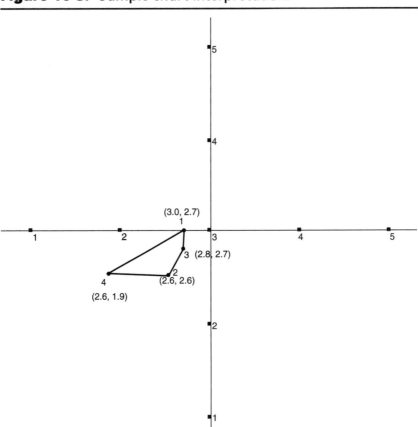

The perception/learning dimension scores close to the center (2.8, 2.7). Many of the statements receive solid scores on individual surveys. The overall score is pulled down by several questions on which only a very creative organization would score well. These statements pose a challenge to reasonably creative organizations that nevertheless are not hothouses. Thus, this coordinate pair indicates a solid professional effort at promoting discussion and insight into how the company is perceived, and good learning initiatives. However, there is likely little challenge to tried-and-true ways of perceiving the work or the industry, and learning is probably task-based albeit useful.

The social/play dimension scores weakest, which seems to affect the entire organization. Or it may be symptomatic of what is *not* happening in the other areas. In either case, the score of (2.6, 1.9) points to a culture most likely split according to position, and with little *esprit de corps*. There is no indication people are at each other's throats, but the social realm probably drains employees' energies rather than sustains them.

I would assess this company to be reasonably successful and well-managed, its strengths being its ability to fulfill contracts in a professional manner. It is less likely to provide innovative solutions in its field. It will do well because of its professionalism and position in a strong industry. It will not fulfill its potential, however, and in rough times may not have the internal resources to avoid taking a major hit. But an important reminder: CHAI-T addresses *creativity*, which is tied to long-term success. As stated before, good, solid companies with a lot of professional integrity and a record of continuing success need not be particularly creative. And many companies are content to remain that way. The problems lie on either side of the spectrum. It is difficult to become a *great* company without a high level of creativity, and it is difficult to withstand crisis—whether within the company or the economy—without significant creative resources. Another problem is that an organization's performance can stay solidly in the black while the entire spectrum of industry activity shifts; suddenly, one's products are obsolete. In other words, do what you've always done in this environment and the world is certain to pass you by.

Noteworthy Responses to Specific Statements

Statement #26, referring to the benefits of continuous learning to one's career, scored by far the highest responses, garnering three 5s, two 4s on surveys that were fairly negative about the company, and one 2. No other statement scored as many 5s or five of six positive responses. The good news is that the company strives to enhance employee knowledge. The bad news, however, is that this response alone boosted the third dimension's score. There seems little indication of follow-through with the learning that does take place or its connection to creativity. Statement #21 also scored well, because most people felt free to address the performance of both leadership and the company. So again, we find solid indications of a willingness to address important issues, but a lack of sustained support for these efforts. There seems to be little context in which learning or corporate critiques are part of an ongoing process of development, and this chills the creative impulse.

A score of 1 was achieved most frequently by Statement #29, with Statements #37 to #39 of the social/play dimension also scoring poorly.

The latter, along with low scores in the dimension's other responses, point to significant discontent within the company. Statement #29 does not indicate major problems, but it is one of the hothouse markers: If the company scores high on Statements #26 to #28 and #30, and low on #29, it is less likely to be a hothouse. In this case, the weak showing of Statement #29 is counterbalanced by the strong showing of Statement #26, which also addresses learning.

Future Considerations

Two employees were much more positive about the company than the others; different stakeholders view the company very differently. The sampling represented about 20 percent of the staff and yet provided an accurate picture of the company's culture. The main point, however, is not how accurate CHAI-T proves to be. Rather, CHAI-T is an early step in rethinking the role creativity plays within a company. What can be done to improve the social/play dimension? Would offering activities related to Statement #29 help? How can the learning function, already a modest strength, be bolstered to enhance the company's intellectual capital? What lies behind the striking disparity in motivation and job satisfaction uncovered by the variations in individual responses? All four dimensions scored close to one another; not only were they in the same quadrant, but in a small area of that quadrant fairly close to the center. In this case, it is a positive because it indicates an across-the-board consistency that we would expect in a fundamentally well-run company solidly in the black. But again, this company's long-term position is not secure because of a lack of the creativity needed to drive growth or cushion the company against unexpected downturns.

17

THE HOTHOUSE CHALLENGE!

The following quiz is a chance to create your own hothouse effect by responding to twenty-one different situations, some of which have more than one best answer. There are not any wrong answers. (I know you've heard that before but, really, who's keeping score?)

1. In a job interview, a vice president tells you that the company is values-driven. Which of the following statements that he makes to prove his point would best indicate a company likely to generate the hothouse effect?

    a. "Our founder has very clear ideas about the type of person he wants working for him and that's the type of person we're looking for."

    b. "We want 'people who like people' because ultimately, management is about sensitivity to the needs of your coworkers."

    c. "We want problem solvers, people who have a passion for finding solutions."

    d. "The people who succeed here value success and their value system is geared toward achieving it."

Discussion: While problem solving is not identical to creativity, a company looking for self-starters *(c)* will likely give people the go-ahead to develop their own creative solutions. And while problem solving is not actually a value, the belief in employees' abilities to enact their own solutions certainly reflects respect and trust. A view of management as being people-centered *(b)* is helpful but doesn't speak as directly to creativity as *(c)* and, taken too far, would lead into the O Zone. The emphasis on the leader's dominance *(a) could* indicate anything but possibly a conformist culture that could bury one in the Dead Zone. And while success *(d)* is a worthy aim, the concept alone does not tell us what the company considers success to be or how it is to be achieved, thus denoting a culture racing its wheels around the I Zone.

2. You've been given the job of retooling your organization to generate the hothouse effect. Every employee is to be involved. Which of the following would be an effective first step?

   a. Hang posters in public areas that reinforce messages about creativity and teamwork.

   b. Begin weekly discussions with managers at the same level of responsibility as one another on topics related to creativity in the workplace.

   c. Have a creativity trainer offer half-day workshops to whoever wants to take them.

   d. Take the entire workforce on a guided tour of a nearby historical area.

Discussion: All responses would contribute to the project, but I would recommend *(b)*, even though the discussions may not seem inclusive. However, it is important to start small and create a group of like-minded stakeholders who support the initiative. Posters *(a)* work best when enthusiasm for the initiative already runs high. Creativity training *(c)* is a wonderful tool but without a strong supporting context, the learning tends to remain highly localized among those who took the course. A cultural event *(d)* that brings employees into the community is a terrific idea, but also works best once you have established an organizational context.

3. In a restaurant, you overhear four friends arguing over whose company has the most beneficial impact on society. Which argument seems most compelling to you?

   a. "Without us, there'd be no plumbing. We make the pipes, the valves, the drains. What's a society without a safe and adequate water supply?"

b. "We donate a generous portion of our net income to numerous community charities."

c. "We have 'service days' in which we go out into the neighborhood and perform helpful tasks for the residents of our community."

d. "Everyone at our company is imbued with the idea that whatever they do, they should consider the most far-reaching impact they can have."

Discussion: I vote for *(d)*. The first suggestion *(a)* makes a good point but does not distinguish *that particular manufacturer* from all other plumbing companies. Community giving and service are fine *(b, c)*, but ultimately, they are add-ons to the actual organizational culture. The mind-set described in *(d)* reflects the hothouse theme of always seeking a creative dimension and more universal impact for one's work.

4. Which of the following do you think is the most damaging preconception about creativity in the workplace?

a. It's one of the flavors of the month that management keeps coming up with.

b. It's basically a soft skill that doesn't have a real impact on the bottom line.

c. Only naturally creative people benefit from attempts to inspire creativity at work.

d. "I'll know they're serious about creativity when they pay us for being more creative."

Discussion: This one is up to you, based on your experience. The flavor-of-the-month syndrome *(a)* is a response to the way initiatives are managed in a company; it doesn't really say anything about the core learning behind the initiative. Rather than arguing against that attitude, let the creative activities speak for themselves. Creativity gave us art, science, government, love, computers, and ice cream, so how soft *(b)* could it be? Boundaries are dissolving throughout the business and economic environment, and creativity is increasingly necessary for survival. The idea that only some people can be creative *(c)* is perhaps most damaging because of its inhibiting effect on creative potential. Only some people can be *highly creative* by definition: whatever the norm, some "creatives" will always stand out, whether it's Leonardo da Vinci in Florence or the first cave person to think, "Hey, food tastes better after sitting in those flames awhile." The problem of compensation *(d)* is not a preconception but a tough truth about creativity: What happens when everyone is being so creative and taking on new responsibilities? You have to find a way to compensate them or else (1) they leave or (2) they turn off and performance declines.

5. Would you rather spend your creative time in a:
   a. Research lab?
   b. Urban café?
   c. Labyrinthine library?
   d. Artist's studio?

If your answer is "all of the above," congratulations, you are a Renaissance woman or man in the spirit of Leonardo. But that's not really the question. This is: What would be the best way to introduce the equivalent of such hotbeds of inquiry as labs, cafés, libraries, and studios into your organization?

   a. Set aside a conference room that anyone can use, equipped with white board, CD player, and multicolored lighting.
   b. Hold salons once a month in which people gather to discuss ideas that excite them.
   c. Establish weekly lunchtime seminars in which outside experts share their research and employees discuss its relevance to their own work.
   d. Create online discussion threads where employees can discuss different company issues and where ideas can be archived.

Discussion: The answer of "all of the above" still works. The conference room outfitted for creativity *(a)* is a great resource but the organization must integrate its use into everyday work life. Salons *(b)* can stimulate on-the-job creativity and raise morale. The weekly seminars *(c)* have the same effect and more directly impact the work-related knowledge base than do salons. Online discussion threads *(d)* stimulate the circulation of ideas and provide contributors more time to think about their responses. This technique requires some investment in time and money, but it is a great source of collaboratively developed insights. Using "all of the above" would stimulate the production of ideas and the establishment of productive links between participating employees.

6. Two midlevel managers with different types of responsibilities are not getting along. One tends to focus on getting all the right paperwork done and following procedure, which is critical to her ability to keep track of the many administrative threads she coordinates. Her colleague is more focused on delivering the goods, which makes him an exceptional asset to customers and the organization. But their duties overlap in important areas and the contrast of styles has turned into a clash of personalities. How can you creatively resolve this situation?

   a. Review with both employees together the cycle of tasks belonging to each and identify the exact points of conflict. Reiterate why these flash points are important to each manager and develop procedures to clarify responsibilities and procedures. Keep the focus on getting the work done in an effective, time-sensible manner.

   b. Put them in a conference room, tell them to work it out within thirty minutes, and leave. If they haven't gotten it resolved by then, tell them that if there are any more sparks, it'll be nothing like the sparks that will fly at their performance reviews.

   c. Speak with them separately and assure them you value their work and ask how you can help. Validate both positions and try to come up with a solution that meets both their needs.

   d. Call a meeting of your entire staff and tell them the current process is not working. Ask for volunteers for a committee that will develop a solution.

Discussion: It may be tempting to tell them to just fix it *(b)*, but the next time the pot boils, it will explode—*conflict exacerbation* rather than *resolution* on this one. Choice *(c)* does not really confront the issues and you allow the two contending parties to define the terms of engagement. And you don't want to bring everyone into the conflict *(d)*. The best choice *(a)* establishes a clear procedure for getting to the bottom of the conflict, defuses personal entanglements, and focuses on establishing a viable and potentially creative solution. Of course, if the two employees just hate each other, move the one you judge to be most invested in the personal conflict; by that point, the situation is on a destructive downward spiral.

7. In meetings, one of your employees contributes particularly thoughtful comments that challenge the common wisdom. Your best policy toward this person should be:

   a. Encourage her to drop in on you anytime she has one of her golden ideas.

   b. The next time she has such an idea, ask her to discuss it, and if you think it worthwhile, tell her to write you a memo stating how to put the idea to practical use.

   c. Get a better sense of the full range of her thinking, and give her more responsibility.

   d. Take her next great idea and present it to *your* boss as your own.

Discussion: Okay, let's drop (*d*) right away, although it probably happens as often as any of the others. Encouraging her to follow up on an idea makes a lot of sense, and in that regard, (*b*) offers more focus than (*a*). Choice (*c*) establishes a mentoring relationship with her, which is an excellent idea, but (*b*) allows you to evaluate her skills more carefully and should precede (*c*).

8. "Ideas matter" is the slogan for the new companywide initiative and *you* have to make that slogan real to the employees in your division. Which of the following should you do?

   a. Start your own "What's the big idea?" campaign, encouraging everyone to come up with at least one big idea per week for submission into a suggestion box.

   b. Divide your employees into groups that meet for one lunch hour per week to discuss such issues as "Getting the most out of our technology" and "Developing an ethical code."

   c. Hand out a short but noteworthy article to each person to read within a week. Set up groups to derive ideas from the articles and quietly implement several of the ideas, and then point out that the suggestions came out of the group's response to the article.

   d. Have everyone brainstorm why ideas *don't* matter. Use the tension implicit in this contrarian approach to develop interesting, off-beat strategies for the campaign.

Discussion: It doesn't pay to substitute your own campaign for the company's *(a)* and the suggestion box never inspires creativity. Seminars targeting company issues *(b)* are less effective in the early stages of a cultural shift; better to use seminars to increase knowledge and refine employee methodologies. The article *(c)* is tricky. Will it be perceived as "homework" or a not-so-subtle attempt to deliver a message? This works best when people actively ask for more ideas and perspectives. The last choice *(d)* directly addresses the company's theme in a way that is at once creative and somewhat ironic. This contrarian approach is a classic creativity technique: One follows a solution path that flies in the face of common wisdom. The irony helps disarm, in an intelligent and respectful way, the inevitable skepticism that many employees feel when asked to rally behind a new campaign. Focusing on why ideas *don't* matter also challenges the theme that ideas *do* matter. If the discussion wards off this challenge, it validates the original theme and, if the theme cannot survive the challenge, you've uncovered its weaknesses. Thus *(d)* may produce the most creative sparks, but *(b)* and *(c)* also have merit.

9. As the president of a manufacturing company, you hope to keep your factories from moving overseas, but competitive pressures are so intense you think you may have to close up shop. If you could only figure out an alternative solution, you would gladly remain in the communities that have given so much to the company. Your best approach would be to:

   a. Establish clear benchmarks that must be met to keep the factories open. Galvanize the entire workforce and community to develop ways to achieve these goals. Publicly rule out downsizing as a possible solution.

   b. Hire a leading consulting firm to help you cut costs.

   c. Halve your own salary and propose salary cutbacks to all employees.

   d. Offer a generous severance package to anyone who wants to retire early, thereby cutting expenses and forcing people to work "smarter" as well as harder.

Discussion: The most ethical choice *(a)* may not always seem the best business decision. Choosing between going broke or heading for the land of fifty-cents-an-hour workers raises serious ethical dilemmas. But often, if we commit to the most ethical course, we force ourselves to develop outstanding creative solutions. Establishing clear criteria in areas such as savings, productivity, and sales offers people clear goals on which to focus.

Ruling out downsizing, while risky, also rules out the quick and easy solution. Hiring consultants *(b)* puts you at the mercy of *their* preconceptions, imposing salary cuts *(c)* has you playing catch-up in a race against sweatshop salaries that you can never win, and early retirement packages *(d)* do the same and guarantee loss of valuable employees just when you need them most.

10. Your goal is to enrich your company's internal educational network to take full advantage of in-house expertise. Which one of these is *not* a good way to proceed?
    a. Create an internal mentorship program wherein all new employees are assigned mentors who stay with them throughout their employ.
    b. Identify the best practices of the company's top performers and use them as the basis for a staff-wide training program.
    c. Establish mutual mentoring relationships between employees with similar levels of responsibility but from different departments.
    d. Publicize the most intelligent actions taken by employees in the past month.

Discussion: The first three choices reflect methods that have been discussed previously. Casey Powell implemented mentorship programs *(a)*, while Cerebyte exemplifies a sophisticated approach to transmitting best practices via training *(b)*. Mutual mentoring *(c)* between people of approximately equal position is a highly effective way for practitioners to exchange and develop ideas and troubleshoot difficult situations. It is fine to acknowledge employees who perform well *(d),* but spotlighting people for so-called intelligence implies everyone else isn't quite that smart and fails to enhance or sustain creativity, so *(d)* is the one *not* to use.

11. You realize that your organization needs a more sophisticated business intelligence system than it currently uses. You want the system to stimulate creativity and analytic thinking, not just provide data. You review four programs and will select the one that has the most useful of the four qualities below, each one unique to a different program.
    a. "Crystal Gazer" offers weekly updated industry data and customized interpretations, based on its 1,024 evaluative criteria developed by leading economists.

b. "Bird Watcher" presents data from a variety of perspectives. Users can compare the company's performance to industry standards, preselect the data most relevant to their position in the company, and establish projections based on several different business models.

c. "Star Sighter" places all the data within a five-stage cycle of "seeding, birthing, blooming, ripening, and harvesting" that opens users' consciousnesses to the underlying energies governing their business strategies.

d. "Number Cruncher" lets users break down every entry into as many as twelve subsets, thus providing the most in-depth look at operations available today.

Discussion: And the winner is Bird Watcher *(b)*! Good business intelligence stimulates the mind and teaches it to process information in a fluid, proactive, analytic way. Bird Watcher's features are the most likely to achieve that. No program can offer customized quality interpretation *(a)* because tasks of such complexity require a specialist's full attention and they are not offering that. Star Sighter's scheme *(c)* may provide insights during a weekend retreat, but it is highly subjective and imposes the same interpretive mold onto widely divergent situations. Number Cruncher's data-proliferating *(d)* approach can be very helpful, but it provides the fuel rather than the engine for business intelligence.

12. Once Bird Watcher is installed, your CEO decides that it's time to look at whether the company is fully utilizing the available technology. "Maybe we've got built-in capacity we never utilize, as if our technology is a Ferrari that we only use to drive to market once a week. Maybe we're not doing the best we can because of inadequate technology, like running the Daytona 500 in an old station wagon." You appreciate his metaphor and think he's right. Which of the following would you suggest?

a. Upgrade all computer systems immediately to give the company the flexibility to implement whatever is necessary.

b. Ask each employee to develop a wish list of the technology that allows them to do their work as effectively as possible.

c. List every task currently done by computer and revamp the system to root out inefficiencies and redundancies.

    d. Have select work groups review (1) the chief outcomes they are responsible for, (2) how technology contributes to each outcome, and (3) how to enhance the outcomes and the procedures that generate them. Bring in a technical specialist to help groups figure out what adjustments to make to their systems to achieve these enhanced outcomes and procedures. If this pilot program works, gradually expand the program throughout the company.

Discussion: Sweeping changes in technology *(a)* are often ill-considered and impulsive and hence risk disaster. Note that your CEO is not responding to a crisis, but seeking to raise the general performance level to transcend the status quo. No one knows whether the technology is being used optimally, so a wish list *(b)* is an expensive way of leaving the same question unanswered. The four-step plan outlined in *(d)* addresses the same questions as *(c)* but more comprehensively and creatively. The review of job outcomes should be conducted in a way that is nonthreatening to employees. The second step *(d)* seeks clarity in how technology contributes to outcomes. Considering that many economists believe computers did not significantly raise productivity in the United States until the 1990s, such reviews should be far more common than they are. The second step reveals lines of demarcation between human and machine, while the third asks employees to visualize the best possible outcomes for their jobs. A good tech consultant can be invaluable and an informed group of employees will get the most out of the consultation. Primary focus is not on the technology but on outcomes, and the gradualism of the program reflects a low-risk approach to achieving high returns.

    13. Which of the following considerations will be least important when integrating creativity training techniques into the workplace?

        a. Employees will feel embarrassed about actually *doing* some of the activities, such as visualization, movement exercises, or even random word exercises.

        b. Managers will be reluctant to allow their staff the time to "sit for ideas" or pursue an unconventional activity that purportedly enhances creativity.

        c. Underneath it all, many people don't really believe that these methods lead to any practical insights or solutions.

d. Creativity by its very nature encourages independence and initiative, which may generate conflict as employees realize they're making decisions formerly reserved for their managers.

e. Some people will use creativity techniques to waste time. "Don't bother me, I'm visualizing!"

f. As people become more creative and effective at their jobs, turnover will increase because they'll be able to find better jobs that reflect their new skills and responsibilities.

g. If we encourage people to meet across departments and job levels, chaos will ensue.

Discussion: Any organization afraid of education because people might leave for better jobs *(f)* is headed for the Dead Zone. Learning can only improve a company's performance, even if it incurs costs in terms of tuitions, fees, and raises. Turnover is more likely to occur in a stultifying, dead-end situation than a dynamic one in which people can develop career skills. Yet *(f) is* in fact an attitude one often confronts in corporations, and while it *should* be least important, it might in fact be very important to disabuse management of this misconception.

The other responses all deserve serious attention. Embarrassment *(a),* reluctance to give up work time *(b),* and a fundamental disbelief that such techniques really work *(c)* are not trivial concerns. They go to the core of widely held feelings that, as we've mentioned, also affect very creative people. These can be alleviated by group leaders modeling the activities, by providing a strong rationale for why they work, and simply by forging ahead with having everyone experience them. Once staff learn such methods, however, it is important to provide additional training that helps people integrate such techniques in the fulfillment of their tasks.

The next three choices, *(d), (e),* and *(g),* address the fear that the hierarchy will be undermined by an effective creativity initiative. Such concerns should be taken seriously because they're accurate: The organization will change. Creativity may indeed mean that a manager supervises less and leads more. Creativity is *not* simply an elixir to cure "tired blood." It is one of life's elemental forces and releasing its power can trigger new social arrangements, which in organizations might well include rethinking the nature of management, job definitions, style of communication, and even compensation.

14. On the next divisional retreat, your vice president wants to celebrate thirty years of die and mold manufacturing. She asks you to

develop the two-day program to have the most powerful creative impact possible. Of the four following ideas, which will be most effective?

a. Display company highlights over the past thirty years and hand out employee appreciation awards. The staff also discusses "The Next 30 Years."

b. Bring in local experts from colleges and museums to demonstrate your industry's early technology. Include materials people can take home. Continue this work with in-house classes for which employees receive training or college credits. Examine the early technology in light of the company's future goals and strategies. Create a pilot group of interested employees who continue to learn about the past and attempt to apply their new knowledge to the workplace.

c. Arrange a "Design Fest" where all employees make models of machine molds out of clay and get to discuss the project with production people.

d. Organize a costume dance party for the evening portion of the retreat. Everyone must come dressed as a work-related piece of equipment or idea. Midway through the dance lead a performance in which everyone enacts a role. Don't be concerned about making a point—trust the experience to energize the retreat and resonate with everyone long after the retreat is over.

Discussion: Learning about the early assumptions, principles, and techniques in any field *(b)* powerfully informs creativity and strategic planning. The Design Fest *(c)* offers everyone a chance to immerse themselves in the company's core activity. It's fun and increases appreciation for the product that all work to support. Production people are notoriously underappreciated and this is a good way to acknowledge them. The performance *(d)* helps establish a creative and festive atmosphere, but is more likely to increase creative momentum than get the ball rolling. The celebration of the company *(a)* shifts the focus away from participants and provides a rather standard experience unlikely to inspire creativity.

15. Which would be least effective in promoting learning by osmosis?

a. Establish an online resource center that includes discussion threads, interactive skill-building programs, and links to Web sites about all aspects of your industry.

b. Set up workplace displays that highlight topics such as local history or general-interest subjects such as Broadway musicals, movies, rock and roll, great sports moments, hobbies or avocations of employees, and art exhibits related to employees' home countries or countries of ancestry.

c. Initiate conversation in the cafeteria, lounge, or even at meetings about hot business or industry topics. Ask people to find and share information about these topics.

d. Establish a dynamic library akin to that of the Rowland Institute and urge employees to utilize it both as a research resource and a place to concentrate and reflect.

Discussion: Try to avoid planting conversations *(c)* because if they don't happen naturally, they can't be forced on people. It's better to establish the activities that will naturally stimulate such conversations, and *(c)* would be the least effective method here. The Web *(a)* is a tremendous resource and the workforce—at all levels—needs to learn how to take advantage of the knowledge environment represented by the Web. The displays *(b)* create a stimulating atmosphere in which people can recharge their minds, a concern that Edwin Land addressed with the indoor garden at the Rowland Institute. The library *(d)* also hearkens back to Land and can enrich intellectual capital, provide a center for creative work, and dramatically reduce stress.

16. You truly believe that crisis keeps people on their toes but you can't simply manufacture a crisis and you don't want everyone in a hyperadrenalized state all the time. So you decide to:

a. Study history and business's best practices in responding to crisis and its aftermath. You realize you don't need to have a crisis to utilize those best practices. Once you establish benchmarks, you can model and promote these behaviors for use in a variety of circumstances.

b. You consistently allude to "the wolf at the door" when speaking with staff, and imply that if everyone doesn't produce more, serious downsizing will take place.

c. Cultivate an *esprit de corps* based on an us-against-the-world attitude. The new motto is "Play mean and play clean, but if you have to choose, make it mean."

d. Arrange crisis management seminars that deliver the message that successful crisis management is informed by more general business and management lessons.

Discussion: It is definitely worthwhile examining the long human experience in responding to crises *(a),* but it is equally important to prepare for real crises *(d),* since they always defy expectations and call upon unique qualities in each individual. "Us against the world" works in certain high-stress, highly focused situations such as a battle or sporting event, especially when one is the underdog. It can motivate but is an inadequate overall strategy for dealing with crisis. And hinting at oncoming disaster *(b)* is a sure-fire way to generate a real crisis—of confidence in leadership!

17. You are fascinated with the idea of using time for your own creative ends. On a personal level, you employ exercises that help you to achieve intense concentration, which makes time seem to slow down and improves your productivity. But getting folks at work to "harvest time" seems likely to result in your being shown the quickest route to the nearest exit. Still, one day you mull over ways to make it work. Which of the following do you think might do the job?

    a. Change all the clocks everyday. Have some run backward. Slow some down and speed others up. Tell people they are now operating on "creative time."

    b. Move to a flex-time schedule based on individual biorhythms so that each person gets the most out of his or her day.

    c. Do nothing. Manipulating time with reason or rhyme is so far beyond humankind that you're just asking for trouble, so never mind. You lose credibility and it won't work anyway.

    d. Bring someone in to teach a course in *alcheringa,* the Australian aborigine term for the "dream time." Establish a group to delve into dream work and apply the new skills to jobs and careers.

Discussion: Don't change the clocks *(a)* unless you are actually running an experiment with human subjects who have signed seventeen separate ethical oversight and nondisclosure release forms and you have trained medical personnel on the premises. Under those conditions, it could actually prove interesting. Biorhythm *(b)* is one way to manage our physiological energy. We are learning enough about brain and nutritional chemistry to sustain high levels of physical energy twenty-four hours a day, even while we sleep. Still, using these methods at work raises serious privacy issues. One might well wonder why we'd waste time experimenting with a dubious perception of time *(c)*. One answer is that that's the point: Time represents a central experience of our lives. Because it is a new frontier, time will attract the more adventurous and experimental among us. Dream work *(d)* provides time-tested methods of going deep into the core of one's perceptions where time is most susceptible to distortion. The people of many cultures harvested knowledge brought to them from that "other world," and this possibility brings us back to the truth about creativity: Its roots lie deep within our unconscious minds and our unconscious brings us back to cognitive modes that predate technology, urban and even settled life, and, indeed, human consciousness itself. The greatest creators are receptive to messages originating in the unconscious. Most of us, however, operate almost entirely in the conscious mind. Enhancing creativity on a broad scale requires a commitment to exploring the unconscious where time itself opens the door to new dimensions of creative technique and discovery. One would not want to turn an organization into a great big dream workshop, but it is possible to make these techniques available to those who want to pursue them in the interests of enhanced creativity.

18. The boss wants a new company logo as the centerpiece of an entirely new corporate image. Guess who is going to lead the way? You, of course! So what do you do?

   a. Go out and hire Brandon Iron, the guru of corporate insignia, who will lead focus groups, work up six preliminary design concepts, and provide in his words "a customized integrated design solution that fuses postmodernist noise theory with a hallowed tradition of endless billing cycles that utilize the most expensive hourly rates embedded in the market today or any day soon. Our motto is, 'If you start with a red circle, we'll give you an even better red circle.'"

   b. Fling paint onto a canvas and randomly select a square foot of canvas to shrink down in size, with the resulting design being your company's new logo. Spend ten minutes writing a rationale for why this array of splatters expresses perfectly the future of your company, the industry, and the entire *zeitgeist,* or "spirit of the age." With the money you save, next quarter's results will be so positive that *any* logo you choose will be accounted a great success.

   c. A parrot—a green and red parrot.

   d. Pull together art books, volumes of poetry, magazines, and in-
      dustry publications. Tell everyone to browse the materials and
      create collages, drawings, and designs for the logo and cam-
      paign. Gather all the ideas and tell your boss that a corporate
      image must be developed along with more general strategic ini-
      tiatives. Meanwhile, present your materials to a good design
      firm known for solid customer service and visual flair.

Discussion: The vocabulary—symbolic, visual, or verbal—that defines
the company should come from the employees, although only a skilled
design professional can really bring the final product to market *(d)*. And *(d)*
makes a good point to your boss. To plunk down money for a new company image without tying it to more long-term developmental strategies
restricts the creative energy applied to the project. Another reason to hire
the design firm *(d, not a)* is that beauty matters: It is persuasive, it triggers
endorphins in the viewer's brain and pheronomes in the body, and it creates
good will. Or you can just go with a parrot framed by a red circle.

   19. You've been invited to participate in a high-powered panel to
       discuss "The Future of Business Leadership: Where Will It Come
       From?" The following ideas are promulgated by various panel
       members. Which one did *you* suggest, with the hothouse effect in
       mind?

       a. Distinguished business schools ought to adopt a service model
          of leadership. Our best and brightest must understand their duty
          to behave ethically and improve society. This type of approach
          will also attract a high-quality person to the ranks of business
          leadership.

       b. Leave it to the market. The top dog will wind up at the head
          of the pack. Besides, leadership is based on innate qualities. You
          might be able to teach management, but you can't teach leader-
          ship—you either have it or you don't.

       c. Leadership reflects the qualities of its community. To ensure a
          steady supply of strong leaders, hire talented, proactive, inde-
          pendent practitioners who will not be threatened by capable,
          far-sighted, confident leadership. The quality of the employees
          regulates leadership, because a healthy community responds to
          outstanding leadership and refuses to tolerate mediocrity.

d. We need people who have been in the trenches and worked their way up by making the tough choices when it counted. They're good, they're tested, and we need to reward them when their time comes rather than importing some fancy MBA.

Discussion: The great Russian writer Leo Tolstoy understood leadership when he said, in effect, "A jockey is only as good as his horse." Leaders don't like to think themselves beholden to those below them, but they are. This doesn't diminish the importance of leadership one bit. The function of the leader, like that of the conscious mind, is limited but crucial. Leaders refine and direct organizational energy and creativity. They motivate but they also have the profound but passive function of becoming a symbol of organizational purpose, mission, and ethical compass. They don't need to provide all the big ideas—that's why they have so many smart, talented people working under them. However, they need to encourage and direct the flow of ideas, decide resource allocation, define overall objectives, and find the right people to make it happen. The leader cannot mold a group of people into something they're not, but he or she can shape a more perfect version of an already existing rough form. Nor should leaders delude themselves into thinking they have all the right answers. Great leaders are notorious for making awful decisions. Churchill made so many military errors that one would imagine England was lucky to survive. He did, however, do one thing very well: lead a beleaguered country by galvanizing the best impulses and greatest strengths of those he led. Thus *(c)* would be the best answer.

It would be nice if the best business schools cultivated a conscience in their graduates *(a)*, but I don't believe that the best leaders emerge from an elite environment because (1) those environments have their own skewed values and criteria for deciding who belongs there, (2) the very act of being preened for leadership from a relatively young age tends to produce outsized egos prone to self-delusion, and (3) I trust the wisdom of a dynamic population over the assessments of self-appointed guardians, even those who set themselves on the moral high road.

As for the leader of the pack *(b)*, successful human groups tend to value leaders who can coordinate collective action rather than dominate a pack of snarling individuals. It's a great idea to reward those who have proven their worth year after year *(d)*, but performance at any given level does not guarantee the ability to succeed at the next level up. Sometimes the prospect of rising through the ranks is just what a company needs, and sometimes it has a tunnel-vision effect. Generally, one's colleagues know best whether a leadership candidate will pass muster.

20. A group of venture capitalists visits your headquarters and in the ensuing discussion two of them express concern that the atmosphere seems too playful and frivolous. How will you ever develop a marketable product in this type of atmosphere? You reply:

a. Hey, we have investors lined up outside the door!

b. Visitors to Edison's labs expressed similar reservations over the number of practical jokes Edison and his men played on one another; one even opined that it was a mistake to call such jokes "practical" as they obviously diverted the men's attention from their work.[1] Then you can add that "Einstein attributed his scientific prowess to what he called a 'vague play' with 'signs,' 'images,' and other elements, both 'visual' and 'muscular.' 'This combinatory play,' Einstein wrote, 'seems to be the essential feature in productive thought.'"[2]

c. You explain that creativity is impossible without the freedom to combine ideas in unexpected ways and an environment that possesses the "unbearable lightness of being" is very stimulating.

d. You hang your head and admit they are right and promise to implement stricter control over your employees immediately, but because you don't want to embarrass your staff, you'll wait until the potential investors leave, I'm sure you understand.

Discussion: Now, now, no need to be so hostile *(a)*. Edison and Einstein *(b)* make a pretty good argument for the value of play, expressing two basic notions of creative play: the type that keeps people loose and brings them closer together (Edison's jokes) and the kind that refers to tinkering, doodling, "mucking about" in Edison's phrase, and just playing around with combinations of ideas, as Einstein and Edison both did. The Czech writer Milan Kundera's title for his most famous work, *The Unbearable Lightness of Being*, *(c)* is a beautiful expression of freedom that is the essence of play, and it would certainly reinforce Edison and Einstein's testimony. The leader's role is to run interference for his people, and if that means placating a perceived threat *(d)*, well, that's certainly one way to preserve a dynamic, open, and creative office. So *(b)*, *(c)*, and *(d)* all have merit.

21. You decide to jolt your organization with creative energy by bringing your employees into contact with an environment so rich

and multilayered that everyone will be inspired by it. But where do you find this type of meta-system? After all, you can't simply conjure up an entire civilization just to provide a challenging creative experience. What do you do?

a. Sponsor employee outings to fascinating but nearby places, such as local caves, nature reserves, industrial plants from other industries, or historical tours of local neighborhoods.

b. Fund employee excursions to various cultural events and sponsor discussions of their experiences during periodic lunchtime salons.

c. Offer lunchtime or Friday afternoon lectures in which visiting luminaries speak about the themes that animate their work, whether it is in an industry-related field or not. If employees are involved in college programs, try to arrange a course for credit or a seminar for CEUs that has a similar impact to that of the World Views course described earlier in Chapter 6.

d. Offer workshops in "scanning" and reading cultural cues. The former can utilize magazines and the World Wide Web, while the latter can include media literacy, qualitative marketing research techniques, and interesting views of popular culture. These types of programs can inspire ideas about product design, marketing, sales, and career development.

Discussion: No meta-systems are readily available to provide revelations to a large group of diverse individuals at reasonable cost. To provide contact with a meta-system, an organization can offer several experiences that engender a shift in worldview among employees. Each of our four choices contributes to a shift in emotional, intellectual, and cultural mind-sets, and together they can approximate the impact of a meta-system.

NOTES

1. Andre Millard, *Edison and the Business of Innovation* (Baltimore: Johns Hopkins University Press, 1990), pp. 32–33.

2. Win Wenger and Richard Poe, *The Einstein Factor* (Rocklin, CA: Prima Publishing, 1996), p. 13.

CONCLUSION

No one can claim to know whether a citizen of ancient Athens lived a better or more balanced life than anyone else in history, be it a member of Attila the Hun's army, a denizen of the rain forest living in Stone Age conditions, a young corporate climber worried over the scratch in his BMW, or an inhabitant of Corinth or Thebes, Athens's most bitter rivals. Indeed, a look at the intimate lives of Athenians would indicate that there were better ways to live one's life than as part of this oppressive, warlike slave state. On the other hand, the Greeks themselves stated, "There is no better place to be a free man than Athens (and no worse place to be a slave than Sparta)." As we've noted, oppressive, warlike slave states appear all across the historical landscape, but there was only one Athens. Doric-style Greek temples similar to the Parthenon also abounded in Greece and Italy, but none came close to the mathematical perfection, perceptual innovation, and sheer aesthetic triumph of Athens's shrine to its presiding deity.

Based on our evidence from the business world, it does appear that employees of highly creative companies find a great deal of job satisfaction that escapes many other people throughout their careers. And from what we have heard from Werner Heisenberg, Ernest Hemingway, Gertrude Stein, the Bauhaus practitioners, and a host of jazz musicians, it appears that being caught up in the excitement of the hothouse effect is a thrilling experience that produces memorable results.

Ultimately, we can only weigh the evidence, and history's verdict—that is, the sum of the judgments of millions of people, of experts, and even of contemporaries—is that communities with highly concentrated creative output seem endowed with a kind of grace or benevolent destiny that bestows upon their members a sense of pride, delight, and liberation.

By now, we have become familiar with the factors that generate the hothouse effect, and we have seen that whether an ancient city or a modern corporation, the factors are identical. Not only *can* the historical factors and techniques be translated into modern organizational terms, they actually *have* been, with great business success as well.

The historical communities show us what works. The thirty-six factors make a clear statement: This is what it takes to generate breakthrough results; this is how it's been done. As noted earlier, the hothouse effect does not claim to be the only template for success. Its focus is on *creativity,* or rather, an exceptional, sustained expression of creativity that results in a substantial record of practical innovation. Many organizations emphasize values, but the hothouse effect requires a profound belief in the ability of one's work to transform the world (even the universe), and to transfigure society's values. Organizations rightfully aspire to become learning companies, but the hothouse effect only takes off when idea development becomes central to group development, and when it pursues knowledge in part for its own sake, as illustrated by Edwin Land's notion that a good research firm must also pursue pure science. While communication is acknowledged as an important business skill, the hothouse always produces an integrated system-wide network exchange of ideas that in turn further fuels the hothouse effect.

Review of procedures with an eye toward streamlining operations and improving quality is standard business practice, but the hothouse effect goes well beyond that by challenging fundamental perceptions and assumptions, whether those shaping an industry, an artistic or scientific field, or human reality. An engagement with the meta-system and the proliferation of creative hubs, to name just two factors, challenge organizations to view their ongoing development in unorthodox and exciting ways. And factors in the social/play dimension, such as vocabulary, crisis, leadership, time, beauty, and play, identify categories of experience that lend themselves to bold organizational initiatives that drive a group beyond modest creative activity into the hothouse effect.

In historical communities, most of the creative impetus comes from a people's culture, while in the business world, the greater part derives from the vision and policies of the founder or CEO and his or her team. But as I've also observed over the years, numerous lower- and mid-level managers make concerted efforts to encourage their employees' creativity because they know the impact creativity has on the workplace and the bottom line. However, as Mike Jahnke's post-Sequent experience illustrates, these efforts only have a local impact within an organization unless they are supported by top leadership. Even with decentralization of many management functions, the dominant culture is determined by leadership. This is less true of historical communities, where cultural elements moving from the bottom to top are just as important, if not more so, as the influence of a ruler or ruling class. The historical experience demonstrates how much potential resides in those lower down the hierarchy, which is why the hothouse effect always seems to rely on a synergy between leadership and the people or, in organizations, the employees. It's simply that in business, the first moves usually come from upper-level management.

The hothouse effect demonstrates that far-reaching and enduring cultural change is most likely to occur when desired patterns of behavior emerge naturally out of individual responses to the organizational environment, rather than when change is imposed from the outside or top of the system. The hothouse effect is not about the quick fix. This book also does not offer a step-by-step approach to implementing the effect, or templates of how a hothouse company is supposed to look like or behave, or how the hothouse manager is supposed to manage. Instead, its purpose is to provide ideas, observations, reflections, examples, evidence, and suggestions—and to stir up the same in those who read it. The experiences of the communities and companies, the hothouse factors, the insights of the extraordinary people interviewed for the book, and the application-oriented sections such as CHAI-T and the Hothouse Challenge, provide a multifaceted view of what it takes to build a culture of creativity within an organization.

The hothouse effect is an efficient generator of highly creative practitioners; it produces its own momentum and generally it takes a series of major setbacks to slow it down or derail it. The hothouse quickly brings its practitioners to a high performance level because whether born or drawn into the hothouse, one immediately becomes immersed in its messages, standards and objectives, techniques, and learning opportunities, and its passion, drive, and desire to achieve something magnificent and lasting. All creativity, all *activity,* begins with the individual. Even the enraged mob can only come about because each individual makes a decision, at some level of consciousness, to yield up his or her will to the pleasures of collectively expressed passion. The hothouse effect is reinforced by countless messages transmitted and received by all group members, yet it relies on each individual to make a choice to leave behind business-as-usual. This spirit is unmistakable: The English poet William Wordsworth, recalling his youthful escapades in revolutionary France, expressed it brilliantly two centuries ago: "Bliss was it in that dawn to be alive, but to be young was very heaven." People know when they are caught up in the hothouse effect. The experience often remains, as Hemingway said about the movable feast of Paris, the most memorable of one's life.

I find it impossible to consider these themes without being reminded that we have entered a new millennium, by our common reckoning. However arbitrary the numbering of years might seem, our civilization has been counting years for a long time, and somehow we recently reached the point where that 1 in front of each year of the previous millennium turned over into a 2. At the same time, we are poised at the edge of a technological revolution whose dimensions we cannot fathom. Nanotechnology, biogenetics, new forms of energy, brain research, virtual reality, holography, and immensely powerful superchips and supercomputers will render our world unrecognizable (were we to leave and return) well before the end of the first century of the new millennium. We are also aware of the various challenges that face us in the political, environmental, and economic arenas as well. The new millennium not only symbolizes change but it arrived with a set of conditions that promises a dramatic, volatile, high-risk future.

These conditions, on the other hand, contain an inherent, unlimited creative potential. Many businesspeople are seeking ways to establish secure careers while doing meaningful work and earning a good living. It is creativity that drives innovation, and innovation that drives growth and development. Creativity also dramatically heightens the commitment and desire to excel among most individuals, and tends to empower them and improve their standing within their communities. Meanwhile, the hothouse effect reinforces broad-based individual success because creativity is simply impossible unless it activates as much of a system's potential energy as possible. It is no accident that Athens was the most democratic of the Greek city-states (despite its flaws), or that the Florentines were a proud, independent people by nature, or that the nickname of jazz's consummate innovator was Bird. And if, for example, we can point to the many Renaissance figures who embodied cruel, ruthless ambition—after all, they tend to get the most press—they are more than offset by the many men and women who worked, ruled, lived, and created with drive, integrity, and a large share of benevolence. The members of creative groups tend to be supportive of one another, despite the occasional back-biting and parting of the ways. Above all, creativity depends on freedom and, in a more mysterious way, freedom depends on creativity. Ultimately, creativity and freedom are likely to be identical, and this equation may perfectly suit the conduct of business in the coming century.

I like to think of the hothouse effect as a landscape akin to those strange aquamarine-tinged worlds one glimpses in the background of Leonardo's paintings, a landscape existing synchronistically in all places and times and within which we discover tools, receive visions, exchange ideas, and inspire one another to enrich and actualize creativity in all areas of our lives, in accordance with those creative gifts that every one of us has been granted the privilege to receive.

BIBLIOGRAPHY

Barabási, Albert-László. *Linked: The New Science of Networks.* Cambridge, MA: Perseus Publishing, 2001.

Bax, Marty. *Bauhaus Lecture Notes, 1930–1933.* Translated by Kist Killian Communications, Michael O'Loughlin, and Robert Ordish. Amsterdam: Architectura and Natura Press, 1991.

Baxandall, Michael. *Painting and Experience in Fifteenth-Century Italy.* Oxford: Oxford University Press, 1972.

Black, Roger, with Sean Elder. *Websites that Work.* San Jose, CA: Adobe Press, 1997.

Blumenfeld, Larry. "Unshrouding the Mysteries of Steve Coleman." *Jazziz,* vol. 15, no. 6 (June 1998).

Bramly, Serge. *Leonardo: Discovering the Life of Leonardo DaVinci.* Translated from the French by Siân Reynolds. New York: HarperCollins, 1991 (1988).

Briggs, John. *Fire in the Crucible: The Self-Creation of Creativity and Genius.* Los Angeles: Jeremy Tarcher, Inc., 1990.

Broderick, Damien. *The Spike: How Our Lives Are Being Transformed by Rapidly Advancing Technologies.* New York: Tom Doherty Associates, 2001.

Buchanan, Mark. *Nexus: Small Worlds and the Groundbreaking Science of Networks.* New York: W.W. Norton and Co., 2002.

Carter, James. *Conversin' with the Elders.* New York: Atlantic Records, 1996.

Courthion, Pierre. *Paris in Our Time.* Translated by Stuart Gilbert. Paris: Skira Press, 1957.

Csikszentmihalyi, Mihalyi. *Creativity: Flow and the Psychology of Discovery and Invention.* New York: HarperCollins, 1996.

Danto, Arthur C. "Reading Leonardo." *The Nation,* vol. 276 (April 7, 2003).

Davis, Miles, with Quincy Troupe. *Miles: The Autobiography.* New York: Simon and Schuster, 1989.

"Defense and the National Interest." http://d-n-i.net/second level/boyd_military.htm# discourse (April 11, 2003).

DeVeaux, Scott. *The Birth of BeBop: A Social and Musical History.* Berkeley: University of California Press, 1997.

Droste, Magdalena, with Bauhaus archive. *Bauhaus: 1919–1933.* Translated from the German by Karen Williams. Cologne: Taschen Verlag, 1990.

Garfield, Charles A., Ph.D., with Hal Zina Bennett. *Peak Performance: Mental Training Techniques of the World's Greatest Athletes.* Los Angeles: Jeremy P. Tarcher, Inc., 1984.

Giddins, Gary. *Visions of Jazz.* New York: Oxford University Press, 1998.

Hall, Edward T. *The Silent Language.* New York: Fawcett Press, 1959.

Harman, Willis, and Rheingold, Howard. *Higher Creativity: Liberating the Unconscious for Breakthrough Insights.* Los Angeles: Jeremy Tarcher, Inc., 1984.

Hauser, Arnold. *The Social History of Art, Volume 2.* Translated by Stanley Goodman with Arnold Hauser. New York: Vintage Books, 1951.

Heisenberg, Werner. *Encounters with Einstein and Other Essays on People, Places, and Particles.* Princeton, NJ: Princeton University Press, 1989 (1983).

Hill, Napoleon. *Think and Grow Rich.* New York: Fawcett Crest, 1960.

Huizinga, Johan. *Homo Ludens.* Translated by Johan Huizinga and publisher. Boston: Beacon Press, 1955.

Hyde, J.K. "Universities and Cities in Medieval Italy." In Bender, Thomas, ed., *The University and the City: From Medieval Origins to the Present.* New York: Oxford University Press, 1988.

Hyde, Lewis. *Imagination and the Erotic Life of Property.* New York: Vintage Books, 1979.

Jardine, Lisa. *Worldly Goods: A New History of the Renaissance.* London: Macmillan, 1996.

Kahn, Ashley. *Kind of Blue: The Making of the Miles Davis Masterpiece.* New York: DaCapo Press, 2000.

Kempers, Bram. *Painting, Power and Patronage: The Rise of the Professional Artist in Renaissance Italy.* Translated by Beverley Jackson. London: Penguin Books, 1987.

King, Jonny. *What Jazz Is.* New York: Walker and Co., 1997.

King, Ross. *Brunelleschi's Dome: How a Renaissance Genius Reinvented Architecture.* New York: Penguin Books, 2000.

Kunda, Gideon. *Engineering Culture: Control and Commitment in a High-Tech Corporation.* Philadelphia: Temple University Press, 1992.

Land, Edwin. "Research by the Business Itself." In *The Future of Industrial Research: Papers and Discussion.* New York: Standard Oil Development Company from a paper presented at the Standard Oil Development Company Forum in New York (October 5, 1944).

———. "Some Conditions for Scientific Profundity in Industrial Research." The Charles F. Kettering Award address, Washington, DC (June 17, 1965).

———. "The Second Great Product of Industry: The Rewarding Working Life." *Science and Human Progress.* Pittsburgh: Mellon Institute, 1963.

———. "Thinking Ahead: Patents and New Enterprises." *Harvard Business Review* (September–October 1959). Paper first presented to the Boston Patent Law Association, 1959.

Láng, Paul Henry. *Music in Western Civilization.* New York: W.W. Norton and Co., 1941.

Lipsey, Roger. *An Art of our Own: The Spiritual in Twentieth Century Art.* Boston: Shambhala, 1988.

Masters, Roger D. *Fortune Is a River: Leonardo da Vinci and Niccolò Machiavelli's Magnificent Dream to Change the Course of Florentine History.* New York: The Free Press, 1998.

McCarthy, Mary. *The Stones of Florence.* New York: Harcourt Brace Jovanovich, 1963 (1959).

Menocal, María Rosa. *The Ornament of the World: How the Muslims, Jews, and Christians Created a Culture of Tolerance in Medieval Spain.* Boston: Little, Brown, 2002.

Meyer-Thoss, Christiane. *Louise Bourgeois: Designing for Free Fall.* Translated by Catherine Schelbert, Jorg Trobitius, and Friederike Mayrocker. Zurich: Ammann Verlag, 1992.

Middleton, W.E. Knowles. *The Scientific Revolution.* Cambridge, MA: Schenkman Publishing, 1963.

Millard, Andre. *Edison and the Business of Innovation.* Baltimore: Johns Hopkins University Press, 1990.

Murphy, Michael, and White, Rhea A. *In the Zone: Transcendent Experience in Sports.* New York: Penguin Books, 1995 (1978).

Neville, Richard. *Footprints of the Future: Handbook for the Third Millennium.* N. Sydney, Australia: Richmond Ventures, 2002.

Nisenson, Eric. *Blue: The Murder of Jazz.* New York: St. Martin's Press, 1997.

Olmert, Michael. *The Smithsonian Book of Books.* Washington, DC: Smithsonian Books, 1992.

Oshry, Barry. The Power and Systems Workshop, a one-week immersion experience in organizational behavior, polished over decades of experience into a leadership training tool. The idea of the *power move* is one tactical technique that Oshry teaches. (The author participated in one workshop but has no connection, professional or personal, to Power and Systems.)

Ostrander, Sheila, and Lynn Schroeder, with Nancy Ostrander. *Super-Learning.* New York: Dell Publishing, 1979.

Overy, Paul. *De Stijl.* London: Thames and Hudson, 1991.

Richter, Paul. *The Notebooks of Leonardo Da Vinci: Compiled and Edited from the Original Manuscripts,* vol. 1. New York: Dover Press, 1970.

Scanlon, Lisa. "No P-N Intended: A Cracked Crystal Launched the Silicon Revolution." *Technology Review* (February 2003).

Steegmuller, Francis. *Apollinaire: Poet Among the Painters.* New York: Farrar, Straus and Company, 1963.

Stein, Gertrude. *The Autobiography of Alice B. Toklas.* New York: Vintage Books, 1990 (1933).

Stewart, Thomas A. *Intellectual Capital: The New Wealth of Organizations.* New York: Doubleday, 1997.

Tufte, Edward R. *The Visual Display of Quantitative Information.* Cheshire, CT: Graphics Press, 1983

Vasari. *Lives of the Artists.* Translated by George Bull. New York: Penguin Books, 1965.

Vezzosi, Alessandro. *Leonardo da Vinci: The Mind of the Renaissance.* Translated from the French by Alexandra Bonfante-Warren. New York: Harry N. Abrams Inc., 1997 (1996).

Weltge, Sigrid Wortmann. *Women's Work: Textile Art from the Bauhaus.* San Francisco: Chronicle Books, 1993.

Wenger, Win, and Richard Poe. *The Einstein Factor.* Rocklin, CA: Prima Publishing, 1996.

Westphal, Uwe. *The Bauhaus.* Translated by John Harrison. New York: W.H. Smith, 1991.

Wingler, Hans M. *The Bauhaus: Weimar, Dessau, Berlin, Chicago.* Translated from the German by Wolfgang Jabs and Basil Gilvert. Edited by Joseph Stein. Cambridge, MA: MIT Press, 1980 (1962).

Woideck, Carl. *The John Coltrane Companion: Five Decades of Commentary.* London: Schirmer Books, 1998.

INDEX